THE BOOK OF REVELATION

MADE CLEAR

THE BOOK OF REVELATION
MADE CLEAR

A User-Friendly Look at the Bible's Most Complicated Book

DOUGLAS CONNELLY

ZONDERVAN

The Book of Revelation Made Clear
Copyright © 2007 by Douglas Connelly

This title is also available as a Zondervan ebook.

Previously published as *The Book of Revelation for Blockheads*.

Requests for information should be addressed to:
Zondervan, 3900 *Sparks Drive SE, Grand Rapids, Michigan* 49546

This edition ISBN: 978-0-310-59713-1

The Library of Congress cataloged the original edition as follows:

Connelly, Douglas, 1949-.
    The book of Revelation for blockheads: a user-friendly look at the Bible's weirdest book / Douglas Connelly.
        p. cm.
    Includes bibliographical references.
    ISBN 978-0-310-24909-2
    1. Bible. N.T. Revelation—Criticism, interpretation, etc. I. Title.
    BS2825.52.C66 2007
    228'.06-dc22   2007006710

Cover design: Halie Culver
Cover image: Shutterstock
Interior design: Mark Sheeres
Interior illustration: Patten Illustrations

Printed in the United States of America

HB 04.16.2024

Contents

Break-Out Sections

- **Heads Up**— Brief overview of what lies ahead in the chapter
- **Access Codes**— Key terms in each chapter defined
- **Help File**— An in-depth look at crucial facts
- **Future FAQs**— Further exploration of a perplexing problem or confounding question
- **Bible Networking**— Illuminating passages from other parts of the Bible
- **In Other Words**— Relevant quotes from Revelation masters
- **Living Wisely**— Insights that help us apply Revelation's truth to life today
- **Revelation 360°**— A look at alternative viewpoints
- **Try, Try Again**— Some famous (and infamous) predictions about the end
- **Points to Remember**— A summary of each chapter's important points

Access:
Understanding a Book That
Has Confused Millions

The book of Revelation makes us nervous. Even a person who has never read a word of the Bible has heard about Revelation (or, as it's usually incorrectly called, "Revelations"). We've heard the words "Antichrist" or the "Beast" or the number 666; we've been told that Revelation talks about the end of the world—and we get nervous just thinking about what the book might say.

When we get enough courage to actually read the book, it starts out pretty mild—instructions to some churches, scenes of God's throne in heaven. But it gets ugly fast. Suddenly we see catastrophic wars and violent earthquakes and huge hailstones! We close the book in a cold sweat and decide to read something a little less threatening.

But our curiosity continues. What does this weird book say about the future—and particularly about *my* future? How many disasters will *I* have to face—and when will the end come? So we go back to Revelation and try again.

The purpose of this Blockheads guide is to help you understand Revelation. I will admit right at the beginning that I don't have all the answers—no one fully understands this book. We all walk away from it with some mysteries still unsolved. My goal is to help you grasp what we can understand and give you some options in the difficult spots. You won't agree with everything I say, and that's OK. Christians have debated the meaning of Revelation for almost two thousand years. In the end, I hope you will at least wrestle through the book with me and come away blessed.

Prepare to Be Blessed!

What prompted me to tackle this book in the first place is that Revelation is the only section of the Bible that promises a blessing on those who read it. The blessing is promised in verse 3 of the very first chapter:

> Blessed is the one who reads aloud the words of this prophecy, and blessed are those who hear it and take to heart what is written in it.
>
> Revelation 1:3

God will bless those who read and heed the book of Revelation. I think there are at least four ways you will be blessed by studying this book.

- First, you will see Jesus in a new, powerful way. Revelation unveils Jesus' majesty and power and greatness like no other New Testament book. Jesus is not some poor, lonely man, desperately trying to find people who will believe his message. He is the conquering King and Lord of all.
- A second blessing is that we see in Revelation the fulfillment of human history. God outlines for us how he will bring everything to completion. There won't be any loose ends. Our world is moving toward a goal. We aren't just a tiny speck in a vast universe; this planet is the center of God's attention. He created it with a plan in mind, and he is guiding it to the completion of that plan.
- Another blessing of reading and understanding Revelation is that the book will show us Christ's final victory over Satan and all that is evil. Sin and rebellion against God seem to have the upper hand in our world right now. Satan is the prince and the god of this age, but Satan will never triumph. His doom is certain, and it is sealed in the pages of Revelation.
- If all *these* blessings aren't enough, Revelation also makes it clear that followers of Christ are the ultimate winners in God's plan. God doesn't tell us this to make us proud; he tells us so we will be confident in God's power to do what he says he will do. God has the future in his control!

Revelation is the only absolutely trustworthy guide to the future that we have. Futurologists may speculate about the future and prophets may claim to see certain events in the future and we may all dream about (or dread) the future at times, but God has given us a totally reliable guide that we can trust with absolute confidence. We may not understand every detail, but we know that, in the end, God wins.

In light of these great blessings, it's amazing that so many people avoid Revelation. I've even heard pastors say with some pride that they never preach from the book! Only Satan could fog us that badly.

But What Does It Mean?

We will talk more about how to interpret what we read in Revelation as we move through the book, but I want to give you a heads up on the various approaches that are used by people who try to understand what Revelation says. I have found four basic approaches to the interpretation of this book.

The make-believe approach. Some interpreters of Revelation believe that John's writings have no connection with any real events, past or present. One writer says the book is simply the "ecstatic musings of an old man." In this view, the book of Revelation is just an ancient fantasy novel.

The John's-own-day approach. Other students of Revelation believe that the author was writing in a secret code about events in the first century. The "beast" described in the book was really the Roman emperor who was persecuting the church. John wanted to assure the early Christians that Christ would ultimately triumph over Roman oppression, but he didn't want to get in trouble by actually naming names.

The spiritual-conflict approach. This view of Revelation claims that John's writing could be applied to any time period in the church age. Christians persecuted by Rome or persecuted in Stalinist Russia or persecuted today in North Korea are all going through a "tribulation"-style experience. Any state-sponsored oppression can be viewed as the Antichrist. According to this approach, the book is an allegory for persecution against Christians in any age.

The future-is-coming approach. The approach I use in this book is that most of the book of Revelation applies to the future. The present age is addressed in chapters 2 and 3 of Revelation; everything after the end of chapter 3 happens in the future. This is the only approach that takes the book in its literal, normal sense. That doesn't mean there aren't symbols used in the book. In chapter 13 John sees a seven-headed beast rise from the sea. That is obviously a symbol. But in my view, the seven-headed beast stands for a real person, an evil world leader who will rise to power in the future.

Let the Journey Begin

The best way to come to a better understanding of the book of Revelation is not to talk about it but to read it for ourselves. Buckle your seatbelts and hold on! You are about to start an incredible journey into God's future.

CHAPTER 1

Falling in Front of Jesus

Falling in Front of Jesus

▶ Be prepared to be blessed!
▶ Dear churches—from Jesus
▶ Catch a glimpse of our Sovereign King.
▶ Lampstands and stars

Key Codes: Level 1

→ Revelation: Uncovering something hidden
→ Angel: A powerful being who serves God; a messenger from God
→ Prophecy: Predictions of future events
→ Province of Asia: Roman state located in the western part of modern Turkey
→ Alpha and Omega: The first and last letters of the Greek alphabet
→ Patmos: An island in the Mediterranean; part of Greece today
→ Seven churches: Groups of believers in seven cities
→ Hades: A place of torment; hell
→ Lampstand: A pedestal that holds an oil lamp

A Book about Jesus (Revelation 1:1–3)

> The revelation from Jesus Christ, which God gave him to show his servants what must soon take place. He made it known by sending his angel to his servant John, who testifies to everything he saw—that is, the word of God and the testimony of Jesus Christ. Blessed is the one who reads aloud the words of this prophecy, and blessed are those who hear it and take to heart what is written in it, because the time is near.

When I read a book, I read it all—the foreword, the footnotes, the thank-yous, the historical notes at the back. I even scan the copyright page! Sometimes you can find important clues about the book in the parts most people skip. Some people are so anxious to get to the prophecy part of Revelation that they just skim through the opening verses. They miss some important clues about the book and why it was written.

Since every passage in the book is part of God's message to us, we should carefully consider it all.

The first thing we discover in verse 1 is that this book is a "revelation." That's where the title comes from, but it is also a description of the book itself. The word means "unwrapping" or "unveiling." In Greek, the word "revelation" is *apokalypsis*, so sometimes the book is called "the Apocalypse." That word in English has come to mean the end of the world, but in Greek it means opening—like opening a present on Christmas morning. The book of Revelation is not a secret book; it's a book that unwraps secrets. God doesn't want its contents sealed up; he wants to tell everyone what he plans to do.

The book is not an unveiling of everything in God's mind. It's a revelation that focuses on Jesus Christ. The subject of this book is not the Antichrist or the War of Armageddon, but Jesus in his majesty and glory. God tears back the curtain and we see Jesus emerge as the Sovereign

SOMETHING ABOUT THAT NAME

Here are the titles and descriptions applied to Jesus in the book of Revelation:

- the faithful witness (1:5)
- the firstborn from the dead (1:5)
- the ruler of the kings of the earth (1:5)
- the Alpha and the Omega (1:8; 21:6; 22:13)
- someone like a son of man (1:13)
- the First and the Last (1:17; 22:13)
- the Living One (1:18)
- him who holds the seven stars in his right hand and walks among the seven golden lampstands (2:1)
- him ... who died and came to life again (2:8)
- him who has the sharp, double-edged sword (2:12)
- the Son of God (2:18)
- him who holds the seven spirits of God and the seven stars (3:1)
- him who is holy and true, who holds the key of David (3:7)
- the Amen (3:14)
- the faithful and true witness (3:14)
- the ruler of God's creation (3:14)
- the Lion of the tribe of Judah (5:5)
- the Root of David (5:5; 22:16)
- the Lamb (5:6) [thirty-two times in Revelation]
- Lord of lords and King of kings (17:14; 19:16)
- Faithful and True (19:11)
- the Word of God (19:13)
- the Beginning and the End (21:6; 22:13)
- the Offspring of David (22:16)
- the bright Morning Star (22:16)
- the Lord Jesus (22:20, 21)

King of history and eternity. If all you see as you read Revelation are beasts and wars and pounding judgments, you have missed Jesus.

Another insight these opening verses give us is how the book came into existence in the first place. Revelation is not just an old man's hallucinations. The revelation came from God the Father—who gave it to Jesus—who sent it by an angel to John—and John stands as a witness to us that the message is true. The point is that the contents of this book came from God to us through a chain of reliable witnesses, and it wasn't corrupted anywhere along the way. The book is the accurate record of what John saw as he was guided by an angel who received direction from Jesus who got it from the Father. God's goal all along was to get this message to us. He wants us to know what will soon take place.

Another crucial insight into the nature of this book comes from one phrase in verse 3 where Revelation is called "the words of this prophecy." The book focuses on *future* events. God's program for our world will come to a powerful conclusion in Jesus' return to earth in majesty and glory. The events leading up to and following the second coming of Christ are spelled out for us in detail. Nowhere else in the Bible do we find such a complete picture of what the future holds.

What we learn in these opening verses helps us keep our bearings all the way through the book:

- It's a book that reveals, not a book that hides.
- It's a book that focuses on Jesus.
- The book's perspective is the future.

God wants us to understand this book. He will bless those who read it and the Holy Spirit will give us understanding if we open our minds and hearts to God's truth revealed in his Word.

John the Revelator

Four times in Revelation the author of this book signs his name. He calls himself John (1:1, 4, 9; 22:8). Five times we find God commanding John to "write" what he sees and hears (1:11, 19; 14:13; 19:9; 21:5). Scholars have debated for a long time about who John is, but the best answer seems to be that this is the apostle John, who was one of the twelve original followers of Jesus. Church tradition and history provide several strong indications that John lived until late in the first century and, during the last decades of his life, lived in Ephesus in the Roman province of Asia.

We learn down in verse 9 of chapter 1 that John received these visions while he was exiled on the island of Patmos. Patmos was a Roman prison island, and John, during a time of persecution against the Christians, was sent into exile there. He was later released and then compiled the book of Revelation in its final form.

An Early Date

Some Christians insist that Revelation was written in the AD 60s—*before* the armies of Rome destroyed the temple in Jerusalem in AD 70. They insist on the early date because they believe that the book of Revelation predicts the fall of Jerusalem, not a future Tribulation. This view, that the prophecies in Revelation were fulfilled in the past, is called the *preterist* view (from the Latin word for "past"). Some prominent advocates of this view are R. C. Sproul, Hank Hanegraaff, and Robert Gentry. If Revelation had been written in the AD 90s, the prophecies would have to apply to a future Tribulation since the destruction of Jerusalem had taken place more than twenty years earlier.

Scholars and students of Revelation also debate about *when* the book of Revelation was written. Some interpreters believe that it was written during the reign of the Roman emperor Nero, around AD 68. Most interpreters believe John was sent into exile during the reign of Domitian in the middle of the AD 90s. I think the evidence points more strongly to this later date. Several early church writers claim that John the apostle lived in Ephesus in his later years and that John was sent into exile during Domitian's reign. One early church leader, Irenaeus, tells us that John returned to Ephesus from exile after Domitian was assassinated in AD 96.

A Letter to Seven Churches (Revelation 1:4–8)

John,

To the seven churches in the province of Asia:

Grace and peace to you from him who is, and who was, and who is to come, and from the seven spirits before his throne, and from Jesus Christ, who is the faithful witness, the firstborn from the dead, and the ruler of the kings of the earth.

To him who loves us and has freed us from our sins by his blood, and has made us to be a kingdom and priests to serve his God and Father—to him be glory and power for ever and ever! Amen.

"Look, he is coming with the clouds,"
    and "every eye will see him,

JOHN'S RÉSUMÉ

- had early career as a fisherman in Galilee
- brother of James, son of Zebedee (Matthew 4:21)
- left promising business to follow Jesus (Matthew 4:22)
- wrote the gospel of John, the three New Testament letters of John, and the book of Revelation—about one-quarter of the New Testament.
- closest friend of Jesus (John 21:20)

- present at Jesus' trial and at the cross (John 18:15–16; 19:26)
- entrusted with the care of Jesus' mother, Mary (John 19:25–27)
- eyewitness of the empty tomb and the risen Christ
- the only one of the original twelve followers of Jesus to die of natural causes

Hint: Do not confuse John the apostle with John the Baptizer, the prophet who announced to Israel the coming of the Messiah (Matthew 3:1–16).

even those who pierced him";
and all peoples on earth "will mourn because of him."
So shall it be! Amen.

"I am the Alpha and the Omega," says the Lord God, "who is, and
who was, and who is to come, the Almighty."

The book of Revelation is not only a book of prophecy; it is also a letter written to seven churches in seven cities in the Roman province of Asia. John lived in one of the cities, Ephesus, and so he knew these seven congregations well. John greets the seven churches in a way that was customary in first-century letters, but he makes it clear (again) that the letter he is writing really came from God. John blessed them with grace and peace "from him who is, and who was, and who is to come"— an obvious reference to God the Father. In God's perspective there is no past or future. He inhabits eternity. Giving us the details of future events is not hard for God. He sees it all and knows it all.

The letter also comes "from the seven spirits before [God's] throne." John is referring to the Holy Spirit, but it seems like a strange way to do it. The number seven often refers to completeness or fullness and may be John's way of describing the full presence of the invisible Holy Spirit.

Sometimes the most comforting words we can say to a person who is hurting or broken are "I love you." Those words have dried more tears and comforted more hearts than any others. In the same way, when I am struggling or sad or in pain, I need the assurance that God loves me—not just that he acted in love in the past to provide salvation for me, but that he loves me now. It's that present-tense love that we find in Revelation 1:5—"To him who *loves* us" (emphasis added). The Christians who first read John's book needed to be reminded of Christ's love too. They were bruised and battered. Some had been arrested or had died for their faith. In grace Jesus reaches out and embraces their hearts (and ours) and assures us that his love is always present tense—I love you, I love you, I love you.

Bible Networking

Isaiah 46:9 – 10

I am God, and there is no other;
    I am God, and there is none like me.
I make known the end from the beginning,
    from ancient times, what is still to come.

1 Peter 4:7

The end of all things is near. Therefore be alert and of sober mind so that you may pray.

The third source of the information revealed in Revelation is Jesus Christ. Three titles establish Jesus' authority and give credibility to his message:

- He is "the faithful witness." Some of the first readers of Revelation were facing arrest and even death for their loyalty to Jesus. He stands with them against evil and oppression.
- He is "the firstborn from the dead." Christians don't have to fear death because Jesus has gone through it before them — and he has triumphed over it.
- He is "the ruler of the kings of the earth." Persecuted Christians don't have to fear powerful rulers either. Above the rulers of the earth sits a Sovereign King, who will one day bring about justice for all who follow him.

As John thinks about the wonders of who Jesus really is, his heart is so filled with adoration that he bursts into a shout of praise to Jesus. This great Jesus loves us and has set us free from our slavery to sin by his death on the cross. The risen, ruling Jesus has made us to be a kingdom and priests before God. We will reign with Jesus. We have direct access to God because a human being has pioneered the way for us, and he sits at God's right hand as our Defender and Savior. To that powerful, compassionate, reigning Jesus be glory and power forever!

It's not just Christians who will recognize Jesus as King. The day is coming, John says, when *every* eye will see him. When Jesus returns to earth in majesty, the whole world will acknowledge his power. For most of them, it will be too late to receive his mercy and forgiveness, but there will be no mistaking who Jesus really is. Jesus will be unveiled— that's what Revelation is all about—as the true Son of God and the Sovereign Ruler of the whole earth.

A Vision of Majesty (Revelation 1:9-20)

I, John, your brother and companion in the suffering and kingdom and patient endurance that are ours in Jesus, was on the island of Patmos because of the word of God and the testimony of Jesus. On the Lord's Day I was in the Spirit, and I heard behind me a loud voice like a trumpet, which said: "Write on a scroll what you see and send it to the seven churches: to Ephesus, Smyrna, Pergamum, Thyatira, Sardis, Philadelphia and Laodicea."

I turned around to see the voice that was speaking to me. And when I turned I saw seven golden lampstands, and among the lampstands was someone like a son of man, dressed in a robe reaching down to his feet and with a golden sash around his chest. The hair on his head was white like wool, as white as snow, and his eyes were like blazing fire. His feet were like bronze glowing in a furnace, and his voice was like the sound of rushing waters. In his right hand he held seven stars, and coming out of his mouth was a sharp, double-edged sword. His face was like the sun shining in all its brilliance.

When I saw him, I fell at his feet as though dead. Then he placed his right hand on me and said: "Do not be afraid. I am the First and the Last. I am the Living One; I was dead, and now look, I am alive for ever and ever! And I hold the keys of death and Hades.

"Write, therefore, what you have seen: both what is now and what will take place later. The mystery of the seven stars that you saw in my right hand and of the seven golden lampstands is this: The seven stars are the angels of the seven churches, and the seven lampstands are the seven churches."

Help File

BANISHMENT

Banishment or exile under Roman law meant the loss of all civil rights. It also meant that the Roman government could confiscate all your property. If that wasn't enough, your sentence had no end. Those exiled stayed in exile until they died or until the emperor who had banished them died. Some early Christian writers say that John survived Domitian (who was assassinated in AD 96) and that he returned to Ephesus and lived into the reign of Trajan (who ruled from AD 98–117).

Bible Networking

Psalm 29:4

> The voice of the LORD is powerful;
> the voice of the LORD is majestic.

Deuteronomy 4:24

For the LORD your God is a consuming fire, a jealous God.

Isaiah 11:4

> He will strike the earth with the rod of his mouth;
> with the breath of his lips he will slay the wicked.

John explains where he was when these visions began. He wasn't at some quiet spiritual retreat or praying at a church altar. John was on a barren, rocky island about ten miles long and six miles wide. He wasn't there voluntarily. He had been sent there by the Roman authorities for his loyalty to Jesus. Patmos was a prison island. Most of the prisoners worked under the whip in the quarries or mines on the island. John probably didn't have to work in the quarries because of his advanced age (close to ninety years old), but he would have been cut off from any contact with the Christians whom he loved and served. No email, no voice mail, not even snail mail.

John was a church leader and so had been singled out for persecution, but he wasn't the only Christian under pressure. He calls himself a "brother ... in the suffering and kingdom and patient endurance." All the Christians were undergoing suffering—or "tribulation," as some versions translate the word. This was not the final Tribulation that will come on the world in the future but the ongoing tribulation that Jesus said would come on those who follow him faithfully.

John found himself "in the Spirit" on the Lord's Day. Perhaps John was engaged in worship on a Sunday, perhaps he was transported by the Spirit "into the Day of the Lord" (another way to translate the phrase), but God put John in a state of prophetic ecstasy where he could hear and see and experience visions from God. If we had been sitting beside John that day, we would not have seen or heard anything except that John would have been unresponsive to anything we would have said or done to him. John was taken by the Holy Spirit into another realm.

His mind and his spirit were able to see into God's realm, and God began to reveal a series of startling visions to this imprisoned apostle. Powerful political forces may lock Christians away and cut them off from any communication, but God can turn the worst mankind can do into blessing for one of his servants. On a prison island, all alone, John was led through some of the most stunning revelations ever given by God.

In that state of prophetic vision, John heard a loud voice. When he turned, his eyes fell, not directly on the speaker, but on seven golden lampstands and, in the middle of those lampstands, on a man clothed in brilliant majesty. John knew immediately that it was Jesus. But this was not the teacher walking the hills of Galilee or even the suffering Savior dying on the cross. This was the risen, ascended Jesus, crowned with glory and majesty. This is how Jesus is today! We don't usually picture him this way in our minds, but this is how he appears in heaven.

Jesus is clothed in the brilliant garments of a priest—a full-length white robe with a golden sash wrapped across his chest. Beginning at Jesus' head and moving down to his feet, John describes what Jesus looked like:

- Hair as white as snow: A picture of the purity and sinlessness of Jesus.
- Eyes like blazing fire: He can see right through us; every hidden thing is visible to him.

Try, Try Again

Richard the Lionheart

As Richard the Lionheart made his way toward Jerusalem in 1190 on the Third Crusade, he conferred with the most famous prophecy scholar of his day, Joachim of Fiore. Joachim told Richard that the Muslim leader Saladin was the Antichrist and that Richard would defeat him—a prophecy that failed to come to pass. He further predicted that Christ's kingdom would begin sometime between 1200 and 1260. Wrong again.

In Other Words

Majesty, worship his majesty,
Unto Jesus be all glory, power, and praise.

Jack Hayford, from the hymn "Majesty" (copyright
© 1981 by Rocksmith Music).

Scripture clearly teaches that God holds the overseers of the church responsible for the spiritual condition of the people, and this responsibility is not only upon the pastors but upon all who hold positions of leadership.

Donald Grey Barnhouse, in *Revelation: An Expository Commentary* (Grand Rapids: Zondervan, 1971), 32.

- Feet like glowing bronze: A symbol of judgment; Jesus' feet are restless as he moves among his people.
- A voice like a thundering waterfall: Jesus' words will block out all other voices; he alone is the supreme authority.
- A face like the sun: A picture of the stunning glory of Jesus.

John was Jesus' closest human friend on earth. It had been sixty years since they had last seen each other. But John doesn't run up and slap Jesus on the back and tell him how good it is to see him. In the face of Jesus' glory, John falls at Jesus' feet like a dead man.

We've come up with a lot of strange ideas about what we will do in heaven when we first see Jesus. Some people think they will shake his hand or give him a hug. Some people have questions they want to ask. I think we will do what John did—fall down in awe and wonder and love at Jesus' feet.

What's in *Your* Hand?

In Jesus' right hand are seven stars. Jesus finally explains what they are in verse 20—"The seven stars are the angels of the seven churches, and the seven lampstands are the seven churches." Jesus, the risen, glorious Lord, walks among his churches. Jesus protects them, cares for them, watches over them, corrects them. He walks past and through and around the church you are part of. He examines the leaders and the hearts of every person. His eyes see every secret. He speaks with the sharp sound of his Word.

Jesus carries the "angel" of your church in his right hand. There could be a holy angel assigned to every body of Christian believers as a special emissary of Christ. The word *angel* can also mean messenger and may refer to the pastor or elder who has responsibility to shepherd God's flock in your local church. If this is the case, Jesus pays special attention to the person who shepherds you week after week. If you are a pastor, be encouraged by that. The Lord Jesus holds you close to his heart. If you receive ministry from a pastor, the fact that Jesus holds pastors so close should encourage you to pray more for your pastor. Support pastors in the work God has called them to do.

Jesus' close presence in our lives is not designed to make us fearful. Jesus tells John not to be afraid (verse 17). He even touches John compassionately. If there's any question about who this person is, Jesus makes it clear that he is the one who was dead but is now alive forever. The keys that unlock death and hell are now in his possession. Jesus is the Creator who began the human story, and he is the One who will bring the human story to its final end.

Jesus then gives John his assignment. He tells his servant to write down what he has seen. Jesus even gives John a simple outline of the whole book of Revelation: John will write:

- what he has seen (the vision of Jesus);
- what is now (the message from Jesus to each of the seven churches in Revelation 2 and 3); and
- what will take place later (events of the future in Revelation 4–22).

Revelation presents a powerful portrait of Jesus. He is much more than a religious teacher or a good man. He is the risen Lord, who

DOMITIAN

The Roman emperor Domitian had demanded worship as a god. His favorite title for himself was *dominus et deus*, "Lord and God." Christians, of course, could not call anyone Lord and God except Jesus Christ. Many of the Christians were arrested and condemned on a charge of atheism—a refusal to worship a visible god.

ascended to heaven and who now reigns in majesty over a kingdom that will never end. He is our future Judge and our conquering King. Those of us who know Jesus certainly need to elevate our image of who he is a few notches. If you don't have a personal relationship with Jesus, the good news is that he is extending a gracious invitation to you right now. He offers you forgiveness and cleansing and mercy if you will believe that he died for you and rose again. If you personally receive Jesus as Savior and King, he will make you his own dear child. Nothing will ever be the same again.

Points to Remember

- ☑ God promises a blessing to those who *read, hear,* and *take to heart* what is written in Revelation.

- ☑ John sees Jesus as he really is—as the exalted, ascended Lord of glory—and he falls at Jesus' feet in adoration.

- ☑ Jesus holds the power of release from death and hell because of his death on the cross and his resurrection.

- ☑ Jesus moves among his people in compassion and care.

CHAPTER 2

Something to Think about in Church

Something to Think about in Church

- ▶ Seven churches in God's headlights
- ▶ Forsaking our love for Jesus
- ▶ Rewards for the faithful
- ▶ Repent or else!

Key Codes: Level 2

→ Apostles: The closest followers of Jesus during his life on earth; key leaders in the early church

→ Nicolaitans: A sect of false teachers

→ Paradise: Heaven

→ Smyrna: City in the Roman province of Asia; pronounced **smur-***nuh*

→ Victor's crown: A wreath given as a reward for faithful service or extraordinary athletic effort

→ Second death: Eternal separation from God

→ Satan: The devil; a powerful angel who fights against God

→ Balaam: A prophet for hire in the Old Testament; pronounced **bay-***lum*

→ Balak: The king of Moab who hired Balaam

→ Manna: White seedlike food that God provided to Israel during their years in the wilderness

→ Jezebel: A wicked queen in the Old Testament

→ Scepter: Symbol of a ruler's authority

To: believers@sevenchurches.org

The book of Revelation is like a group email. It was sent to seven Christian congregations that were clustered near the city of Ephesus in western Asia Minor (modern Turkey). The apostle John had helped to

Map of the Seven Churches

lead the church in Ephesus, and he was also well known in the other six churches. Tucked inside the book are seven letters—one to each church—but all the churches got to read each other's mail. John (and Jesus, who dictated these letters to John) wanted all the churches to hear what Jesus had to say.

The seven churches, then, were actual groups of Christian believers who met in seven different cities to worship God and to learn from God's Word, the Bible. But the interesting thing is that you can still find seven churches like these today. Wherever you live, in your extended community somewhere, you could find an Ephesus-style church or a Laodicean church or a Smyrna-like church. In every era of the church, in times of expansion and in times of decline, all seven types of churches have existed.

That's important to remember as we read these letters. This is not just what Jesus said a long time ago to a group of long-forgotten churches; this is what Jesus is still saying to churches today. Outward setting and circumstances may have changed, but inwardly the church you attend is a lot like one of these seven churches. Get ready for some honest evaluation of your spiritual condition—and the condition of the people worshiping with you. You may not like what you hear, but Jesus speaks as the Lord of the church.

What to Look For

The seven letters to the seven churches follow a distinct pattern.

- Each letter opens as the *church* is identified by the city where it was located. John wrote these letters long before there were several different congregations in each city. If you were a Christian in the first century, you belonged to the single church in your city.

- The second element in each letter is a description of *Christ* that is particularly suited to that church—or that kind of church.
- Then comes *commendation* from the Lord—a pat on the back for a job well done. In some letters the commendation is long; in some it is short; in one there is none.
- Approval is followed by discipline. *Condemnation* is the fourth element. A couple of churches are severely chastised, but in two of the letters, no words of disapproval are spoken.
- Jesus follows evaluation with clear direction. He gives them his *counsel* as the Lord of the church.
- The letters close with words of *challenge.* Jesus urges the believers to new levels of obedience and faithfulness.

It would be a mistake to read these chapters only as historical documents or even as spiritual instructions to whole congregations. The letters are more practical and personal than that. The seven churches also represent seven kinds of Christians in every church.

Some of us need to hear Jesus' words of approval. Others need to take Jesus' words of correction seriously. All of us need to hear his wisdom and challenge. I found myself sitting in all seven churches! These are Jesus' last instructions to Christians who are looking eagerly for his return. Jesus is speaking to you!

AN OUTLINE OF HISTORY?

Some interpreters of Revelation believe that the seven churches of Revelation 2 and 3 represent seven distinct ages in the almost two-thousand-year history of the church. The fifth church, for example, the church in the city of Sardis, represents (in their view) the Reformation church that started with great spiritual zeal but soon fell into apathy and deadness.

The seventh church, the church at Laodicea, represents the church in the last days of the church age—a compromising church—on the verge of apostasy and denial of biblical truth. You will sometimes hear preachers or prophecy buffs say that we are living in the "Laodicean age." The seven churches/seven ages view is interesting but difficult to prove. Revelation doesn't give any indication that the churches outline church history. We're on more solid ground, I think, to see these seven churches as representative of churches in every age of the church's story.

In Other Words

In each of the seven letters which follow, the risen Christ lays emphasis, either in rebuke or in condemnation, on one particular characteristic of an ideal church. Put together, these characteristics constitute the seven marks of a true and living church. They tell us what Christ thinks of his church, both as it is and as it should be.

John R. W. Stott, in *What Christ Thinks of the Church*
(Grand Rapids: Eerdmans, 1958), 20.

If [German pastor Dietrich] Bonhoeffer was correct in describing the church as "God's redeemed piece of the world," looking at ourselves with honesty becomes important. Sometimes that is only possible by looking at ourselves reflected in others. Let the churches of Revelation, then, be our mirror. And again, let us dare to believe that there are important challenges in these chapters.

Terence Kelshaw, in *Send This Message to My Church*
(Nashville: Nelson, 1984), 18.

Ephesus: Neglecting God's Priorities (Revelation 2:1–7)

"To the angel of the church in Ephesus write:

These are the words of him who holds the seven stars in his right hand and walks among the seven golden lampstands. I know your deeds, your hard work and your perseverance. I know that you cannot tolerate wicked people, that you have tested those who claim to be apostles but are not, and have found them false. You have persevered and have endured hardships for my name, and have not grown weary.

Yet I hold this against you: You have forsaken the love you had at first. Consider how far you have fallen! Repent and do the things you did at first. If you do not repent, I will come to you and remove your lampstand from its place. But you have this in your favor: You hate the practices of the Nicolaitans, which I also hate.

Whoever has ears, let them hear what the Spirit says to the churches. To those who are victorious, I will give the right to eat from the tree of life, which is in the paradise of God."

One of the great assurances found in the book of Revelation is that Jesus is close to his people—he moves among his churches. Even within the churches he criticizes most severely, Jesus' presence can be found. If you are a pastor or church leader, that fact is both comforting (in times of trouble) and challenging (when compromise seeps in). If you are a believer who goes to church week after week with little expectation of something significant happening, look around next Sunday—you may catch a glimpse of Jesus passing by. If you are hit-and-miss with your participation in a church, you may miss the Sunday that Jesus shows up in power.

Given a choice, almost everyone wanted to live in Ephesus. It was the "big city" in the whole region. A guy or gal could make it big in Ephesus—wealth, power, influence, a good time. Ephesus had it all.

Ephesus also had a church—a good church, an active church. Any Christian would have been proud to be a member. Jesus commends the church for four things;

- Their *activity* is first—"I know your deeds, your hard work." These Christians toiled to the point of exhaustion in doing God's work. If you are in an Ephesian-style church, plenty of people are involved in ministry. They aren't looking to be entertained; they want to be in the trenches, touching lives.

- Their *purity* as a church also receives praise from Jesus—"I know that you cannot tolerate wicked people." The Christians at Ephesus were not afraid to deal with moral impurity in the church. They went to people who were out of line and confronted them in humility and grace. They weren't looking to kick people out but to restore people to lives of holiness and obedience. Ephesian churches in any age and in any place have a concern for purity.

- Jesus next commends their *loyalty* to him and to the truth of God's Word. This was a doctrinally sound church. They were well-read and well taught in biblical truth. When some teachers showed up and claimed to be apostles of Jesus who spoke with Jesus' authority, these Christians didn't just take their word for it. They put the teachers to the test and found them false. If you find an Ephesian-style church, God's Word is central in all they do. An Ephesian-style Christian loves Bible study and sound Bible teaching.

- Finally, Jesus commends the Ephesian Christians for their rock-solid *consistency* — "You have persevered and have endured hardship for my name, and have not grown weary." Jesus loves that in a church. The Ephesians had held their ground under persecution. Instead of wiping out the church, opposition from the world made the church grow.

If you had been transferred to Ephesus in the first century, you would have had no trouble settling into the church in that city. You probably would have said on the first Sunday, "*This* is the church we've been looking for!" — active, biblically based, loyal to Jesus, rock-solid. You wouldn't have sensed anything wrong. But Jesus — the one who walks among the churches and who knows the heart of every Christian in the church — found something wrong. It was hidden from the eyes of people, but it wasn't hidden from him.

When Love Grows Cold

Jesus' evaluation is this: "You have forsaken the love you had at first" (verse 4). Jesus looks at an Ephesian church today and sees a church falling out of love with him. Their hearts are cooling down. The fire of pure devotion to Christ is going out — and Jesus is concerned. He holds that against them.

In Other Words

Activity in the King's business will not make up for neglect of the King.

G. Campbell Morgan, in *The Letters of Our Lord* (London: Pickering & Inglis, 1945), 28.

Jesus makes this point: the continual blessing of God on a given church is not guaranteed. Unless they continue in or return to "first love attitudes" and "first deed acts," they are in danger of Christ "darkening" the life of the church.

Richard Mayhue, in *What Would Jesus Say About Your Church?* (Fearn, Scotland: Christian Focus, 1995), 52.

In light of his criticism, maybe we need to reevaluate Jesus' commendation—and look more closely at our own church and our own lives. The church at Ephesus was a hardworking church, but without the hot fire of love for Christ, their work was simply a performance. The services were well planned, the pews were packed, and the pastor's sermons were polished, but Jesus says, "I miss the love you had at first." He misses the extravagance of love poured out; he misses the spontaneous expressions of praise; he misses the full sacrifice of their hearts. The ministry at the Ephesian church in your neighborhood is very impressive, but Jesus is not pleased.

The remedy to revive the fire involves three steps:

- Step one in that spiritual turnaround is to *remember* the high place of devotion to Jesus that you have left behind. Go back and remind yourself of what it was like when you first met Christ. Remember what it was like when the song in your heart was a *new* song. Remember when you couldn't get enough of Jesus.

- Step two is to *repent*. Jesus wants us to see the seriousness of the situation. It's sin to be cold toward Christ. It grieves God's heart when his children fall out of love with him. Instead of drifting further away, we turn around and head back. That's what genuine repentance is—a change of mind that always leads to a change of direction.

- The third step is to *repeat* the things we did at first. Back when we were first saved, we focused on the simplest, most basic areas of the Christian life. We came to the Bible eager to hear from God, and we read it with hearts that longed to know him more deeply. God's Word was like cool water to our parched souls. In the

Try, Try Again

Cotton Mather

This highly influential Puritan in colonial America set several dates as the time of Christ's return—1697, then 1716, finally 1736. All were wrong, of course, but that didn't deter old Cotton from trying again. Maybe it was growing up with a name like Cotton.

(His father's name, by the way, was Increase Mather.)

Bible Networking

1 Corinthians 13:2

If I have the gift of prophecy and can fathom all mysteries and all knowledge, and if I have a faith that can move mountains, but do not have love, I am nothing.

John 14:15

"If you love me [Jesus], keep my commands."

Ephesians 5:18

Do not get drunk on wine, which leads to debauchery. Instead, be filled with the Spirit.

---

first rush of love for Jesus, we found it easy to pray—repeatedly, constantly through the day. Now, if the truth were told, we can go days without a word between us. Revival in our hearts does not come through some slick new seminar; it comes when we, in genuine faith and burning love, do the simple basics of the Christian life.

Repent — or Else

Jesus adds a warning that we can't ignore: "If you do not repent, I will come to you and remove your lampstand" (verse 5). If our coldness toward Jesus continues, he will blow the light out. The choice for an Ephesian church is repentance, or removal. If a congregation grows cold and worship becomes dead ritual, not many generations have to pass until the church is gone. The building or denomination may still be there; people may still come; someone may stand in the pulpit—but the light, the power, is gone. The lamp has been blown out by Jesus himself.

If you're saying as you read those words, "That won't happen to us! We are too active, too well taught, too well grounded"—if you are saying that, let me tell you about the church at Ephesus. According to the ancient church historian Ignatius, the church did repent. The fire of devotion to Christ was revived. But within another generation, it had begun to cool again. In the end, Jesus did what he promised to do.

Today there is no church in Ephesus. The light in Ephesus went out, and it has never been rekindled.

Smyrna: Dying for Jesus (Revelation 2:8 – 11)

"To the angel of the church in Smyrna write:

These are the words of him who is the First and the Last, who died and came to life again. I know your afflictions and your poverty—yet you are rich! I know about the slander of those who say they are Jews and are not, but are a synagogue of Satan. Do not be afraid of what you are about to suffer. I tell you, the devil will put some of you in prison to test you, and you will suffer persecution for ten days. Be faithful, even to the point of death, and I will give you life as your victor's crown.

Whoever has ears, let them hear what the Spirit says to the churches. Those who are victorious will not be hurt at all by the second death."

Thirty-five miles north of Ephesus in the Roman province of Asia stood the city of Smyrna. It was an amazingly beautiful place marked by wide streets, a magnificent athletic stadium, and the largest open-air theater in the eastern Roman Empire. The city claimed to be the birthplace of the Greek poet Homer, who wrote the *Odyssey* and the *Iliad*. (Think back to that eleventh-grade world lit course.)

Smyrna was well known for other qualities:

- The people were *fanatically loyal* to Rome. They loved all things Roman!

Help File

A FAITHFUL PASTOR

Just fifty or sixty years after this letter was written, one of the ten "days" of suffering was breaking over Smyrna in full force. The pastor of the congregation in Smyrna was a man named Polycarp. Arrested and shackled, Polycarp was taken before the Roman proconsul of Smyrna and given a choice—curse Christ and sacrifice to Caesar, or die. Polycarp's response has become one of the classic quotations of Christian history: "Eighty-six years have I served him, and he has done me no wrong. How then can I blaspheme my King who saved me? Hear my free confession—I am a Christian."

The proconsul condemned Polycarp to be burned at the stake. One of the Christians wrote later: "[As Polycarp's body was consumed] we perceived a sweet smell as the aroma of myrrh being crushed." Polycarp died at the hands of a Roman proconsul, but he received a victor's crown from the hands of his true King.

1 Peter 1:6 – 7

In all this you greatly rejoice, though now for a little while you may have had to suffer grief in all kinds of trials. These have come so that your faith—of greater worth than gold, which perishes even though refined by fire—may be proved genuine and may result in praise, glory and honor when Jesus Christ is revealed.

2 Corinthians 4:16 – 17

Therefore we do not lose heart. Though outwardly we are wasting away, yet inwardly we are being renewed day by day. For our light and momentary troubles are achieving for us an eternal glory that far outweighs them all.

- The religious life of the city was *completely pagan*. A hill called the Pagos overlooked Smyrna, and it was crowded with temples and shrines to Greek and Roman deities.
- The people were also *extremely prosperous*. No downsizing or outsourcing in Smyrna. The chief source of wealth was the production of myrrh—the perfume of the ancient world. Myrrh was also used to embalm dead bodies. The Greek word for myrrh is *smyrna*, the name of the city itself.

Myrrh was an oily, fragrant gum produced by a thorny tree that grew in the region around Smyrna. To extract the gum, the plant had to be crushed. The more thoroughly it was crushed, the more pressure that was applied, the more myrrh was produced. That is precisely what was happening to the church in Smyrna. This was a suffering church, a church under pressure. But as these Christians endured the crushing weight of persecution, the more the sweet perfume of their love for Christ was released. The more they were oppressed, the sweeter they smelled to God.

Jesus says that the Christians in Smyrna were suffering under three things:

- "I know your *afflictions*." The Greek word Jesus uses here (translated "affliction" or "tribulation") means "pressure." In its basic form it means "to crush." Instead of driving people away from

Bible Networking

Romans 6:1 – 2

What shall we say, then? Shall we go on sinning so that grace may increase? By no means! We are those who have died to sin; how can we live in it any longer?

Jude 4 (The Message)

What has happened is that some people have infiltrated our ranks (our Scriptures warned us this would happen), who beneath their pious skin are shameless scoundrels. Their design is to replace the sheer grace of our God with sheer license — which means doing away with Jesus Christ, our one and only Master.

Jesus, however, the pressure pushed them closer to him. Persecution came in Smyrna because the Christians refused to worship the Roman emperor. Once a year, every Roman subject was required to offer incense at the altar to the emperor and say publicly, "Caesar is Lord." A certificate was issued, and the person was considered a loyal Roman. Christians were loyal citizens, but they could not say those words. Only one person was Lord to them, and it was *not* Caesar. Their refusal meant arrest and imprisonment and, for some, execution — which may be why Jesus introduces himself in this letter as the one "who died and came to life again" (verse 8).

- Jesus also knew their *poverty*. The Christians in Smyrna had nothing — probably the direct result of their persecution. Homes of criminals became the property of Rome. Without a certificate of loyalty, they couldn't get a job. In Jesus' eyes, the Christians were rich, but from a human perspective, they were destitute.
- If that wasn't enough, the Christians also had to face *slander* from the Jewish community in Smyrna. These were Jews who had rejected Jesus as their promised Messiah and King. They named their house of worship "the synagogue of the Lord," but Jesus called it "a synagogue of Satan." The Jews in Smyrna weren't doing God's work; they were standing in God's way.

What a price these Christians had to pay! Their loyalty to Jesus had cost them everything. That's why there is no condemnation or criticism from Jesus in this letter. You couldn't be a hypocrite and survive in Smyrna. No one is willing to die for something or someone they don't believe in. When persecution came, the halfhearted believers left. Those who stayed behind were so committed to Jesus that they were willing to die for him.

Jesus issues two commands to the suffering and persecuted church—and the commands are as relevant today to the church in North Korea or Sudan as they were to the first-century Christians in Smyrna. First, Jesus tells them not to be afraid of the suffering that lies ahead. He does *not* say, "You won't suffer anymore." Instead he tells these Christians that their suffering has a purpose and, in time, will come to an end. They would suffer ten days of persecution. It's possible to take that as ten twenty-four-hour days. More likely Jesus is telling them that there would be ten periods of time when the church at Smyrna would say, "This is a day—a time—of persecution." Historians count ten periods of intense persecution in the Roman Empire from the time this letter was written until persecution officially ended in AD 312.

Jesus' second word of counsel to the suffering church is to stay faithful, even to the point of death. Jesus would deliver some of them out of the persecution by allowing them to die, and after death they would receive an overcomer's crown of reward and blessing.

Jesus said that the world would always hate him and his followers (John 15:18–19). Yet most of us can't identify with the persecuted church in Smyrna because we haven't had to suffer for our faith. The world around us hasn't changed much. I think it's the church that has changed. Our loyalty to Christ isn't distinctive enough to produce that kind of outrage from the world. The day may come when we will have to take a stand that leads to persecution or poverty or even death. I wonder what kind of courage we will have.

Pergamum: The Church Next to Satan's Throne (Revelation 2:12–17)

"To the angel of the church in Pergamum write:
These are the words of him who has the sharp, double-edged sword. I know where you live—where Satan has his throne. Yet you remain true to my name. You did not renounce your faith in me, not even in the days of Antipas, my faithful witness, who was put to death in your city—where Satan lives.

1 John 5:4 – 5

Everyone born of God overcomes the world. This is the victory that has overcome the world, even our faith. Who is it that overcomes the world? Only the one who believes that Jesus is the Son of God.

Isaiah 55:3

Give ear and come to me;
listen, that you may live.

Nevertheless, I have a few things against you: There are some among you who hold to the teaching of Balaam, who taught Balak to entice the Israelites to sin so that they ate food sacrificed to idols and committed sexual immorality. Likewise, you also have those who hold to the teaching of the Nicolaitans. Repent therefore! Otherwise, I will soon come to you and will fight against them with the sword of my mouth.

Whoever has ears, let them hear what the Spirit says to the churches. To those who are victorious, I will give some of the hidden manna. I will also give each of them a white stone with a new name written on it, known only to the one who receives it."

Here's an assignment for you: start a Bible study group in the city where Satan has his throne. I'm not sure where that city is today (although several "sin cities" come to mind), but in the first century, Satan's throne was in Pergamum. The devil's base of operations on earth was the capital city of the Roman province of Asia, a city of wealth, culture, religion—and spiritual darkness. On a hillside above the city stood an immense altar to the Greek god Zeus. It dominated the city. No one could miss it. The altar looked (from down below) like a giant throne. In Jesus' eyes, it was Satan's throne.

The amazing thing is that in the city where the forces of evil were so powerful, there was a church—a body of believers in Jesus. You would think that if the church were persecuted anywhere, it would be persecuted in Pergamum. But Satan had found a much more effective weapon. Instead of attacking the church from the outside, Satan cor-

In Other Words

We may not be called upon to die for Christ. There would be quite a thinning out of church members if we were.

Vance Havner, in *Repent or Else!* (Westwood, N.J.: Revell, 1958), 37.

Chains are the only fitting ornament for believers.

Polycarp, pastor in Smyrna, AD 155.

rupted the church from the inside. It was fashionable in Pergamum to be a church member. Offerings were up, attendance was way up, but the church had compromised its stand to make peace with the world. The name *Pergamum* means "to be joined in marriage"—and that's what was happening to the church. That's what happens in every Pergamum-style church. The demands of God's Word for spiritual and moral purity are lowered for the sake of popularity or acceptance. The pure church marries the harlot world.

Some of the people in the Pergamum church truly loved the Lord—and Jesus commends them—"you remain true to my name." These genuine Christians had stood firm in earlier days of persecution. We don't know who Antipas was (mentioned in verse 13), but he was killed right before their eyes. The Christians didn't back away from their commitment, even in the face of death. But that was in the past. Things were different. Jesus had a few things against them.

Two issues bothered Jesus—or perhaps it was two sides to the same issue. First, the church tolerated some people who held to the teaching of Balaam. The true Christians hadn't embraced that teaching yet, but they put up with people in the church who held to false teaching. Jesus makes a clear distinction between the true believers and the false. He refers to "you" (believers) and "them" (those who hold to the false teaching). Unless there's a change, Jesus will soon come to the true believers in correction, and he will fight against the false teachers who are allowed to function inside the church.

Understanding the doctrine of Balaam requires some background from the Old Testament. Balaam was a prophet who sold himself and who sold out God's people for money. The people of Israel had escaped from slavery in Egypt and had wandered for forty years in the wilderness. Now they were on their way to claim the land God had promised their forefathers. As they passed through the land of Moab, the Moabite king, Balak, hired Balaam to curse Israel. Several times Balaam tried, but when he opened his mouth, only words of blessing came out. Finally Balaam went home—without his money.

Then he was struck with a great idea. He sent an email to Balak and said, "If you want to see Israel suffer, get them involved in sin. You won't have to lift a finger against them because their God will bring judgment on them." Balak sent Moabite prostitutes into the Israelite camp, and before they knew it, a full-fledged sex party was going on. The women brought Moabite idols with them too. They seduced the people sexually and they seduced them spiritually—and it worked. Judgment came from God, and 24,000 people died at the hands of a holy God. (You can read Balaam's story in Numbers 22–24 and 31.)

The "teaching of Balaam" in the church at Pergamum said, "As long as you believe in God, as long as you go to church, as long as you keep up some superficial commitment as a Christian, you can live any way you want." The false teachers lured the Christians into the same sins that Israel was lured into—associating with idolatry (eating food sacrificed to idols) and sexual immorality. That teaching is still around, by the way.

OLD TESTAMENT INSIGHTS

The book of Revelation quotes and refers to the Old Testament more than any other New Testament book. Of the 404 verses in Revelation, 278 (69 percent) allude to or quote the Old Testament. John refers most to Daniel, Isaiah, Ezekiel, and the Psalms. Here in chapter 2, for example, Balaam and Balak are mentioned along with Jezebel and manna. In verse 27, Psalm 2:9 is quoted. The writer usually quotes rather loosely. John wasn't allowed to have his Old Testament scrolls in prison, so he quotes or paraphrases from memory.

If you want to learn more about Balaam, read Numbers 22–24 and 31. You will find a talking donkey in those chapters. Balaam is mentioned two other times in the New Testament: 2 Peter 2:15 and Jude 11.

For gruesome reading about Jezebel, check out 1 Kings 16:18–19, 21, 29–33 and 2 Kings 9.

If you want to know more about manna, read Exodus 16:11–35. Manna burgers anyone?

It says to immature Christians that their life on Sunday is different from their life on Monday. What you are at home or on a business trip doesn't have to match up with what you sing or say or profess at church.

We certainly are not saved by how we live. We are made right with God by grace alone. But how we live will demonstrate whether we really are God's child. It's not enough to have correct doctrines; we are also called to holy living.

We don't know much about "the teaching of the Nicolaitans" (verse 15), but what we do know suggests that it was similar in emphasis to the teaching of Balaam. They called themselves Christians but lived like the unbelieving world.

Jesus' words of counsel are few, but forceful:"Repent — repent, or else!" If they didn't take a different path — God's path — Jesus would come to them in chastening and would fight against those in the church who taught false doctrine. Either the believers cleaned things up or Jesus would.

His promise to those who faithfully follow his direction is "hidden manna" and "a white stone." Hidden manna pictures daily provision. Manna was the food God provided to Israel every day in the wilderness. In the same way, God will provide for those who follow him. The second gift is a white stone with a new name on it. The name may be God's name engraved on our hearts, or it may be a new name we receive in heaven; the white stone pictures our purity before God. We will be given entrance into God's presence forever.

Pergamum Christians in the twenty-first century look pretty convincing. They know the right words; they show up for church; they claim to be Christians. Upon closer examination, however, you will find things in their lives that shouldn't be there. They tolerate habits or relationships or attitudes that don't please God. If Pergamum Christians and Pergamum churches don't repent, they will find themselves in a fight. Jesus will fight against them, not for them. The Lord of the church is a holy Lord.

Thyatira: A Church in Trouble (Revelation 2:18 – 29)

"To the angel of the church in Thyatira write:

These are the words of the Son of God, whose eyes are like blazing fire and whose feet are like burnished bronze. I know your deeds, your love and faith, your service and perseverance, and that you are now doing more than you did at first.

Nevertheless, I have this against you: You tolerate that woman Jezebel, who calls herself a prophet. By her teaching she misleads my servants into sexual immorality and the eating of food sacrificed to idols. I have given her time to repent of her immorality, but she is unwilling. So I will cast her on a bed of suffering, and I will make those who commit adultery with her suffer intensely, unless they repent of her ways. I will strike her children dead. Then all the churches will know that I am he who searches hearts and minds, and I will repay each of you according to your deeds. Now I say to the rest of you in Thyatira, to you who do not hold to her teaching and have not learned Satan's so-called deep secrets, 'I will not impose any other burden on you, except to hold on to what you have until I come.'

To those who are victorious and do my will to the end, I will give authority over the nations—they 'will rule them with an iron scepter and will dash them to pieces like pottery'—just as I have received authority from my Father. I will also give them the morning star. Whoever has ears, let them hear what the Spirit says to the churches."

If you were to attend a Thyatira-style church in your community next Sunday, you would not suspect that anything was wrong—at first. Jesus even praises this church for their love and faith and ministry. They kept at it too. Jesus says they were doing more now than they did at first. The Thyatira Community Church where you live is a busy place. Every day of the week something is going on.

But if we've learned anything from the letters Jesus wrote to these seven churches, we've learned that things are not always as good as they appear on the surface. If you push a little deeper at Thyatira, you find rottenness on the inside. Thyatira is the wicked church. It's not just on the brink of embracing the world, like the church at Pergamum did; this church has married the world and moved in. Thyatira is an illustration of what happens to a Pergamum church that doesn't repent. Everything Jesus threatened against the Pergamum church he is ready to carry out against the Thyatira church. If you are a member of a corrupt church, you best get out before judgment falls.

The problem at the church at Thyatira centered on a woman—a woman in the church who should have been removed but wasn't. The Christians winked at a witch in their presence. Jesus calls her Jezebel (verse 20). I don't think that was her real name, but it describes her character. The real Jezebel was a non-Jewish woman in the Old Testament who married a king of Israel. Ahab took a foreign wife and welcomed her false gods into Israel. The immoral worship of the Canaanite god Baal and his consort Asherah soon replaced the worship of the Lord.

That's the kind of activity the woman at Thyatira was promoting. Jesus says that she was luring genuine Christians ("my servants") into sexual immorality. The church dinners were nothing more than hook-up opportunities for sexual sin. This Jezebel-like woman was also pushing the Christians to identify more closely with idolatry by persuading them to eat food that had been offered in sacrifice to false gods. The food itself was not contaminated, but buying it and eating it put these Christians too close to the pagan life from which Jesus had delivered them.

Jesus' third accusation against the woman was that she claimed to have access to secret knowledge. She called herself a prophet and said that God had given her special information that no one else had. Her so-called secret knowledge was nothing more than Satan's "deep secrets" (verse 24). So this was a cultish church, centered not on the Word of God but on the teaching of a persuasive leader.

The problem in Thyatira was that the Christians had tolerated this woman's presence and teaching far too long. So Jesus steps in to protect his people. Jesus begins to cleanse his church first with suffering. The woman is cast on a bed of suffering. Sickness or physical disability takes her out of commission. The Christians who have followed her teaching will suffer too — unless they repent. Jesus even uses death to purify his church. He says in verse 23: "I will strike her children dead." I think Jesus means her spiritual children, her most loyal followers. Those who refuse God's gracious invitation to repent will find their lives cut short.

The church that tolerates sin, the Christians who refuse to deal with open disobedience in their lives, will find themselves facing catastrophe at Jesus' hands. Jesus fights against them. All you can do for a wicked church is pray for repentance. If the leaders refuse and the people continue on in disobedience, find a new place to worship. Get out of Dodge.

In Other Words

I believe that every conceivable church trouble is covered in these letters of our Lord in Revelation and by them any church can be examined, the trouble diagnosed, and the remedy prescribed.

Vance Havner, in *Repent Or Else!* (Westwood, N.J.: Revell, 1958), 50.

Jesus closes the letter with some words of encouragement to the little group of faithful believers in Thyatira. He tells them to hold tight—not to some new secret wisdom but to the old truth they had been taught long before. Those who remain loyal to Jesus will receive authority and responsibility in Jesus' kingdom—and they will receive Jesus himself, the Morning Star.

Jesus ends every letter the same way: "Whoever has ears, let them hear what the Spirit says to the churches" (verses 7, 11, 17, 29). Jesus wants a pure church, but it will only be as pure as the people in it. Have you looked through the closets of your life lately? Whatever you find that dishonors or displeases Jesus should be carried to the curb and left there. Jesus is searching our hearts and minds right now.

Points to Remember

☑ The seven letters to the seven churches were written to seven actual first-century congregations—and still speak to churches and Christians today.

☑ In Ephesus, the Christians had lost the hot fire of love for Jesus.

☑ The Christians in Smyrna were being crushed by persecution and, in the process, released a sweet fragrance of loyalty to Jesus.

☑ Pergamum-style churches tolerate false teachers and put themselves on shaky ground.

☑ The church at Thyatira had an appealing outward appearance but a rotten heart.

CHAPTER 3

Something *Else* to Think about in Church

Something *Else* to Think about in Church

▶ Three more churches face Jesus' evaluation.
▶ Watch for a promise of escape from the Tribulation.
▶ Can you hear Jesus knocking?

MR. BLOCKHEAD
HEADS UP

Access Codes

Key Codes: Level 3

→ Sardis: A city in the Roman province of Asia
→ The book of life: The record in heaven of those who are genuine believers in Jesus
→ Philadelphia: Ancient Roman city of brotherly love
→ Synagogue: Worship center for Jewish people
→ Jews: Descendants of Abraham, Isaac, and Jacob; John and Paul were Jews, so was Jesus
→ Hour of trial: The future seven-year Tribulation
→ Laodicea: A city, pronounced *lay-od-i-see-uh*
→ Salve: A famous product produced in Laodicea

Sardis: Dead Church Walking (Revelation 3:1 – 6)

"To the angel of the church in Sardis write:

These are the words of him who holds the seven spirits of God and the seven stars. I know your deeds; you have a reputation of being alive, but you are dead. Wake up! Strengthen what remains and is about to die, for I have found your deeds unfinished in the sight of my God. Remember, therefore, what you have received and heard; hold it fast, and repent. But if you do not wake up, I will come like a thief, and you will not know at what time I will come to you.

Yet you have a few people in Sardis who have not soiled their clothes. They will walk with me, dressed in white, for they are worthy. Those who are victorious will, like them, be dressed in white. I will never blot out their names from the book of life, but will acknowledge their names before my Father and his angels. Whoever has ears, let them hear what the Spirit says to the churches."

Jesus finds nothing to praise in the church at Sardis. He commends a faithful few, but to the church as a whole he says, "You have a reputation of being alive, but you are dead." Don't get the impression from Jesus' statement that the church at Sardis was ready to fall apart. It was a busy place. The church had a reputation as a going, growing congregation. Other Christians looked at Sardis and wished they could have a program like that in their church. Church leaders throughout the region held Sardis up as a model for other churches. But in Jesus' eyes, the life the church once had was gone.

The organization at Sardis still functioned, but the organism was dead. It needed CPR. Sardis-style churches today seem to be alive, but they are just going through the motions. Jesus calls them to repent—and wake up.

Jesus put his finger on the problem: "I have found your deeds unfinished in the sight of my God" (verse 2). The people in the church at Sardis prayed, but their prayers never connected with the Lord. Prayer was just empty words—beautifully spoken but powerless. The worship at Sardis was well planned, masterfully performed, but it never went higher than the ceiling. The offering plates overflowed, but the people gave in order to impress others, not as a sacrifice to God. If you've ever been in a dead church, the program runs well. It's just empty and mechanical, with no connection to the life and power of the Holy Spirit.

Jesus rattles off five commands to this lifeless church and none of them are easy to obey. The only remedy for a dead church is resurrection in the power of the Spirit. So Jesus stands at the tomb of the Sardis church and shouts commands designed to jolt them back to life.

- *"Wake up"*: The church was asleep to what was really going on. Probably, when the church at Sardis first read this letter, they were shocked. "How can Jesus say we are dead? There must be some mistake. Just look at all that's going on. How can we be dead?" Lifeless Sardis churches never want to admit that genuine life is gone. Death has been so subtle that no one was aware it was happening. The first step back to life is admitting you are dead.
- *"Strengthen what remains"*: Jesus wasn't asking this church to toss out everything they were doing. He just wants them to infuse genuine spiritual life back into the outward motions. Worship

services should continue at Sardis—even beautifully planned and performed worship services—but make it more than performance. Make your praise to God the genuine expression of your heart to him. Continue to pray, but with new passion. Continue to give, but with a desire to see God use and multiply what is given to accomplish far more than you can imagine. Don't simply drop your money in the offering plate; put yourself in the plate. Give all you are and all you have to God.

- *"Remember what you have received and heard"*: Jesus wants the lifeless church to get back to the basics. He wants them to think back to the foundational truths of the faith. He wants them to reaffirm their love and commitment to Jesus. They need to learn again what it means to pray and to trust God and to serve others. Dead churches get that way because they forget the basics.

- *"Hold it fast"*: Once the people at Sardis remembered the basic truths of the Christian life, they were to cling to them. Jesus certainly isn't telling us to stay immature. We should be growing in knowledge. We should be exploring the deeper things of God's truth. It's great to scrape the theological Milky Way in high-flying doctrinal discussion. But never forget the simple, fundamental aspects of what it means to be a Christian. Loving God with all our hearts and loving others are still the greatest commands.

- *"Repent"*: The only hope for a lifeless church is change. Change your mind about the condition you are in—dead, not alive. Change your mind about what it will take to come alive again—God's power, not your efforts. Change your mind about what's really important as a church—God's glory, not your reputation.

Or I Will Come Like a Thief

Jesus adds a warning to his advice to the Sardis church: either repent, or you will receive a sudden, unexpected visit—a visit that will bring loss and judgment, like the visit of a thief.

The lifeless church or the lifeless Christian just going through the motions of worship every Sunday is in for a big shock. Jesus will show up when you least expect him and it won't be pleasant.

What's interesting to me is that a few people at Sardis had watched the church slowly die, and they had grieved over its path. They may have been in leadership at one time, but they were gradually moved out.

Occasionally they spoke up about the spiritual drift in the congregation, but their pleas and protests were ignored. Finally all they could do was pour out their hearts in prayer to God.

Jesus commends those faithful few—and makes some amazing promises to them.

- *"They will walk with me"*: Jesus promises close friendship with those who follow him in a difficult church. It's only the Lord's sustaining presence that keeps a faithful pastor or a faithful Christian church member going. He stays close to those who stay close to him.
- *They will be "dressed in white"*: These faithful few have not soiled their garments with compromise or disobedience. They will be clothed in the pure white garments of Christ's purity and goodness. That's Jesus' promise to all who believe in him and live in obedience to his Word.
- *"I will never blot out their names"*: The genuine Christians at Sardis have demonstrated their faith by remaining loyal to Jesus even when others have drifted away. They are secure in Christ's love and grace.
- *"I ... will acknowledge their names"*: Jesus promises that he will publicly affirm those who are faithful to him. The affirmation may not come in the arena of this life. The dead church may never listen to your pleas and may continue to write you off. But someday,

In Other Words

The hope of revival lies with the few.

Vance Havner, in *Repent or Else!* (Westwood, N.J.: Revell, 1958), 66.

One would hope that there are few churches like Sardis today, but there are many.... In such churches the righteous few must stand up and be counted. They must consider themselves missionaries to their own church and wake up those who are about to die while there is still time.

Grant Osborne, in *Revelation* (Grand Rapids: Baker, 2002), 181–82.

Jesus will acknowledge your loyalty in a much larger setting—before God the Father and all the angels. You may not find much affirmation on earth for your spiritual faithfulness, but this life is not all there is.

I'm not suggesting that you stand up in a lifeless church and pronounce some sentence of doom. People really will ignore you—or escort you out. I think the better path is to stay faithful to Christ and model by your life what a follower of Jesus really acts like. Then pray that God by his Spirit will call the lifeless church out of its sleep. Pray also that the church will hear his call and repent.

Philadelphia: Standing at an Open Door (Revelation 3:7–13)

"To the angel of the church in Philadelphia write:

These are the words of him who is holy and true, who holds the key of David. What he opens no one can shut, and what he shuts no one can open. I know your deeds. See, I have placed before you an open door that no one can shut. I know that you have little strength, yet you have kept my word and have not denied my name. I will make those who are of the synagogue of Satan, who claim to be Jews though they are not, but are liars—I will make them come and fall down at your feet and acknowledge that I have loved you. Since you have kept my command to endure patiently, I will also keep you from the hour of trial that is going to come upon the whole world to test those who live on the earth.

I am coming soon. Hold on to what you have, so that no one will take your crown. Those who are victorious I will make pillars in the temple of my God. Never again will they leave it. I will write on them the name of my God and the name of the city of my God, the new Jerusalem, which is coming down out of heaven from my God; and I will also write on them my new name. Whoever has ears, let them hear what the Spirit says to the churches."

The city of Philadelphia (in Asia, not in Pennsylvania) was founded as a missionary city. Around 140 BC a Greek ruler named Attalus saw how barbaric the people in this region were, and he determined to do something about it. He built Philadelphia to bring Greek culture and the Greek language to barbarians—and it worked. The whole region in John's day had become highly sophisticated and fiercely loyal to Rome.

Two hundred fifty years after Attalus, another door of opportunity opened in Philadelphia—a door not for the gospel of the Greeks but for the gospel of Christ. A small band of rather weak, unimpressive Christians stood before a door of great opportunity, a door Jesus had opened and a door no one could ever shut.

The letter to the church in Philadelphia is a letter of pure praise. There's no criticism or condemnation found anywhere in the letter. You won't find the word "repent" anywhere in Jesus' words. Philadelphia is the fruitful church. This is the letter I would want to receive from Jesus. These are the words any Christian wants to hear from the Lord. Jesus found in Philadelphia a small group of believers who were absolutely obedient to God's Word ("you have kept my word") and who were fiercely loyal to Jesus as Lord ("and have not denied my name"). When opposition arose, when persecution came, when it would have been easier to deny Jesus and confess that Caesar was Lord, these men and women stood firm.

In response to that kind of faithfulness, Jesus promises some amazing blessings. First he promises exaltation of the church before their enemies. We heard about "the synagogue of Satan" back in chapter 2. The reference is to Jews who aren't *true* Jews because they refuse to believe in Jesus as Messiah. The Jews in Philadelphia had opposed the Christians and done everything in their power to quash their movement. Someday, Jesus says, they will bow down to you and acknowledge Christ's love for his church. But not willingly. Jesus said, "I will *make* them come and fall down" (emphasis added).

I don't know when that happened. There may have been a day when the Jews of Philadelphia really did bow down to the Christians. But it *will* happen in the future. At the final judgment of unbelievers, every knee will bow to Christ. When unbelievers bow to Christ, they also acknowledge that Christ loves those who follow him. That is a great promise. The enemies of the church will someday acknowledge the authority of the very church they tried to destroy.

Jesus also promises a glorious exit from the world to the faithful church: "Since you have kept my command to endure patiently, I will also keep you from the hour of trial that is going to come on the whole world to test those who live on the earth" (verse 10). That is the clearest promise (I believe) in the Bible that the church will *not* enter the Tribulation. God is going to send seven years of judgment on the earth in the future. Revelation describes those years in detail in chapters 6–19. But Jesus says that genuine Christians will not experience that hour or time of trial.

Jesus does not say he will preserve us *through* the trial; he says he will take us *out* of the trial. He will keep us out of it by means of the rapture. Jesus will return in the air to take genuine Christians away—out of the earth and out of the time of testing. Jesus even adds in verse 11: "I am coming soon [or suddenly]." The faithful church lives in expectation of the rapture. Jesus could return at any moment. In that light, Jesus calls us to "hold on" to what we have. He challenges us to stay faithful, to stay loyal. Compromising our commitment doesn't mean we will miss out on the rapture; it means we will lose our reward, our crown of recognition, given by Jesus to those who hold fast to him in faithful obedience to the end.

If exaltation and rapture and rewards aren't enough, Jesus promises three gifts to those who are victorious:

July 1999

Nostradamus was a sixteenth-century French physician and astrologer. He's famous for his cryptic four-line poems that claim to be prophecies about the future. Supposedly he has accurately predicted the rise of Adolf Hitler, the mysterious death of Pope John Paul 1, and the September 11th attack on the twin towers of the World Trade Center. One of his clearest predictions centered on the year 1999:

> The year 1999, seven months,
> From the sky will come a great King of Terror;
> To bring back to life the great King of the Mongols,
> Before and after Mars to reign by good luck.

July 1999 is about the only thing that *is* clear in that weird little verse, but the seventh month of 1999 passed with very little activity on or around Mars and no sightings of the King of the Mongols.

August did make some end-of-the-world news that year. The surviving Branch Davidians (remember Waco, Texas?) were convinced that their former leader, David Koresh, would rise from the dead and judge the world. August 6, 1999, was 2,300 days after his death—a number the Davidians found in Daniel 8:14 and thought predicted their Messiah's return. This prediction proved false

1 Thessalonians 5:9

For God did not appoint us to suffer wrath but to receive salvation through our Lord Jesus Christ.

1 Thessalonians 5:23 – 24

May your whole spirit, soul and body be kept blameless at the coming of our Lord Jesus Christ. The one who calls you is faithful, and he will do it.

- *Stability*: Jesus will make us pillars in the temple of God (verse 12). In Philadelphia, when a person served as a faithful civic leader or ruler, the city would erect a pillar in one of its temples with the person's name on it. Everyone who passed by would remember the honored person. Those who are faithful to Jesus will become a pillar in God's temple. God will remember us and honor us.
- *Safety*: Once we are established in that temple, we will never leave it (verse 12). Philadelphia was famous for its earthquakes. Whenever the earth began to shake, the people would run from their homes and from the city to avoid being crushed by crumbling buildings. They were always leaving and coming. To those Christians, Jesus promises a city where they are safe. We will never have to leave the heavenly city.
- *Security*: Jesus will write three names on us—marks of ownership and protection. The first name tells who we belong to—"the name of my God"; the second name tells where we belong—"the name of the city of my God"; the third name tells who we are with— Jesus will write on us his own "new name" (verse 12).

What doors of spiritual opportunity stand open in your life? If you see an open door, don't hesitate. Step through it. The door was put there by Jesus. The door may seem small and unimpressive, but as you are faithful in small things, God will give you opportunity for larger things. God is absolutely loyal to us. How can we be less than wholeheartedly loyal to him?

Laodicea: The Disgusting Church (Revelation 3:14 – 22)

"To the angel of the church in Laodicea write:

These are the words of the Amen, the faithful and true witness, the ruler of God's creation. I know your deeds, that you are neither cold nor hot. I wish you were either one or the other! So, because you are lukewarm — neither hot nor cold — I am about to spit you out of my mouth. You say, 'I am rich; I have acquired wealth and do not need a thing.' But you do not realize that you are wretched, pitiful, poor, blind and naked. I counsel you to buy from me gold refined in the fire, so you can become rich; and white clothes to wear, so you can cover your shameful nakedness; and salve to put on your eyes, so you can see.

Those whom I love I rebuke and discipline. So be earnest, and repent. Here I am! I stand at the door and knock. If anyone hears my voice and opens the door, I will come in and eat with them, and they with me.

To those who are victorious, I will give the right to sit with me on my throne, just as I was victorious and sat down with my Father on his throne. Whoever has ears, let them hear what the Spirit says to the churches."

You would leave a Sunday service with the believers in the faithful church at Philadelphia feeling encouraged and strengthened and more deeply committed to Christ. If you went the next Sunday to the church in Laodicea, you would leave feeling sick — at least that's how Jesus felt when he came into the Laodicean church. What he saw nauseated him.

The big question I have when I read this letter is, Were these people in the church at Laodicea saved or not? Were they genuine believers in Jesus or just religious worldlings? I want to say they were not genuine

A FAMOUS PAINTING

In a painting seen around the world in churches and in homes, artist Holman Hunt captured the picture of Jesus standing at the door. He painted Jesus, wearing a crown of thorns, standing outside the bolted dark door of the human heart, patiently knocking. The original painting hangs in St. Paul's Cathedral in London. When it was first displayed, one art critic said, "Mr. Hunt, you have painted a masterpiece, but you have made a serious mistake. You have painted a door with no handle." The artist replied, "That is no mistake. The handle to the door of the human heart is on the inside."

believers, but Jesus identifies them as a church and gives some indication that a few in the church were saved. Sadly, even the handful of true believers were shallow and indifferent to Jesus. Most of the people filling the pews at Laodicea were lost.

The majority of people in Laodicean-type churches aren't genuine Christians, but they are very religious. That's the problem. The people attend services, pledge money, serve on church boards—but it's only an outward religion. The church is a club. It is the place to be on a Sunday morning. But there is no heartfelt devotion to Christ. The name of Christ is over the door; the people in the pews are comfortable; but Jesus is locked out. He is standing at the door of a Laodicean church— or of a Laodicean heart—and knocking.

The other six churches all receive at least some words of commendation from Jesus, but not this church. There's *nothing* to commend! I'm sure this letter upset a lot of people at Laodicea. They had listened to the other churches being evaluated, and they must have thought that Jesus was saving the best for last. Instead they hear this condemnation: "So because you are lukewarm—neither hot nor cold—I am about to spit you out of my mouth." The word "spit" is a polite translation; the original is actually the word for "vomit."

What makes Jesus sick is when people rely on themselves and their own good deeds to make them right with God. The hardest people to talk with about Jesus are not the people who are far from God and who know they are far from God. Those people are often eager to hear

Material prosperity can lead to spiritual poverty—a lesson the affluent Western church needs to take seriously. The church at Laodicea was proud and self-sufficient. They didn't need anyone's help, including the Lord's. The Laodicean church also came in for stern rebuke. The Philadelphian church had little strength and was desperate for God's power. That church received some of Jesus' greatest promises. I'm not anxious for the church to go through a time of oppression or persecution, but that may be what it takes to focus our attention once more on the things that matter most to Jesus.

about Jesus' love and forgiveness. The hardest people to talk with about Jesus are religious people—baptized but not born again, members of an earthly church but not members of Christ by faith. When you talk to religious people about Jesus, they say, "Don't worry about me. I'm OK. I've been baptized or confirmed or I'm a member of First Church"—and they shut out the gospel.

That's why Jesus says to the Laodiceans: "I wish you were either one or the other!—that you were either far from God and willing to admit it, because then you might listen to the gospel and believe, or that you were white-hot in love with me." Laodicean churches are *self-righteous*. They are resting their eternal destiny on their own good works.

Laodicean churches are also *self-deceived*. They *say*, "[We are] rich," but the reality is that they are wretched, pitiful, poor, blind and naked (verse 17). The *only* solution for a Laodicean is to receive from Jesus what he offers by grace—true riches, white garments, and eye salve for his or her blind eyes.

Then Jesus uses one of the most powerful pictures in the Bible of his seeking love for lost people. He portrays himself standing at the door of the church or standing at the door of a human heart and knocking. It's unlikely that the entire religious crowd at Laodicea would repent, but

In Other Words

The Laodicean church was a halfhearted church. Perhaps none of the seven letters is more appropriate to the [modern] church than this. It describes vividly the respectable, sentimental, nominal, skin-deep religiosity which is so widespread among us today. Our Christianity is flabby and anemic. We appear to have taken a lukewarm bath of religion.

> John R. W. Stott, in *What Christ Thinks of the Church*
> (Grand Rapids: Eerdmans, 1958), 116.

Here is the key to the sad state of many Christians and churches. There is a cheap, easy believism that does not believe and a receivism that does not receive. There is no real confession of Christ Jesus as Lord. It is significant that the word "Savior" occurs only twenty-four times in the New Testament, while the word "Lord" is found 433 times.

> Vance Havner, in *Repent or Else!* (Westwood, N.J.:
> Revell, 1958), 118

Jesus is hopeful that at least one will hear his knock or his voice calling. If *anyone* responds and opens the door, Jesus will enter that heart and change that life.

Before you shake your head in disgust at the Laodicean church, ask yourself one question: Would I be comfortable in the pews at Laodicea? It's possible to do all the right religious things and still be lost. You can pray and read the Bible and attend church. You may even be in the leadership of your church, but you have never believed in Jesus as Savior and Lord. What pleases God is not all our religious baggage but faith alone in his Son alone. If you are trusting in your religious activities to make you right with God, it won't work.

Points to Remember

- ☑ A few committed believers can wake up a sleeping church.

- ☑ Jesus promises to remove the faithful church from the time of Tribulation.

- ☑ Jesus stands outside the door of the human heart, knocking and calling for a response of faith.

- ☑ "Whoever has ears, let them hear what the Spirit says to the churches."

CHAPTER 4

On the Throne in Heaven

On the Throne in Heaven

- ▶ Glimpse an open door into heaven.
- ▶ God reigns in majesty!
- ▶ Powerful angels shout their adoration.
- ▶ The redeemed church falls down in worship.

Key Codes: Level 4

→ Elders: Spiritually mature leaders
→ Seven spirits of God: A picture of the fullness of God's Holy Spirit
→ Four living creatures: Majestic angels
→ Holy: Separate from all other beings; unique—and separate from all evil; pure
→ Worship: To ascribe worth

"Come Up Here"

After recording his vision of Jesus as the glorified King in chapter 1 and Jesus' words to his church in chapters 2 and 3, John now focuses on the future, beginning in chapter 4. This is the beginning of the prophetic section of Revelation. The present church age is addressed in chapters 2 and 3, but from this point on the church is pictured in heaven, not on earth. The events recorded in Revelation after this point occur (I believe) *after* the rapture, after all the believers in Jesus are taken out of the world.

We even have a hint of the rapture in John's own experience. In verse 1 of chapter 4 he sees a door into heaven standing open, and a voice says, "Come up here." From this point on, John sees events on earth from the perspective of heaven—just like the church will see the events of the Tribulation unfold. The church does not appear again on earth until Jesus' return is told about in Revelation 19. Believers or saints are mentioned in the intervening chapters, but these are references to people who believe in Jesus during the Tribulation. The church-age

Why can't I find the word "rapture" in the Bible?

If you pull a Bible concordance off the shelf (or use an online one) and look up "rapture," you will find—well—nothing. The word "rapture" is not found anywhere in the Bible. The word comes from a Latin word that an early church translator named Jerome used when he translated the Greek New Testament into Latin (around AD 400). In 1 Thessalonians 4:17, where our English Bible says we are "caught up" to be with Christ, Jerome used the Latin verb *rapere*. Eventually Christians coined the word "rapture."

The word may not appear in Scripture, but the *fact* of a future rapture is certainly taught in the Bible. (The key passage is 1 Thessalonians 4:13–18.) The word "trinity" doesn't appear in Scripture either—or "deity" or "omniscience"—but we use these words to identify truths that are taught there. The word "rapture" is a shorthand way of referring to Christ's return in the air to snatch away genuine believers.

believers are taken to heaven in the rapture *before* the Tribulation begins.

The Throne in Heaven (Revelation 4:1 – 6a)

> After this I looked, and there before me was a door standing open in heaven. And the voice I had first heard speaking to me like a trumpet said, "Come up here, and I will show you what must take place after this." At once I was in the Spirit, and there before me was a throne in heaven with someone sitting on it. And the one who sat there had the appearance of jasper and ruby. A rainbow that shone like an emerald encircled the throne. Surrounding the throne were twenty-four other thrones, and seated on them were twenty-four elders. They were dressed in white and had crowns of gold on their heads. From the throne came flashes of lightning, rumblings and peals of thunder. Before the throne, seven lamps were blazing. These are the seven spirits of God. Also before the throne there was what looked like a sea of glass, clear as crystal.

John enters heaven and is ushered into the throne room of God. It's a dazzling sight that John can hardly describe in words. In the center of everything is an enormous throne, and the person sitting on the throne shines with brilliant light. The person is obviously God the Father, the Ruler of all.

We know from other Scripture references that God the Father has no visible body. He is pure spirit. So what John sees is a representation of God, a visible outshining of the invisible God. That's why John sees powerful light and a majestic rainbow. God centers his being on this throne, but he is not confined to a body, like human beings or angelic beings are. He is not confined to heaven either. He is infinite and eternal; his presence encompasses all of creation.

Rapture.alt

Not every Christian agrees with the view that the rapture will occur before the Tribulation begins. Alternative positions can be found all over the Christian bookstore or the Internet or from church pulpits. Let me summarize some of the other views:

- *The end-of-the-Tribulation rapture*: Some Christians believe that the church will go through the Tribulation. God will protect some, but many church-age believers will die for their faith. They believe that the rapture occurs at the end of the Tribulation, just before Jesus returns in power to reign. Christians are removed, glorified, and immediately return with Christ. This view is called the post-Tribulation rapture.
- *The middle-of-the-Tribulation rapture*: Other Christians hold to a mid-Tribulation rapture view (or, as it is sometimes called, the pre-wrath rapture view). They believe that the rapture occurs at about the middle of the Tribulation, before the most intense judgment falls on humanity—before the time of God's wrath.
- *The not-everyone-will-go rapture*: The partial rapture view is based on a parable Jesus told about ten virgins waiting for the coming of the groom to receive his bride. Five of the virgins were ready; five were unprepared (Matthew 25:1–13). The prepared believers were taken into the feast, but the unprepared believers were left outside. In this view, obedient, expectant Christians will be taken at the rapture; unprepared, carnal Christians will be left behind to face the Tribulation.
- *The before-the-Tribulation rapture*: The view I hold and that is presented in this book (called the pre-Tribulation rapture view) says that all church-age believers will be removed from the earth before the Tribulation begins.

As John's eyes adjust to the stunning brilliance of heaven, he sees something else. Around God's throne, twenty-four smaller thrones are arranged, and seated on those thrones are beings John calls elders. John doesn't tell us who the elders are, so we have to try to interpret who they are based on other clues.

The fact that John calls them "elders" seems to indicate that they are humans and not angels. The word "elder" is used in the Bible to point to people who have spiritual authority in Israel or in the church. Angels are never called "elders" in the Scripture. (The only possible exception is in Isaiah 24:23, but even there it's not clearly a reference to angels.)

Another clue is that the elders possess items that Jesus has promised to those who are overcomers in the church: white garments (Revelation 3:5), crowns (Revelation 2:10; 3:11), and a throne (Revelation 3:21). The crowns the elders wear are not kingly crowns (diadems) but victor's crowns, the kind promised throughout the New Testament to Christians who faithfully follow Jesus.

I think the best view of who these elders are is that they are leaders or representatives of the entire church. All church-age believers were taken to heaven in the rapture, and now John sees them represented in the twenty-four elders. We are resurrected in glorified bodies and have been rewarded for our faithfulness. At this point, the church has faced the judgment-seat evaluation before Jesus, and we have received crowns of reward. Now we are clothed in garments of purity and are seated in majesty around God's throne to see and to participate in the next phase of God's plan.

Help File

OTHER BIBLICAL "RAPTURES"

There are several "catching up" events in Scripture:

- *Enoch* was taken up to heaven without experiencing death (Genesis 5:24; Hebrews 11:5).
- *Elijah* was taken up to heaven in a whirlwind and chariot of fire (2 Kings 2:11).
- *Jesus* was taken up to heaven in a cloud (Acts 1:9).
- *Paul* was caught up to heaven and then later returned (2 Corinthians 12:1–4).
- *Two witnesses* later in Revelation will be killed, rise from the dead, and be snatched into heaven (Revelation 11:3–12).

2 Corinthians 5:10

For we must all appear before the judgment seat of Christ, that everyone may receive what is due them for the things done while in the body, whether good or bad.

1 Timothy 6:15 – 16

God, the blessed and only Ruler, the King of kings and Lord of lords, who alone is immortal and who lives in unapproachable light, whom no one has seen or can see. To him be honor and might forever.

Four Living Creatures (Revelation 4:6b – 8)

In the center, around the throne, were four living creatures, and they were covered with eyes, in front and in back. The first living creature was like a lion, the second was like an ox, the third had a face like a man, the fourth was like a flying eagle. Each of the four living creatures had six wings and was covered with eyes all around, even under his wings. Day and night they never stop saying:

"'Holy, holy, holy
is the Lord God Almighty,'
who was, and is, and is to come."

Everything in Revelation 4 centers on the throne. Fourteen times in one short chapter the word "throne" appears.

- *On the throne*, John sees the inapproachable light of the invisible God.
- *Above the throne*, John sees a radiant glowing emerald rainbow.
- *Circling the throne* were twenty-four thrones on which representatives of the church were seated.
- *From the throne* came flashes of lightning and booms of thunder.
- *In front of the throne* were seven lamps, a representation of the fullness of the presence of the Holy Spirit.
- *Surrounding the throne* was a smooth brilliant "sea" of crystal, reflecting and magnifying the light.

The central image of Revelation is in chapter 4, the scene that meets John's eyes when he passes through the heavenly door: God seated on a great throne and surrounded by perpetual worship. This is the core reality, more real than everything else we know. Next to it, all other things become strangely unreal.

> Paul Spilsbury, in *The Throne, the Lamb and the Dragon: A Reader's Guide to the Book of Revelation* (Downers Grove, Ill.: InterVarsity, 2002), 51.

Worship is the essential and central act of the Christian. We do many things in preparation for and as a result of worship: sing, write, witness, heal, teach, paint, serve, help, build, clean, smile. But the centering act is worship.

> Eugene Peterson, in *Reversed Thunder: The Revelation of John and the Praying Imagination* (New York: HarperSanFrancisco, 1988), 140.

CROWNS

The word used in the Bible for a Christian's rewards is not the word for a king's crown but the word for the wreath given to the winner in an athletic contest. The rewards will be visible evidence of faithfulness to the Lord. But we won't wear these crowns for long! We will lay them before the Lord in recognition of his grace and his love for us (Revelation 4:10).

Here are the different crowns mentioned in the Bible:

- *Crown of life* for enduring through trial (James 1:12; Revelation 2:10)
- *Crown of righteousness* for those who eagerly look for Jesus' return and live obedient lives in light of his coming (2 Timothy 4:8)
- *Crown of glory* for servant-leaders (1 Peter 5:4)
- *The incorruptible crown* for consistent self-discipline (1 Corinthians 9:24–27)
- *Crown of rejoicing* for faithfully sharing the gospel and bringing people to faith in Jesus Christ (1 Thessalonians 2:19)

Next, at the four corners of the throne, John sees four magnificent creatures—powerful angels who stand in readiness before God. In John's vision the angels are covered with eyes—a picture of their attention and watchfulness. From John's vantage point each angel seems to have a different face—one is a lion, the second an ox, the third a human face, and the fourth an eagle's form. Most likely all four creatures each had four different faces, but they stood so that only one was visible from each direction. (Compare the living beings Ezekiel saw in Ezekiel 1:4–14.) To four faces and many eyes we have to add six wings (just like the six-winged seraphs that Isaiah saw in Isaiah 6)—a picture of their swiftness and power.

The four creatures around God's throne have one job, one compelling desire. Day and night, constantly, they speak words of adoration and honor to God—"Holy, holy, holy is the Lord God Almighty." Worship is announcing God's worth, God's worthiness, to him and to all who will listen. These angels exist to proclaim God's worth, to exalt and honor God's character. They say back to God what they have come to learn about his nature, and they praise him and thank him that he is the way he is.

These magnificent angels have seen firsthand the holiness of God. He is pure, totally free from sin, deceit, trickery, or evil. God is light, with no darkness mixed in at all. God doesn't have a dark side or a hidden agenda. He's never in a bad mood. God is and has always been and will always be the same—absolutely perfect in every aspect of his character.

Falling-Down Worship (Revelation 4:9–11)

Whenever the living creatures give glory, honor and thanks to him who sits on the throne and who lives for ever and ever, the twenty-four

FOUR FACES — FOUR GOSPELS

Help File

The early church fathers saw the four faces of the four living creatures as representations of the four gospels in the New Testament. Even today on church banners or in stained glass, you will see the four gospels pictured as the four faces or forms of Revelation 4:7—Matthew as a lion (representing Jesus' royalty), Mark as an ox (Jesus' servanthood), Luke as a man (Jesus' humanity), and John as an eagle (Jesus' deity). Most interpreters reject the idea that John intended for us to see the biblical gospels in these faces. It was just a fanciful idea of some early Christian writers who wanted to see a Christian symbol in every word of Revelation.

Bible Networking

Isaiah 6:1 – 3

In the year that King Uzziah died, I saw the Lord seated on a throne, high and exalted, and the train of his robe filled the temple. Above him were seraphs, each with six wings: With two wings they covered their faces, with two they covered their feet, and with two they were flying. And they were calling to one another:

> "Holy, holy, holy is the LORD Almighty:
> the whole earth is full of his glory."

Ezekiel 10:11 – 12

The cherubim [a rank of mighty angels] went in whatever direction the head faced, without turning as they went. Their entire bodies, including their backs, their hands and their wings, were completely full of eyes.

Jeremiah 17:12

> A glorious throne, exalted from the beginning,
> is the place of our sanctuary.

---

elders fall down before him who sits on the throne and worship him who lives for ever and ever. They lay their crowns before the throne and say:

> "You are worthy, our Lord and God,
> to receive glory and honor and power,
> for you created all things,
> and by your will they were created
> and have their being."

The "holy, holy, holy" that the four living creatures speak to God is the first of several hymns or psalms in the book of Revelation. As these angels give adoration to God, the twenty-four elders (who I believe represent the redeemed and raptured church in heaven) fall down in humble worship to God. We won't just bow down or even kneel down; we will fall down in praise and joy and thankfulness to God. Our worship in

In the ancient world, a vassal king or a conquered ruler would show submission to his conqueror by removing his own crown and laying it at the victor's feet. In heaven, we will take the tokens of our faithfulness and loyalty to Christ and lay them before the Father's throne. We have been conquered—not by overwhelming power but by the compelling love and grace of God. We lay our crowns down, not as a sign of disrespect for them but as an acknowledgment that whatever we were able to accomplish in life emerged from the abundance of God's mercy to us. It's surrender, but in the words of the old hymn, it's "sweet surrender"—a sense of yieldedness to God that can mark our lives each day. We remove our control over our own lives and yield that authority to our King. His will, not our own desires, sets the agenda for our lives.

Bringing on the Final Judgment

Jim Jones started the People's Temple in Indianapolis in the 1950s as an urban mission to the poor. By the 1970s, Jones had proclaimed himself to be the Messiah and had predicted that the United States would be destroyed in either a racial war or a nuclear holocaust. Jones and his followers moved to a four-thousand-acre colony in Guyana, South America. When congressman Leo Ryan and some journalists went down to investigate charges of abuse in 1978, security guards opened fire. The congressman and a few others were killed. Knowing that troops would be on the way, Jones called his followers to mass suicide by drinking poison-laced Kool-Aid. Those who resisted were forcibly injected with poison or were shot. A total of 638 adults and 276 children died.

heaven will not be boring or repetitious. It will be genuine and immediate and ongoing—without fatigue, without concern for when the worship service will end. We will be lost in wonder before God.

We will take the crowns of reward that we received at the judgment seat of Christ and lay those crowns before our God. It's not that we don't value God's rewards; it's just that we value God more! We realize that, even though Jesus gave us crowns as rewards for faithfulness and obedience to him and even martyrdom, every act of faith and loyalty came from God's empowering Spirit within us. Our greatest acts of sacrifice and commitment to the Lord are only small expressions of gratitude for God's grace to us. We will lay our crowns at his feet in humble recognition that he is worthy of our complete obedience and love forever.

And that's the song we sing to him—"You are worthy, our Lord and God, to receive glory and honor and power." Heaven will be a place of spontaneous, joyful worship to God. Maybe that's why our lives aren't more heavenly right now. We attend worship services, we sing worship

Help File

CHRISTIAN RECONSTRUCTION

Postmillennialism is the view that, through the gradual spread of the gospel message, the world will become more and more Christianized until humanity enters a golden age of peace. Jesus returns *after* this millennial age for the final judgment, and then eternity begins. Believers in postmillennialism were fairly abundant at the end of the nineteenth century, but World Wars I and II produced dramatic declines in their numbers.

The view is experiencing a resurgence, however, through two groups. Some Pentecostal leaders are advocates of Dominion Theology, which teaches that the charismatic movement is God's way of reclaiming the earth from Satan. Once believers understand the dominion God has given them over culture and politics, they can begin to exercise greater and greater influence for God in those arenas.

Televangelists Pat Robertson and Kenneth Copeland are prominent advocates of the dominion view.

A related view arises out of Presbyterian soil. Christian Reconstruction teaches that the church is responsible to bring about a theocracy in America and a gradual return to biblical law as the basis for our society and government. The Bible becomes the Constitution of the nation. Authors Gary DeMar and Gary North are well-known Christian Reconstructionists.

The goal of both groups is to make God's rule a reality on earth. They believe that this goal can be accomplished through human effort and gradual change. Premillennialists (the view taught in this book) believe that God's direct rule will come only through God's initiative and Jesus' presence when he returns in power and glory.

Bible Networking

1 Kings 22:19

I saw the LORD sitting on his throne with all the host of heaven standing around him on his right and on his left.

Psalm 96:9

Worship the LORD in the splendor of his holiness;
tremble before him, all the earth.

The title "the Lord God Almighty" appears seven times in Revelation (1:8; 4:8; 11:17; 15:3; 16:7; 19:6; 21:22).

songs, we talk about personal worship, but we so rarely engage our minds and hearts and bodies in true worship.

Here's an exercise you can try: The next time you go to church, envision Jesus above the platform or altar. As you pray, pray to him. As you sing words of adoration, sing them to him. It doesn't matter if you go to a church that uses a formal worship style or one that encourages people to dance in the aisles. The focus of worship is not ourselves or the people around us or the people in leadership; the focus of worship is always the Lord.

You can even worship the Lord right now. Read the words of Revelation 4:11, but read them to the Lord as a genuine expression of how you feel about him in your heart. Pray the words. Sing the words. Be concerned with only one thing—that the Lord knows how much you love him.

Points to Remember

- ☑ John is called up to heaven to see what God has planned for the future.

- ☑ John is ushered into the throne room of heaven where God reigns in majesty.

- ☑ The raptured church sings praise to God and falls down in humble worship before him, laying their crowns of reward at his feet.

A Slain Lamb and a Sealed Scroll Revelation 5

CHAPTER 5

A Slain Lamb and a Sealed Scroll

A Slain Lamb and a Sealed Scroll

▶ A sealed scroll in God's hand—and a great search for someone to open it
▶ A lamb appears in heaven.
▶ Jesus alone is worthy!
▶ More singing and shouting

Access Codes

Key Codes: Level 5

→ Scroll: Leather or papyrus, written on and rolled up
→ Elders: Representatives of the raptured church; introduced in chapter 4
→ Tribe of Judah: One of the extended families that made up the people of Israel; Judah was one of Jacob's sons
→ David: The greatest earthly king of Israel
→ Seven spirits of God: The Holy Spirit in his full presence; seven is the number of completeness
→ Angels: Powerful personal beings created by God as his servants and messengers

Watch the Lamb!

The exaltation of God the Father in chapter 4 leads to the exaltation of God the Son in chapter 5. This is one of the great passages of the Bible—a chapter that opens our understanding in several directions and changes everything before and after. Jesus is pictured in this passage as the one person toward which all history is moving. He is also the one who will set events in motion that will bring human history to its final end. The key character in the human drama, the central person in God's future plan, the one figure who brings the entire biblical story together, is Jesus. He's the Lion, and he's the Lamb. You can't read this chapter and not feel your heart fill with praise and adoration for Jesus—and some of it may burst from your lips before we are done! Go ahead and let that praise out. It's good practice for heaven.

Scene 1: A Sealed Scroll (Revelation 5:1)

Then I saw in the right hand of him who sat on the throne a scroll with writing on both sides and sealed with seven seals.

As John looks more closely at God the Father seated on the throne in heaven, he sees a scroll in God's right hand. The scroll has two interesting features: it is sealed, and it is written on both sides. God has filled the scroll with words. There is no room left for John's additions—and the scroll is sealed so no one can tamper with it.

The seals were blobs of soft wax or clay pressed over the edges of the scroll to keep it closed. As the wax dried or the clay hardened, the seals served as protection for the scroll. Obviously anyone could break wax or clay fairly easily, but it would be impossible to reseal the document once the seals were broken. The owner of the scroll would know immediately that someone had opened the scroll and likely changed or compromised the contents.

The scroll probably was not sealed along the outside edge with all seven seals. Later when Jesus begins to break the seals, as each seal is broken, a portion of the scroll is opened and its contents explored. It's better, I think, to see the scroll as sealed along the upper or lower edge at various places. Breaking the first seal allows a person to read part of the scroll but not all of it. Before anyone can read more, the second seal has to be broken and so on through all seven seals.

The big question is, What is written on this scroll? Lots of good suggestions have been made, but I think it's clear that the scroll contains

TWO-SIDED SCROLLS

Most scrolls were written on only one side, the inside. Two-sided scrolls are called "opisthographs" (from a Greek word meaning "on the other side"). The scroll John saw was made either of papyrus (an ancient form of paper) or parchment (smooth leather from sheep or goats).

Most scrolls were about ten meters (twenty-five feet) long and usually had ornate wooden rollers attached at each end to make rolling and unrolling easier.

the rest of the book of Revelation. God's plan for defeating and judging evil and for reclaiming his creation is laid out in Revelation 6 through 22. What John sees about the future from this point on emerges from the scroll. As each section is opened, John doesn't simply read that section; it comes to life right in front of him.

God's plan to end sin's day is complete. Nothing needs to be added. The only problem is that the scroll is sealed. Unless someone is found who has the authority and power to open the scroll, God's plan will never be carried out. Unless someone worthy enough to open the scroll steps up, God's kingdom will not come. So the search begins.

Scene 2: The Search (Revelation 5:2 – 5)

> And I saw a mighty angel proclaiming in a loud voice, "Who is worthy to break the seals and open the scroll?" But no one in heaven or on earth or under the earth could open the scroll or even look inside it. I wept and wept because no one was found who was worthy to open the scroll or look inside. Then one of the elders said to me, "Do not weep! See, the Lion of the tribe of Judah, the Root of David, has triumphed. He is able to open the scroll and its seven seals."

To John's astonishment, a mighty angel steps up and makes a proclamation to the universe: "Who is worthy to open the scroll?" The person God looks for must have the authority to open the scroll. The idea is that whoever breaks the seals must also have the power to carry out God's final plan. This is not a job for the curious or the weak. Whoever opens

Bible Networking

Daniel 12:4

But you, Daniel, close up and seal the words of the scroll until the time of the end.

Isaiah 29:11

For you this whole vision is nothing but words sealed in a scroll. And if you give the scroll to someone who can read, and say, "Read this, please," they will answer, "I can't; it is sealed."

Future FAQs

Will we really play harps in heaven?

While we sometimes joke about sitting on a cloud and strumming on a harp in heaven, here in Revelation 5 we are pictured as holding a harp in one hand and a bowl of incense in the other.

Obviously, you can't play a harp with both hands full! The implication, however, is that we will use the harps to accompany the new song we sing. The harp John refers to is a ten- or twelve-string lyre often used in the Jewish temple as an accompaniment to worship. The harp was King David's instrument of choice. First Samuel 16:16 and several psalms mention harps as the primary musical instrument that accompanied the singing of the psalms (Psalms 33:2; 57:8; 98:5). Harps added a sense of festive joy to the worship of the Lord. The book of Revelation mentions harps on two other occasions (14:2 and 15:2), both depicting times of joy-filled worship to the Lord. So it looks as though we *will* play harps. The real question is: Will we have to attend harp *practice* in heaven?

the scroll must have sufficient moral weight to see the plan through to the end.

As the call goes out, no one steps up to volunteer. No angel, no human, no demon—no one has the right and no one has the might to open the scroll and complete God's plan. If you were listening to the sound track of Revelation 5, it would begin with a loud cry from a powerful angel. That would be followed by a loud silence—and then you would hear an old man crying. John began to weep.

John is not crying simply because he was curious and wants to know what is in the scroll. He is crying because, if no one is found to open the scroll, God's redemption of his world will never be carried out and God's kingdom will never come. He's weeping over an unredeemed world and unjudged evil. John cries and cries until a hand touches his shoulder.

One of the elders, a representative of the church, tells John to stop crying. The elder knows someone who is worthy to open the scroll, someone with all the authority of God himself. "The Lion of the tribe of Judah, John. He has triumphed. He is the victor. He is able to open the scroll."

As John turns to see this mighty Conqueror, this great Lion, his eyes fall instead on a lamb.

Bible Networking

Genesis 49:8 – 10

"Judah, your brothers will praise you;
  your hand will be on the neck of your enemies;
  your father's sons will bow down to you.
You are a lion's cub, Judah;
  you return from the prey, my son.
Like a lion he crouches and lies down,
  like a lioness—who dares to rouse him?
The scepter will not depart from Judah,
  nor the ruler's staff from between his feet,
until he to whom it belongs shall come
  and the obedience of the nations be his."

Romans 8:34

Christ Jesus who died—more than that, who was raised to life—is at the right hand of God and is also interceding for us.

Scene 3: The Savior (Revelation 5:6 – 7)

Then I saw a Lamb, looking as if it had been slain, standing in the center before the throne, encircled by the four living creatures and the elders. The Lamb had seven horns and seven eyes, which are the seven spirits of God sent out into all the earth. He went and took the scroll from the right hand of him who sat on the throne.

Probably no animal seems more powerless to us than a lamb—soft, cuddly, cute. But the lamb John sees standing right in front of God's throne, within the circle of the four living creatures, is a very unusual animal. First of all, it has seven horns and seven eyes! The horns picture power, and the number seven conveys the idea of completeness. This gentle-looking lamb possesses absolute power. Seven eyes portray the lamb's wisdom and knowledge—an all-knowing lamb.

The most unusual aspect of this lamb is that it looks "as if it had been slain"—literally the lamb stands there "with its throat cut." When an animal was brought as a sacrifice to the temple in the Old Testament, the worshiper would confess his sins over the animal, and then, with a swift flash of the knife, the animal's throat was cut. The animal died in place of the guilty sinner. The lamb John sees in Revelation 5 has its throat cut just like a sacrifice—but the lamb is not dead! The lamb standing in the center of everything is very much alive!

The lamb is obviously a picture, a symbol, for the true Lion of Judah and the final sacrifice for human sin, Jesus Christ. Jesus died a violent, cruel death, but he rose again as proof that sin's debt was fully paid. He is the Conqueror, the Lamb slain but alive forever. Jesus is the one who is worthy to open the scroll. He has the *right* to reclaim the world because he died to redeem it. He also has the *might* to reclaim the world since he is the all-powerful Son of God. Jesus is the only person in all the universe who is qualified to open the scroll.

Scene 4: The Song (Revelation 5:8–14)

> And when he had taken it, the four living creatures and the twenty-four elders fell down before the Lamb. Each one had a harp and they

Jesus' victory came at the cost of death. He stands alive in heaven but marked by his cruel death. Jesus taught the same principle of "dying so we can live" to his disciples:

> Unless a kernel of wheat falls to the ground and dies, it remains only a single seed. But if it dies, it produces many seeds. Those who love their life will lose it, while those who hate their life in this world will keep it for eternal life.
>
> John 12:24–25

The rules in Christ's kingdom are almost always the reverse of the rules in the world's kingdom. Success on Wall Street or in Washington comes to those who are strongest and who have the most clout. Success in Jesus' kingdom comes through sacrifice and weakness. Jesus didn't just tell us that this is the way it is; he modeled it by enduring the cross.

were holding golden bowls full of incense, which are the prayers of God's people. And they sang a new song, saying:

> "You are worthy to take the scroll
>   and to open its seals,
> because you were slain,
>   and with your blood you purchased for God
>   members of every tribe and language and people and
>   nation.
> You have made them to be a kingdom and priests to serve our
>   God,
>   and they will reign on the earth."

Then I looked and heard the voice of many angels, numbering thousands upon thousands, and ten thousand times ten thousand. They encircled the throne and the living creatures and the elders. In a loud voice they were saying:

> "Worthy is the Lamb, who was slain,
>   to receive power and wealth and wisdom and strength
>   and honor and glory and praise!"

Then I heard every creature in heaven and on earth and under the earth and on the sea, and all that is in them, saying:

> "To him who sits on the throne and to the Lamb
>   be praise and honor and glory and power,
>   for ever and ever!"

The four living creatures said, "Amen," and the elders fell down and worshiped.

The Lamb takes decisive action. He takes the scroll from the Father's hand, and by that

Try, Try Again

February 4, 1962

The unusual alignment of planets on this day had a lot of end-of the-world people going crazy. A solar eclipse added to the tension. People in Bombay held a prayer vigil. Folks in America stocked up on food and headed for those little-used fallout shelters. The planetary episodes passed without incident. But according to the now-deceased psychic Jeane Dixon, the Antichrist was born the next day somewhere in the Middle East. What was Osama's birthday again?

act he sets in motion the final redemption of all creation. God's plan *will* be carried out! God's kingdom on earth *will* come! Jesus will see to it that all of God's promises are fulfilled!

At that point, a great wave of praise rolls out from the throne through the whole universe. First, those closest to the throne fall down in worship to the Lamb. The Lamb receives exactly the same worship as God the Father received back in chapter 4. The Lamb is God, just as the Father is God. The representatives of the church each have a harp and a bowl of incense, which pictures the prayers of believers rising up to God. (If you've ever wondered where the popular idea came from that we will sit around strumming harps in heaven, this is the place.) In joyful adoration the church and the four living creatures chant a new song of worship and praise to the Lamb.

The hymn has three parts:

- A *declaration of the worthiness of Jesus*: "You are worthy to take the scroll."
- An *announcement of the work Jesus accomplished* in order to qualify as our Redeemer: "You were slain!"
- A *list of the wonderful results* that come to the followers of the Lamb: "You have made them to be a kingdom and priests."

In Other Words

God desired a multicultural body of Christ from the very start. . . . Billy Graham notes that he grew up on a small southern farm where he rarely considered the situation of African-Americans; but once he realized the implications the gospel had for race relations, he took down the ropes separating blacks and whites in a southern crusade in 1952. From then on, he refused ever to preach at a segregated crusade.

Craig Keener, in *Revelation* (NIV Application Commentary;
Grand Rapids: Zondervan, 2000), 195.

The only place you find the church in Revelation 4 – 19 is in heaven, as the twenty-four elders who are seated on thrones, dressed in white, crowned with crowns, worshiping the Lamb.

Mark Hitchcock, in *Could the Rapture Happen Today?*
(Sisters, Ore.: Multnomah, 2005), 77.

Bible Networking

Isaiah 42:10

> Sing to the LORD a new song,
>   his praise from the ends of the earth.

Psalm 40:3

> [The LORD] put a new song in my mouth,
>   a hymn of praise to our God.

Daniel 7:9 – 10

> "As I looked,
>
> "thrones were set in place,
>   and the Ancient of Days took his seat.
> His clothing was as white as snow;
>   the hair of his head was white like wool.
> His throne was flaming with fire,
>   and its wheels were all ablaze.
> A river of fire was flowing,
>   coming out from before him.
> Thousands upon thousands attended him;
>   ten thousand times ten thousand stood before him."

Jesus' saving work has embraced the whole world—"every tribe and language and people and nation" are represented in the raptured church. Our ethnic distinctions and racial features will not disappear in heaven. Our languages will remain as well, although we will certainly be able to understand each other and sing with one voice to God. But all the diversity of the human race will be celebrated in heaven without prejudice or fear or misunderstanding. As his redeemed people, we will sing a new song to Jesus as we begin to see God's promises fulfilled.

As the words of the hymn echo through the throne room, suddenly the house lights come on, and John sees an enormous host of angels surrounding the throne and the living creatures and the redeemed church. Millions of angels are standing on tiptoe to watch this magnificent moment unfold. They have been waiting for this day to come for a long time. Angels have existed since the beginning of creation, and they have witnessed mankind's corruption and rebellion over long centuries of time. They have also witnessed God's patience and his willingness to provide his Son as a sacrifice for lost men and women. But now mankind's day is coming to an end, and Jesus will take back all that Adam and Eve and their descendants had lost.

So the angels, in a loud voice, extend the wave of praise outward: "Worthy is the Lamb, who was slain, to receive power and wealth and wisdom and strength and honor and glory and praise!" Jesus didn't have those things when he came to earth to grow up unnoticed in Galilee and to die under a curse on a Roman cross. But, praise God, he has all those things in his control now—and he is worthy of them all.

Then the wave of adoration moves out to every creature in heaven and on earth and in the sea. The whole created universe joins in a shout of praise that God's plan to reclaim his world is about to begin. Birds will sing, sea lions will bark God's glory, elephants will trumpet—the entire universal chorus will give honor and glory and power to God and to the Lamb. That's one praise gathering none of us will want to miss.

The four living creatures respond to the universe's song with one word—"Amen!" It means "so be it," or we might say, "Yes, Lord!" The church is so overcome that we don't say a word. We fall down—and worship. We cannot begin to fathom the wonder of that experience. As moving as our worship may be at times on earth, our deepest experiences here will all fade in the power of that day in heaven when Jesus steps up to take the scroll from the Father. All we can do right now is imagine what that moment will be like.

Points to Remember

- ☑ God's plan for the final redemption of his world is all laid out—but someone must be found who is qualified to carry it out to the end.

- ☑ John weeps when no one steps forward, but then he is told that Jesus, the Lamb, is worthy to open the sealed scroll and carry out God's plan.

- ☑ When Jesus takes the scroll from the Father, a great wave of praise sweeps through heaven and earth as angels, redeemed human beings, and all creation sings praise to the Lamb.

CHAPTER 6

Storm Riders

Storm Riders

▶ Jesus begins to open the end-times scroll.
▶ As each seal is broken, a new judgment sweeps over the world.
▶ The people who live on earth during the Tribulation will *not* be atheists.
▶ Some people would rather die than face God's judgment!

MR. BLOCKHEAD
HEADS UP

Access Codes

Key Codes: Level 6

→ The Lamb: Jesus
→ Scroll: God's plan for the wrap-up of history; the scroll was given to Jesus in chapter 5
→ Seals: Soft wax or clay pressed over the edges of a document and allowed to dry; prevents tampering or unauthorized access
→ Four living creatures: Powerful angels who stand around God's heavenly throne
→ Four horsemen of the Apocalypse: The four riders revealed as Jesus breaks the first four seals on the scroll
→ Hades: Temporary dwelling place of the spirits of unrighteous people; they go there at death and remain until the final judgment

And So It Begins . . .

Revelation 6 marks the beginning of the Tribulation on earth — seven years of relentless judgment from God. Everything up to this point has been preparation. In chapter 1 John is prepared to receive the prophecy. In chapters 2 and 3 the church is prepared to escape the horrors that will come on the rest of humanity. In chapters 5 and 6 heaven is prepared as the place from which the judgments are sent.

John stands at the edge of heaven and, as each seal on the scroll is broken, he turns to see the judgment unfold on the earth. John doesn't simply read a new section of the scroll each time. As the seal is broken and a fresh section of the scroll is unrolled, the scene springs to life in front of him. He literally "sees" each judgment emerge and play itself out on the world stage.

As Jesus breaks the first four seals, four riders on four different colored horses burst from the scroll. Each rider is called out by one of the four living creatures around God's throne. They say "Come!" or "Go forth!" John's readers would immediately connect this shout to a scene in the amphitheaters of the Roman Empire. A herald (think "stadium announcer") would call each chariot and driver into the arena at the beginning of a race with the same word—"Come!"

The four horsemen of the Apocalypse (as these gents are known) are a widely used symbol in literature and popular culture to refer to forces that signal the end of human history. The riders and the destructive power they exercise over the earth picture the chaos and collapse that will mark the entire span of the Tribulation.

First Seal Broken (Revelation 6:1 – 2)

I watched as the Lamb opened the first of the seven seals. Then I heard one of the four living creatures say in a voice like thunder, "Come!" I looked, and there before me was a white horse! Its rider held a bow, and he was given a crown, and he rode out as a conqueror bent on conquest.

Help File

THE FOUR HORSEMEN

Horses and riders are mentioned three hundred times in the Bible, but none of those references are as famous as these four riders. I punched "four horsemen of the apocalypse" into GooglePrint, and it gave me almost 3,500 references to these guys in the books that search engines can scan (in .05 seconds I might add). These four riders introduce the dreadful period of the Tribulation. Three groups of judgments will sweep over the world as the Tribulation unfolds—seven seal judgments, seven trumpet judgments, seven bowl judgments—but the horsemen start it all. Each horse and rider gallops across the world stage, but not one says a single word. They speak by their actions and plunge the world into chaos.

A Postmillennial Viewpoint

Some postmillennial Christians (those who believe that the reign of Christ on earth will come about gradually as the Christian faith is universally embraced) believe that the first horseman represents the message of the gospel. The message of Christ's love will eventually (in their view) conquer the world. That sounds nice, but those who hold this view have a very difficult time explaining why the other three horsemen bring devastating judgment on the earth and why these judgments come *after* the gospel's conquest and the projected beginning of the golden age of Christ's reign on earth.

When Jesus breaks the first seal, a rider on a white horse emerges from the opened scroll. He has a bow and crown and rides out as a conquering king. John's original readers would have thought immediately of a political or military leader riding in triumph. Victorious Roman generals rode white horses. The horse and the bow were instruments of war. What's interesting is that no arrows are mentioned. The rider may have expended all his ammunition to gain his victory, or he may have conquered by the threat of war alone. The big questions are, Who is this rider, and what does he represent?

Most interpreters of Revelation have seen this rider as an actual person—and they are pretty evenly divided about who it is—Christ or Antichrist.

SADDLE UP

Horses in the Bible frequently represent God's activity on earth. The Old Testament prophet Zechariah saw four riders in a vision—one on a red horse with three other horses behind him. These four riders are sent out to patrol the earth (Zechariah 1:7–13). In Zechariah 6:1–8 the prophet sees four chariots, each one pulled by different colored horses—red, black, white, and dappled. These chariots are sent out in judgment against the enemies of God's people.

Future FAQs

What's holding him back?

All that keeps the rider on the white horse from thundering across the earth is the power of God.

> And now you know what is holding him back, so that he may be revealed at the proper time. For the secret power of lawlessness is already at work; but the one who now holds it back will continue to do so till he is taken out of the way. And then the lawless one will be revealed.
>
> 2 Thessalonians 2:6–8

The *spirit* of the Antichrist is already at work in our world, but God the Holy Spirit is restraining the *person* of the Antichrist until the right time in God's plan. Once the Restrainer is taken out of the way, the Antichrist will ride onto the center of the world stage and will be welcomed with a worldwide sigh of relief.

If You Think It's Jesus ...

Those who think that the first rider is Jesus have some decent evidence for their position:

- This is Christ returning in victory to rapture the church from the earth.
- The white color of the horse fits heaven, not the Antichrist.
- The rider receives a crown and goes out to conquer—descriptions that fit Jesus very well.
- In Revelation 19 Christ is pictured on a white horse, so why not here?
- Psalm 45, a psalm about the Messiah, talks about a rider equipped with weapons of war (a sword and arrows; verses 3–5)—obviously fulfilled here in Revelation 6.

But the view that the first rider is Christ also has some problems:

- A white horse simply portrays a military leader, not necessarily purity or heaven.

- The "crown" the rider wears is a victor's crown (the kind awarded to an athlete who wins the race). In Revelation 19 Jesus wears a diadem (from the Greek *diadēma*), a kingly crown.
- Jesus isn't the only person crowned in Revelation. The Antichrist is also pictured with crowns and as a conqueror.
- The rider here is unnamed; the rider in Revelation 19 is clearly identified as Jesus.
- Psalm 45 celebrates the King's marriage, while Revelation 6 focuses on judgment in the Tribulation—two events not necessarily connected.
- Since Jesus is opening the seals in Revelation 6, it seems unlikely that he would also be the rider who enters the scene at the command of the living creature.

If You Think It's the Antichrist ...

I think we have much stronger evidence that the first rider is the Antichrist, the future evil world ruler.

- The Antichrist is consistently pictured in Scripture as a ruler who relies on the use or threat of military power to get his way (Daniel 7:7–8, 15–22; 11:36–45; Revelation 13:1–10; 17:9–13).
- The parallels between Jesus' predictions about the Tribulation in Matthew 24:4–8 and John's prophecies in Revelation 6 make it clear that the first rider is the Antichrist. Jesus said that the early years of the Tribulation would be marked by the rise of false messiahs—leaders who would claim to have the answers to the world's problems. But among the counterfeit Christs, one man will

Help File

WAR AND PEACE

From 1500 BC to AD 1861, the world endured 3,130 years of war—and only 227 years of peace.

In the same time period, European nations signed more than 8,000 peace treaties. On average they remained in effect just two years.

In the twentieth century, more than 37 million people died in World War I and 45 million in World War II. Countless hundreds of thousands died in regional wars—and the twenty-first century has started the same way.

stand above the rest—the future world leader we call the Antichrist.

- This picture of a peaceful conqueror fits with what we know from the rest of Scripture about the Antichrist. Daniel predicted that he "will confirm a covenant with many" (Daniel 9:27). The world's first glimpse of the Antichrist will be as a great peacemaker. He will broker a covenant between Israel and her enemies that will finally bring a time of peace to that war-torn land. He will succeed where a long list of presidents and diplomats have failed. He will bring (or at least promise to bring) what the world wants—peace and security.

- The rider is not identified as the Antichrist because this world leader is not revealed as the "Beast" until the middle of the Tribulation when he takes over Israel's temple. But he will be on the scene in the early years and will be very influential in world affairs.

Second Seal Broken (Revelation 6:3–4)

When the Lamb opened the second seal, I heard the second living creature say, "Come!" Then another horse came out, a fiery red one. Its rider was given power to take peace from the earth and to make people slay each other. To him was given a large sword.

1914 ... or Thereabout

Probably no religious group has made more "official" predictions about the end of the world than the Jehovah's Witnesses. The founder of the JWs, Charles Taze Russell, predicted that the War of Armageddon would begin in 1914. When the Great War began (called World War I today), Russell's prediction looked pretty good. Only one problem: Jesus didn't return. Then 1915 looked like the year Jesus would come back—then 1916. Russell died on Halloween in 1916, but not before he had moved the date again to 1918. By 1920 the Watchtower folks began to declare that Jesus *did* return in 1914, as Russell had said, but Jesus had come invisibly. There were just not an adequate number of Jehovah's Witnesses around to run his kingdom on earth, so he is still waiting for the group to get big enough—and *then* things will really start happening.

Bible Networking

Ezekiel 14:21

For this is what the Sovereign LORD says: How much worse will it be when I send against Jerusalem my four dreadful judgments—sword and famine and wild beasts and plague—to kill its men and their animals!

Ezekiel 14:21 mentions the same four judgments listed in Revelation 6:8, just in a slightly different order:

No sooner has the rider on the white horse brought a sense of safety and peace to the world than a second rider sweeps it all away. Jesus breaks the second seal on the scroll, and a bloodred warhorse leaps into John's view. War will rule the world. This rider is given a large sword—the same sword carried by Roman legionnaires into battle, but super-sized. The fact that he is "given" the sword indicates that God is allowing the rider to exercise this kind of power within God's sovereign control and plan. This cruel rider is not outside of God's authority. To people caught up in the chaos of war it will seem as though the world is out of control, but God is working out his plan perfectly.

Some students of prophecy suggest that the time of warfare connected with the second seal judgment fits Ezekiel's description of an attack on Israel from her enemies from the north—Magog, Meshek, and Tubal (Ezekiel 38–39). It's possible that this battle fits here, especially since

Help File

HADES

The term *Hades* appears ten times in the New Testament. Before Jesus' death and resurrection, Hades was the place where all human spirits dwelled after death. The righteous who died lived in peace in paradise or by Abraham's side (see Luke 16:22). Unrighteous people who died found themselves in a place of torment (Luke 16:23). Both places were located in Hades.

When Jesus ascended into heaven after his resurrection, he took the spirits of righteous men and women into heaven with him (Ephesians 4:8). Hades today is a place for only the unrighteous, a temporary place of torment and separation from the conscious presence of God. Ultimately, Hades and its inhabitants will be thrown into the lake of burning sulfur, the final hell of Scripture (Revelation 20:14).

In Other Words

In my view, the shadows of all four horsemen can already be seen galloping throughout the world at this moment; therefore, I want not only to apply these four symbols of events yet to come, but also to put our ears to the ground and hear their hoofbeats growing louder by the day.

Billy Graham, in *Approaching Hoofbeats: The Four Horsemen of the Apocalypse* (Waco: Word, 1983), 9.

the people of Israel are said to use the weapons of the slain as "fuel" for seven years—the length of the Tribulation period (Ezekiel 39:9–10).

War will spread beyond the Middle East, however. New conflicts and the threat of such conflicts will spring up every day. Multinational organizations like the United Nations and NATO will be powerless to stop the spread of violence. When he appears, the Antichrist will be a prince of peace—but a false one.

The apostle Paul predicted that the day of the Lord would begin exactly as Revelation 6 describes it:

> While people are saying, "Peace and safety," destruction will come on them suddenly, as labor pains on a pregnant woman, and they will not escape.
>
> 1 Thessalonians 5:3

Billy Graham adds:

> Mankind may have always had war, but never on the scale that Jesus predicted in Matthew 24 and Revelation 6. Never before has man had the potential to totally obliterate the human race.
> Billy Graham, in *Approaching Hoofbeats*, 128.

Third Seal Broken (Revelation 6:5–6)

> When the Lamb opened the third seal, I heard the third living creature say, "Come!" I looked, and there before me was a black horse! Its rider was holding a pair of scales in his hand. Then I heard what sounded like a voice among the four living creatures, saying, "Two

A TRIBULATION BY ANY OTHER NAME

Here are some of the terms and phrases used in the Bible to refer to the Tribulation:

Jeremiah 30:7	A time of trouble for Jacob
Zephaniah 1:14–16	The great day of the LORD A day of wrath A day of distress and anguish A day of trouble and ruin A day of darkness and gloom A day of clouds and blackness A day of trumpet and battle cry
Zephaniah 1:18	The day of the LORD's wrath The fire of the LORD's jealousy
Isaiah 34:8	A day of vengeance
Daniel 9:24–27	The final "seven"
Daniel 12:1	A time of distress such as has not happened from the beginning of nations until then
Joel 1:15	Destruction from the Almighty
Malachi 4:5	The great and dreadful day of the LORD
Matthew 24:8	Birth pains
1 Thessalonians 1:10	The coming wrath
Revelation 3:10	The hour of trial that is going to come on the whole world
Revelation 6:17	The great day of God's wrath

Help File

MODERN PLAGUES

It's not just fourteenth-century plagues that could kill large numbers of people. Thirty new diseases have cropped up since the emergence of AIDS in the mid-1970s. We now have Ebola, mad cow disease, West Nile virus, hantavirus, SARS, and the list keeps growing. For most of these diseases there is no treatment, no vaccine, and no cure. Every year public health officials hold their breath, fearing a new flu epidemic. An outbreak of the Spanish flu at the end of World War I killed twenty million people worldwide in eighteen months—distant hoofbeats of the pale horse.

pounds of wheat for a day's wages, and six pounds of barley for a day's wages, and do not damage the oil and the wine!"

The second horseman bathed the world in blood. The rider on the third horse, a black horse, spreads the scourge of famine. The haunting pictures we see today of swollen-bellied children in Sudan or Somalia will be broadcast then from the streets of New York and Paris. As the third horseman emerges from the scroll, hunger and poverty sweep the earth. Jesus had predicted famine as an element in the Tribulation scenario, but this will be more than a temporary shortage of our favorite breakfast cereal. The areas of the world devastated by war will see their food supplies evaporate, and the rest of the world will search desperately for enough food to stay alive.

What strikes us as we read John's description of the third horseman is that suddenly a voice speaks from the center of the four living creatures. This is the only time that someone associated with the four horsemen speaks, other than the living creatures who call each horse and rider out. So who is speaking—who announces the cost of wheat and barley and oil? It could be Jesus, since he is the one breaking each seal and opening the scroll. More likely, it is the voice of God the Father, offering his commentary on the events on earth.

God's brief statement opens a window on how devastating the famine will be. Life will be reduced to using all our resources to secure the barest of life's necessities. As is always the case when supplies are short, the price of food will escalate out of sight. It will take a day's wages (literally, a denarius) to buy a day's food. A measure or quart of wheat was the single day's ration for a Roman soldier. It will take everything a person

In Other Words

The most destructive creature on earth, so far as mankind is concerned, is not the lion or the bear, but the rat.... It has killed more people than all the wars in history, and it makes its home wherever man is found. Rats carry as many as thirty-five different diseases. Their fleas carry bubonic plague, which killed a third of the population of Europe in the fourteenth century.

John Phillips, in *Exploring Revelation* (Neptune, N.J.: Loizeaux, 1991), 105.

earns to buy just enough food for himself. Forget feeding a family. Forget paying the mortgage or putting gas in the car. In some parts of the world, people will hand over their whole paycheck for a loaf of bread.

Since it will take more and more money to buy less and less food, people will resort to purchasing lower quality food just to feed their families. For the price of one meal of wheat bread, a family could eat three meals of barley soup—a cheaper, less nutritious grain. Barley is largely relegated today to being animal food, but if a person is hungry enough, even dog food can be choked down.

The famine will not affect everyone in the same way. The voice from the throne adds, "Do not damage the oil and the wine." Luxuries like oil and wine will still be available—for the right price. The rich will continue to enjoy their comfortable lifestyle for a while, but they won't escape God's judgment for long. By the end of chapter 6, the rich and the famous are fleeing to the caves in the mountains right along with the poor and homeless. Everyone will be trying to escape God's wrath.

Fourth Seal Broken (Revelation 6:7 – 8)

> When the Lamb opened the fourth seal, I heard the voice of the fourth living creature say, "Come!" I looked, and there before me was a pale horse! Its rider was named Death, and Hades was following close behind him. They were given power over a fourth of the earth to kill by sword, famine and plague, and by the wild beasts of the earth.

The color of the fourth horse that springs to life from the scroll in Jesus' hand is ashen, the sickening green color of a decaying corpse. Two unusual features of the fourth rider startle us—he has a name, and he has a companion. The rider's name is Death, the grim reaper. The rider's shadow is Hades. Death strikes down the people, and Hades scoops them up. Death claims each body; Hades swallows the soul.

Help File

WHAT'S IN YOUR WALLET?

One measure of wheat for a denarius amounts to a 1200 percent inflation rate in John's day. Imagine paying $30 for a loaf of bread or $24 for a gallon of milk or $15 for a box of macaroni and cheese—on sale! It won't take long at those prices before people are measuring out food with a scale.

In Other Words

War will remain a part of man's history until the Prince of Peace returns.

Mark Hitchcock, in *The Four Horsemen of the Apocalypse*
(Sisters, Ore.: Multnomah, 2004), 54.

"You will hear of wars and rumors of wars, but see to it that you are not alarmed. Such things must happen, but the end is still to come. Nation will rise against nation, and kingdom against kingdom."

Jesus, in Matthew 24:6–7.

This gruesome pair is given authority to kill one-fourth of the world's population—one and a half billion people if this were to happen today. This will be unbelievable carnage! The population of China or India—or five times the population of the United States—will be gone in one Tribulation judgment.

The final horseman will have four weapons at his disposal. The sword refers again to brutal, devastating warfare and weapons of warfare. Several scholars believe that the use of nuclear weapons is the only way that so many people can be killed in such a short time.

Famine is the second weapon in Death's arsenal—a continuation of the third rider's deadly work. Plague or pestilence or disease is the third means of bringing death on humanity. Biological agents such as anthrax or smallpox or even bubonic plague could wipe out millions.

Even wild beasts emerge as killers. John might mean that wild animals, disturbed from their normal habitat and food supplies by war and famine, will turn to attacking human beings. Or he may be using "wild beasts" to refer to military and political leaders who massacre their enemies and even their own people as an exercise of power and terror. You will find the word for wild beast thirty-eight times in Revelation, and every other time it refers to the Antichrist or his sidekick, the False Prophet—ruthless world leaders who kill people simply for political advantage.

What will we remember in heaven?

Most Christians are under the impression that we won't remember much about earth when we get to heaven, but Revelation 6:9–11 seems to contradict that idea. These people remembered that they had died a violent, unjust death, and they ask God to take vengeance on those who did it. We may remember a lot about earth after we die—even some of the most unpleasant things. Eventually we will focus totally on the new things of eternity, but for a while, the inhabitants of heaven are very aware of what is unfolding in the plan of God on earth.

Fifth Seal Broken (Revelation 6:9 – 11)

> When he opened the fifth seal, I saw under the altar the souls of those who had been slain because of the word of God and the testimony they had maintained. They called out in a loud voice, "How long, Sovereign Lord, holy and true, until you judge the inhabitants of the earth and avenge our blood?" Then each of them was given a white robe, and they were told to wait a little longer, until the full number of their fellow servants and brothers and sisters were killed just as they had been.

John's attention has been glued to earth as he has watched four horsemen thunder out of heaven and over the earth. Now he hears a shout behind him. As Jesus breaks the fifth seal, John turns away from the scene on earth to see souls under an altar in heaven. John doesn't have to ask or be told who they are. He knows immediately that they are men and women who had been killed on earth for the "word of God and the testimony they had maintained" (verse 9). In Christian-talk, they are martyrs—not simply followers of Christ who died in the war and devastation of the first four judgments but people who had deliberately been killed for their faith in and commitment to Jesus.

But here's the problem: if all the Christians were taken out of the world at the rapture and if this event happens sometime in the first part of the Tribulation, how did these people come to be followers of Jesus during the Tribulation?

We will see the full answer to that question when we explore chapter 7, but I can give you part of the answer now. I think that these are men and women who had heard about Jesus before the rapture but had never believed in him or committed their lives to him. When the Christians disappear at the rapture, these folks will know what happened. They will know for certain that God's Word is true. So they will believe in Jesus right then. The sad part is that they will miss the rapture and will now face the Tribulation.

Thousands of people will believe in Jesus during the years of the Tribulation — and most of them will die for their faith. As the war and famine and plague take their toll on the world, followers of Christ will be hated and hunted and killed. These are the men and women who cry out for God's justice against their murderers when the fifth seal is broken.

The altar John sees is most likely the altar of incense — a small golden altar that stood in Israel's worship center in the Old Testament. The original altar stands in the heavenly tabernacle (Hebrews 9:11, 24). The altar in the Old Testament was used twice each day in Israel's worship. Oil-soaked wood chips were sprinkled over hot coals, and a cloud of fragrant smoke rose up before the Lord. It pictured the prayers of God's people rising before the Lord, just as the prayers of these martyrs in Revelation 6 rise up to fill the throne room of God.

Each martyr is given a white robe to wear. Even though these are "souls," they have some form and substance — a temporary body to inhabit until their physical body is resurrected at the end of the

Bible Networking

Psalm 94:1 – 3

The prayer of these Tribulation martyrs echoes Psalm 94:1 – 3:

> The LORD is a God who avenges.
>   O God who avenges, shine forth.
> Rise up, Judge of the earth;
>   pay back to the proud what they deserve.
> How long, LORD, will the wicked,
>   how long will the wicked be jubilant?

Tribulation. The white robe pictures their purity before God and their reward for faithfulness. They are told, perhaps by Jesus himself, to wait a while longer. God is in the process of avenging their blood and bringing judgment on their murderers, and even more righteous people will have to die before God's final crushing judgment will fall. Their prayer for God's justice is answered as the rest of Revelation unfolds.

What kind of body will we have after we die?

Our human bodies will experience radical changes in the future. In this present life, we have an earthly, physical body of flesh and bone. The immaterial part of us—our spirit or soul—dwells in what Paul calls the "earthly tent" (2 Corinthians 5:1). At death, our spirit goes into the presence of Christ if we are believers (2 Corinthians 5:8), or to the torment of Hades if we are not believers in Christ (Luke 16:23–24). But our spirits after death are not immaterial "ghosts." Even in death, our spirits are "clothed" with a temporary body that can wear a white robe in heaven (Revelation 6:11) or feel the pain of torment in hell (Luke 16:24). At the resurrection, redeemed people will receive eternal, glorified bodies like the resurrected human body of Jesus (1 John 3:2). The bodies of unbelievers are raised too, but not to glory. Those who have rejected God's grace spend eternity in a body that will not die but that will experience pain and dishonor (Mark 9:47–48; Revelation 20:12–14).

In Other Words

The world is looking for a man on a white horse.

David Jeremiah, in *Escape the Coming Night* (Dallas: Word, 1997), 113.

Sixth Seal Broken (Revelation 6:12 – 17)

> I watched as he opened the sixth seal. There was a great earthquake. The sun turned black like sackcloth made of goat hair, the whole moon turned blood red, and the stars in the sky fell to earth, as figs drop from a fig tree when shaken by a strong wind. The sky receded like a scroll, rolling up, and every mountain and island was removed from its place.
>
> Then the kings of the earth, the princes, the generals, the rich, the mighty, and everyone else, both slave and free, hid in caves and among the rocks of the mountains. They called to the mountains and the rocks, "Fall on us and hide us from the face of him who sits on the throne and from the wrath of the Lamb! For the great day of their wrath has come, and who can withstand it?"

It doesn't take long for God to keep his promise of judgment. The broken sixth seal unleashes environmental disaster unlike anything the world has ever seen. John turns back to the earth as Jesus opens the next section of the scroll, and he stares in stunned silence as the universe begins to unravel. Hollywood disaster movies will seem pretty tame compared to what happens next — six rapid-fire disasters!

The ravages of war, famine, and disaster are not just future scenarios. Innocent people, including many godly Christians, experience on a limited scale today what the whole world will experience in the future — Tribulation. Those of us living in peaceful democracies don't know that kind of deadly terror, but we can make ourselves aware of what is happening in other areas of the world and use some of our resources to try to alleviate the suffering. Maybe you should be the person who spearheads a famine relief project in your church or who calls attention to the annual day of prayer for the persecuted church. A simple Web search will bring you face-to-face with the pain and loss others are experiencing — and with some organizations that are trying to bring help to the oppressed in the name of Jesus. Merely shaking our heads at injustice or starvation is not an option for committed followers of Jesus.

Bible Networking

Joel 2:30 - 31

> I will show wonders in the heavens
>   and on the earth,
>   blood and fire and billows of smoke.
> The sun will be turned to darkness
>   and the moon to blood
>   before the coming of the great and dreadful day of the LORD.

Isaiah 13:9 - 10, 13

> See, the day of the LORD is coming....
> The stars of heaven and their constellations
>   will not show their light.
> The rising sun will be darkened
>   and the moon will not give its light....
> I will make the heavens tremble;
>   and the earth will shake from its place
> at the wrath of the LORD Almighty,
>   in the day of his burning anger.

Help File

KILLER METEORS

On June 30, 1903, a meteor or comet fragment at least 130 feet wide flashed through the sky in a remote region of Siberia near the Tunguska River. The fragment never hit the earth. Instead it seems to have exploded and vaporized above ground level. A thousand square miles of Russian forest were flattened by the blast. Scientists estimate the power of the explosion to have been 700 times the force of the atomic bomb that destroyed Hiroshima, Japan, at the end of World War II. If the cosmic fragment had exploded over Chicago or London, the city below would have disappeared in the blast.

The Pre-Wrath Rapture

Some Christians believe that the rapture of Christians out of the world will not take place until sometime near the middle of the Tribulation. The church will experience part of the day of God's judgment but will be rescued from the last and most intense part of the Tribulation.

The problem with this view is that John clearly refers to the *whole* time of the Tribulation as the time of God's wrath. The seal judgments recorded in Revelation 6 take place during the first part of the Tribulation, and yet Revelation 6:16–17 reads, "Hide us from the face of him who sits on the throne and from the wrath of the Lamb! For the great day of their wrath has come." If the rapture is "pre-wrath"—before the time of God's wrath—it must come before the Tribulation begins, not halfway through it.

Disaster 1: Earthquake

Both Jesus and the prophet Joel had predicted earthquakes in their prophecies about the last days (Matthew 24:7; Joel 2:10). What John sees is a megaquake—a massive shifting of the earth's surface.

Disaster 2: Sun Turns Black

Dust and smoke from the earthquake could block out the sun for a while. A black shroud covers the earth.

Disaster 3: Moon Turns Red

The same debris in the air makes the moon look as red as blood.

Disaster 4: Stars Fall

John sees stars—heavenly bodies such as asteroids or comets—fall to the earth. Not all the stars fall because some are still in place later in Revelation (8:12). But enough meteors and comets bombard the earth to fulfill Jesus' words in Luke 21:11 about "great signs from heaven."

Disaster 5: The Sky Rolls Up

The universe begins to come apart at its hinges. The signs in the heavens send shock waves throughout human society. Some interpreters believe that this violent upheaval in the atmosphere will be caused

Points to Remember

- ☑ As Jesus breaks each seal on the scroll he received from the Father, a new judgment leaps off the page and sweeps over the earth.

- ☑ The four horsemen of the Apocalypse bring unbelievable devastation on an unsuspecting world.

- ☑ The men and women dwelling on earth will recognize that these judgments come from God—but they will refuse to honor him and seek his mercy.

by either nuclear explosions or the impact of meteors.

Disaster 6: Mountains Move and Islands Disappear

The earthquake and the likely volcanic eruptions that result change the surface of the earth. The most stable of earth's features—huge mountains—are moved or destroyed. Nothing is secure.

In the days of the sixth seal judgment, men and women will want to die. They will beg to die. They will prefer being crushed under the crumbling mountains than facing the anger and justice of God. By this point in the Tribulation, the people on earth will know that these disasters are the powerful work of God. But rather than turn to God and seek his mercy, the inhabitants of earth will curse God and do whatever they can to escape. No social or economic group will be exempt. Kings and slaves will share the same feelings of panic and horror—no one will escape.

John ends chapter 6 with the people on earth believing that the world is about to end, but it's not the end. In fact, things will get much worse before the end. Human beings will see the universe collapsing but will refuse to face their Creator. The dwellers on earth during the Tribulation will not be atheists. They will know beyond a doubt that God really exists, but they will hate him.

CHAPTER 7

Great Revival
Sweeps the World

Great Revival Sweeps the World

- ▶ John pushes the "pause" button to give us some vital important information.
- ▶ 144,000 Jewish believers receive God's seal on their foreheads.
- ▶ A huge throng in heaven shouts praise to God!

Access Codes

Key Codes: Level 7

- → Winds of the earth: A picture of God's judgment
- → Seal of God: A mark of ownership and protection
- → Tribes of Israel: Extended families that make up the biblical nation of Israel and the Jews today
- → Elders: Representatives of the raptured church; first introduced in Revelation 4 and 5

Time Out

It's why they have halftime in football and the seventh-inning stretch at a baseball game. A pause in the action gives everyone a chance to regroup and take a deep breath. John inserts several "breathers" into the action of the book of Revelation. The action gets so intense that we need a chance to regroup and clear our heads.

This isn't just a rest time, however. John puts the break to good use by filling in some important details. We've been marching along from one judgment to the next, but now we stop and listen to the coach explain some things we wondered about as we moved through chapter 6. He explains, for example, how those martyrs under the altar in heaven had come to believe in Jesus in the first place. He also shows us God's mercy to human beings, even in the middle of his judgment.

How are people saved after the rapture?

Some Christians are under the impression that no one can be saved after Jesus returns for his people at the rapture. They think that if you are "left behind," it's too late to believe in Jesus. The fact is that thousands of people will believe in Christ and be saved during the Tribulation. These seven years of intense judgment will also bring times of wonderful revival.

But how are people saved after the rapture? The same way they are saved today—by believing the Bible's message about Jesus Christ and by the powerful work of the Holy Spirit called the "new birth." People in the Tribulation will believe in Jesus and will be born again.

Another belief some Christians hold is that the Holy Spirit is removed from the world at the rapture. That is not correct. The Holy Spirit's restraining power on the Antichrist and evil is taken out of the way at the rapture, but the Spirit is not taken out of the world (2 Thessalonians 2:7). He will still be actively empowering the proclamation of the message about Jesus and graciously drawing men and women to faith.

Revelation 7 is not here to advance the action of the Tribulation; it's here to provide important insight. We are introduced to two groups of people who come to believe in Jesus during those horrible months of war and famine and death.

Revelation 7 also answers the question raised in verse 17 of chapter 6: Who can stand in the time of God's wrath? Who will possibly survive physically or spiritually when the world starts crashing down around us? We find out that God in his grace does save thousands and thousands of people during the Tribulation. Some will survive physically because of God's special protection; all will survive spiritually and enter heaven as God's people.

John's words must have encouraged the persecuted Christians who first read this book. They were not going through the final Tribulation, but at times it must have felt like it. It must have strengthened them to be assured that God would ultimately be victorious over his enemies but also that God was intimately aware of their suffering. Those who died for their faith in the early centuries of the church have been joined by a long line of faithful men and women who remained true to Christ under incredible opposition and even through death. Jesus welcomed them into heaven.

Restraining Angels (Revelation 7:1–3)

> After this I saw four angels standing at the four corners of the earth, holding back the four winds of the earth to prevent any wind from blowing on the land or on the sea or on any tree. Then I saw another angel coming up from the east, having the seal of the living God. He called out in a loud voice to the four angels who had been given power to harm the land and the sea: "Do not harm the land or the sea or the trees until we put a seal on the foreheads of the servants of our God."

John identifies two groups of people dwelling in two different places—a group of 144,000 on earth still alive, and a great multitude of people who have died and are now in heaven. But first John sees four powerful angels restraining the wind.

The reference to "the winds" in these verses seems to be a picture of God's judgments on the earth. The angels hold back God's judgment for a time while other matters are handled on earth. The issue of "the winds" in Revelation 7 raises an important point for how we interpret the book of Revelation. Why can't we just take this as a literal reference to the wind? Why make it a symbol of God's judgment? There are several answers to those questions:

- First, if it is the literal wind that is restrained, we have to ask why. What is God's purpose for holding back the movement of air across

FOUR CORNERS OF THE EARTH

I attended a lecture in college in which the speaker used Revelation 7:1 as an example of an error in the Bible. "We now know what John did not know," he announced. "The earth is not square and flat, but round." During the question-and-answer time at the end of the lecture, I told the speaker that the weather report I had listened to that morning had given the exact times for "sunrise" and "sunset." I wondered (out loud) if the weatherman still believed that the sun moved around the earth and why he wasn't more precise in his language. John was simply using a metaphor for every direction on earth. The angels restrained "the wind" over the entire planet for a time.

the planet? Nothing is said in these verses about why this happens. If the angels restrain God's judgment for a time, however, God's purpose becomes more clear. Judgment is restrained until the servants of God are sealed (verse 3).

- Second, the wind is clearly used in other places in Scripture as a picture of God's judgment or actions in the world (Daniel 7:2; Hosea 13:15; Jeremiah 49:36).
- Third answer: The fifth angel in Revelation 7 tells the other angels to "not harm the land or the sea or the trees" (verse 3). When the restraint is lifted and the next wave of judgments begins, the first one falls on the land and trees (8:7) while the second one falls on the sea (8:8–9).

So why doesn't John just say, "The angels held back the judgment of God"? Why bring in the wind at all? I think God has John write it this way because the image of strong angels holding back the wind is

The position that the Tribulation happened in the past during the Roman destruction of Jerusalem in AD 70 is called the *preterist* view. The term comes from the Latin word *praeteritus*, which means "gone by" or "past." Some prominent Christian leaders who have held this view are John Calvin (1509–1564) and Matthew Henry (1662–1714). The modern Christian Reconstructionist movement has been a strong advocate of the preterist view. The main contemporary defenders of the "Tribulation is past" view are R. C. Sproul, Kenneth Gentry, Gary DeMar, and Hank Hanegraaff.

Christians who hold to the preterist interpretation of Revelation believe that the 144,000 represent the Jewish Christians who escaped from Jerusalem before the final destruction of the city. The ancient historian Eusebius confirms that the Christians in Jerusalem were warned of the city's fate by divine revelation and that the whole church family fled to a city across the Jordan River. The vast multitude in Revelation 7 in the preterist view represents, as quoted in the book *Revelation: Four Views: A Parallel Commentary* (edited by Steve Gregg [Nashville: Nelson, 1997], 134), "the great throng of Gentiles who will be saved as a result of God's disowning his rebellious wife and children [Israel] and seeking a new family [the church]."

far more powerful and memorable for those of us who read the book. It rivets our attention on John's account and makes us think harder and longer about what God is trying to communicate to us.

A fifth angel now comes out of the east (from Israel, or Jerusalem; a place east of the island of Patmos where John was). He's probably a more powerful angel than the other four, since he commands them. This additional angel has in his possession the seal of God. Think of this as a signet ring, entrusted to the angel by God himself. The same ring that was pressed into the wax or clay of the seals on the scroll is now used to mark God's servants on their foreheads.

The seal indicates *ownership* (these people are God's own possession) and *authenticity* (they are the genuine item—true servants of God) and is also a mark of God's *protection* over them. The seal is probably not visible to human eyes, but it is clearly visible to angels and demons. Those sealed by God will be protected from harm during the Tribulation. They will not be hurt by the judgments poured out on the earth and (apparently) will escape the Antichrist's attempts to destroy and kill them.

Twelve x Twelve Thousand (Revelation 7:4 – 8)

> Then I heard the number of those who were sealed: 144,000 from all the tribes of Israel.
>
> From the tribe of Judah 12,000 were sealed,
> from the tribe of Reuben 12,000,
> from the tribe of Gad 12,000,
> from the tribe of Asher 12,000,
> from the tribe of Naphtali 12,000,
> from the tribe of Manasseh 12,000,
> from the tribe of Simeon 12,000,

Help File

WATCHTOWER WITNESSES

The Jehovah's Witnesses view Revelation 7 as a reference to their particular group. The founder of the group, Charles Taze Russell, taught that when 144,000 people had become Jehovah's Witnesses, Jesus would return and take them to heaven. Today Jehovah's Witnesses believe that the 144,000 are a select band of "spirit brothers" who will be chosen to reign with Christ in heaven for a thousand years. Less committed Witnesses will have to enjoy the kingdom on a renewed earth. Nice, but not the best.

Jonathan Edwards

The Massachusetts preacher Jonathan Edwards (1703–1758) was convinced that the golden age of God's kingdom was just around the corner. He believed that he was living in the days of the bowl judgments described in Revelation 16. The Protestant Reformation (it was clear to him) represented the fifth bowl, and the world of his day was experiencing the sixth bowl—the last judgment before the perfect age of grace and peace would dawn on the world. He saw the Great Awakening, a spiritual revival in America and Britain, as the prelude to a worldwide spread of the gospel. He was also convinced that the new age would begin in America.

> from the tribe of Levi 12,000,
> from the tribe of Issachar 12,000,
> from the tribe of Zebulun 12,000,
> from the tribe of Joseph 12,000,
> from the tribe of Benjamin 12,000.

God's seal is applied 144,000 times. John is very clear and very specific about who is sealed and protected by God—12,000 people from each of twelve different tribes of Israel. One hundred forty-four thousand Jews—not church-age Christians, not the supersaints of the Jehovah's Witnesses, not the followers of David Koresh or some other false messiah—but Jews, descendants of Abraham, Isaac, and Jacob.

This group is converted to faith in Jesus as the Messiah after the rapture, are supernaturally protected throughout the Tribulation, and are God's witnesses about Jesus to the whole world. The great revivals that rock the world in the Tribulation come about as God uses the faithful testimony of these Jewish believers to tell a frantic, panic-stricken society about Jesus. They don't give people the wonderful hope of the rapture ahead, as we can today. All they can promise is that followers of Christ will likely be killed for their faith. But they can promise those who trust in Christ that when they die, they will be with Christ in heaven and that, when it's all over, Christ will fully avenge their blood on the evil people who killed them.

Some interpreters of Revelation believe that John is talking in this passage about "spiritual Israel" (the church, Christians today), not about physical Israel (actual descendants of Jacob through his sons). In their view, a large number of Christians become God's witnesses in the last days before Jesus' return and proclaim the gospel message to the world.

There are two big problems with that view:

- *Big problem #1*: John says that these people are from the tribes of Israel. God gave very specific covenant promises to Abraham and repeated those promises to Abraham's son, Isaac, and to Isaac's son, Jacob. Their descendants would be God's covenant people. Those who blessed them would find themselves blessed, and those who cursed them would in turn be cursed.

  To read the covenant promises made to Abraham, go to Genesis 12:1–3; 17:1–8.

  To Isaac: Genesis 17:19

  To Jacob: Genesis 35:9–13

  Jacob's sons became the fathers (patriarchs) of the "tribes" or extended families that made up the nation of Israel. To be considered a true Jew (or Israelite) you had to be able to trace your family line back to one of Jacob's sons.

FALLING FROM THE FAMILY TREE

What could be simpler than figuring out the twelve tribes of Israel? Old Testament Jacob had twelve sons; each fathered a large extended family, and presto— twelve tribes of Israel.

It sounds simple, but actually it gets pretty complicated. One son, Joseph, was so pivotal in rescuing his people from famine and starvation that God gave him a double blessing. Joseph's two sons, Ephraim and Manasseh, each had a tribe named after them. So we are at thirteen tribes. The descendants of Levi became the priests and worship leaders in Israel. They didn't receive a section of land when the Promised Land of Canaan was divided up. So we are back to twelve tribes with land and one tribe of priests.

There are nineteen or twenty lists of Israel's tribes in the Old Testament, with minor differences between them, and none of those lists agree with John's list in Revelation 7. Here are the differences and how these differences are explained:

- Judah is listed first (as happens often in the Old Testament too) because Jesus, the Messiah, came from that tribe.
- Dan is not mentioned in John's list, probably because they were

- *Big problem #2*: The church today is not a spiritual Israel. Christians share in many of God's promises to Israel, but we are not Israel. During this age, God's program is focused on the church and Christians are drawn from every nation, including Israel. But in the Tribulation, God will again focus on the people of Israel. These 144,000 witnesses will finally fulfill God's desire that Israel would be a nation of priests to the world. The witnesses of Revelation 7 will do what the church has been trying to do for nearly two thousand years—reach the world with the message of Christ. Jesus said, "This gospel of the kingdom will be preached in the whole world as a testimony to all nations, and then the end will come" (Matthew 24:14). Hal Lindsey says that these chosen witnesses will be "144,000 Jewish Billy Grahams."

In all fairness, I need to say that the Bible never specifically says that the 144,000 are evangelists or that they are the ones who preach the gospel to the whole world. Maybe God protects and preserves these Jewish believers simply to guarantee that a remnant of Israel survives the Tribulation. We assume that the 144,000 are evangelists because we are told about them just before John sees a huge multitude of people in heaven from every nation

FALLING FROM THE FAMILY TREE (CONTINUED)

a tribe that allowed idolatry to flourish long before other tribes in Israel fell into that sin (Judges 18:30).

- Levi is mentioned, although they did not receive an allotment of land in Israel.
- John lists a tribe of Joseph but also lists Joseph's son Manasseh. Ephraim is not listed (or is represented by Joseph), perhaps again because of their involvement in idolatry.
- The order John follows seems to be the order of the son's birth according to their mothers. All were sons of Jacob, but through four women—Leah, Bilhah, Zilpah, and Rachel.

One other issue about the family tree: No Jew today knows for sure what tribe or family they belong to. Conquests in the Old Testament, the destruction of records in the temple by the Romans in AD 70, and the forced migrations and oppression of the Jews since then have wiped out any Jew's ability to identify their tribe. What is impossible with human beings, however, is not impossible with God. He has the genealogies all straight—and at the right time he will select believers from every tribe, exactly as John promised.

One popular early Christian (and Jewish) explanation of why the tribe of Dan is excluded from John's list is that the Antichrist will come from that tribe. The Jewish rabbis based this view on Jacob's prophecy about Dan in Genesis 49:17: "Dan will be a snake by the roadside, a viper along the path." That is not a widely held view today because Revelation 13 makes it clear that the Antichrist will arise from the sea of nations, not from Israel. He will likely be a Gentile, not a Jew.

who have "come out of the great tribulation" (Revelation 7:14). These are people who are killed for their faith in Christ after the rapture. They hear about Jesus and come to believe (we assume) through the testimony of the 144,000 Jewish believers who are sealed by God's angel.

A Vast Multitude (Revelation 7:9 – 17)

After this I looked, and there before me was a great multitude that no one could count, from every nation, tribe, people and language, standing before the throne and in front of the Lamb. They were wearing white robes and were holding palm branches in their hands. And they cried out in a loud voice:

"Salvation belongs to our God,
who sits on the throne,
and to the Lamb."

All the angels were standing around the throne and around the elders and the four living creatures. They fell down on their faces before the throne and worshiped God, saying:

"Amen!
Praise and glory
and wisdom and thanks and honor
and power and strength
be to our God for ever and ever.
Amen!"

Then one of the elders asked me, "These in white robes—who are they, and where did they come from?"

I answered, "Sir, you know."

And he said, "These are they who have come out of the great tribulation; they have washed their robes and made them white in the blood of the Lamb. Therefore,

> "they are before the throne of God
>   and serve him day and night in his temple;
> and he who sits on the throne
>   will spread his tent over them.
> 'Never again will they hunger;
>   never again will they thirst.
> The sun will not beat on them,'
>   nor any scorching heat.
> For the Lamb at the center before the throne
>   will be their shepherd;
> 'he will lead them to springs of living water.'
> 'And God will wipe away every tear from their eyes.'"

John turns from the scene of sealing on earth and sees a new scene unfold in heaven. Before this, he saw under the altar souls of believers who had died (Revelation 6:9–11); now he sees the vast multitude that those souls represented. Not only will the 144,000 Jewish believers stand through the Tribulation because of God's protection; a huge throng of people will also turn to Christ in faith and will stand in God's presence in heaven.

The distinctions between the 144,000 and the huge multitude in Revelation 7 are significant.

- The first group has a definite number; the second group is unnumbered.

PALM BRANCHES

The multitude in heaven wave palm branches as they shout words of praise and honor to God and to the Lamb. When Jesus entered Jerusalem as Israel's Messiah, the people waved palms and laid them in Jesus' path (Matthew 21:8; John 12:13). Jewish coins from the New Testament age were frequently decorated with palms and the inscription "the redemption of Zion." John's readers would recognize this image as a picture of victory over evil and as an expression of great joy. Maybe we should occasionally pass out palm branches in our worship services today.

Future FAQs

Is there only one way to be saved?

I am one of the Christians who believes that the Bible makes distinctions between different groups of God's people—Old Testament believers, church-age believers, Tribulation believers. We are sometimes accused of believing that people down through history have been saved in different ways—that Old Testament believers were saved by obeying the law of Moses, for example. But that is not correct. There is only one way to enter into a right relationship with God: we are saved by God's grace through personal faith in God's promises.

What changes from age to age is the content and emphasis of God's message. In the Old Testament, salvation came to those who believed that the God of Israel was the one true God and who demonstrated their faith by obeying God's Word. Today in the church age, we are saved by believing that Jesus died for our sins and rose again as Lord, and we demonstrate that faith by walking under the direction of God's Word and God's Spirit. In the Tribulation, men and women will be saved by believing the gospel of the kingdom—that Jesus died, rose again, and will come again, not to rapture Christians out, but to set up a kingdom of glory.

In Revelation 7:9–17, John sees a multitude of Tribulation believers alongside the twenty-four elders, representing church-age believers. Church-age Christians aren't "more" saved than other groups; we just have different roles to play in the unfolding of God's purpose.

- The first group came from Israel; the second group is from every nation and language and ethnic group.
- The first group is marked out by God for protection on earth; the second group has died and stands in the protection of heaven.
- The 144,000 are protected in a time of danger; the multitude comes out of the Tribulation and is in a place of security.

The connection between the two groups is not specifically stated, but the implication seems to be that the 144,000 Jews will proclaim the message of Jesus to every nation and thousands of people will believe. Those who believe are soon arrested and executed by the Antichrist and by those on the earth who hate God and his people. That company of martyred Tribulation believers is the group John sees and hears in Revelation 7. Their shout rings throughout heaven: "Salvation belongs to our God, who sits on the throne, and to the Lamb" (verse 10).

Praise and Worship

The triumphant shout of the multitude in heaven triggers a worship service that rocks the golden halls. Four distinct groups join in:

- the multitude of Tribulation believers
- the twenty-four elders (whom we met in chapter 4), who represent raptured and glorified church-age believers
- the angels
- the four living creatures

All of us will fall down and offer seven words of adoration to God—praise, glory, wisdom, thanks, honor, power, and strength. Dictators and Caesars may oppress and even kill us, but above all earthly powers a sovereign God "sits on the throne" of the universe.

In Other Words

The greatest revival the world has ever known is yet to come.

Tim LaHaye, in *Revelation Unveiled* (Grand Rapids: Zondervan, 1999), 148.

The Lord at present, by the power of the Holy Spirit on earth, bridles the passions of men, but let the presence and power of the Spirit be withdrawn, and the world's enmity to Christ and those who are His shall burst out in fierce and bitter persecution even unto death.

Walter Scott, in *Exposition of the Revelation of Jesus Christ* (reprint, Grand Rapids: Kregel, 1982), 154.

Rather than being devoid of religion, the Tribulation period will be one of the most religious periods of world history. It will be a time of worldwide revival. Possibly the latter rain of the Spirit will be even more potent than the former rain of the Spirit at Pentecost.

Walter K. Price, in *The Coming Antichrist* (Chicago: Moody, 1974), 178.

John 12:12 – 13

The next day the great crowd that had come for the Festival heard that Jesus was on his way to Jerusalem. They took palm branches and went out to meet him, shouting,

> "Hosanna!"
> "Blessed is he who comes in the name of the Lord!"
> "Blessed is the king of Israel!"

Leviticus 23:40

On the first day [of the Festival of Tabernacles] you are to take branches from luxuriant trees—from palms, willows and other leafy trees—and rejoice before the LORD your God for seven days.

John sees a glimpse of what is ahead in these verses. The "Great Tribulation," the last half of the seven-year time of testing, is about to begin. The six seal judgments were scattered through the early years of the Tribulation, but things will get much worse in the later years. Most of the Tribulation believers will die in the last three and a half years when the Antichrist's power is at its height. But John sees that multitude of martyred believers already in heaven. John can witness the rest of God's judgment, knowing that some of God's people will be protected through it and that the thousands who do die will find safety and rest with the Lord.

An Identity Crisis

One of the elders in heaven surprises John with two questions: "Who are they, and where did they come from?" The elder knows the answers but wants to draw John's attention to the response he is about to make.

The elder explains that these people from every nation were in the process of coming out of "the great tribulation." Jesus applied the phrase "great tribulation" to the last three and a half years of the Tribulation period in Matthew 24:21 (see the King James Version rendering

Some Christians think that the message of the gospel obliterates human culture. Since we are all one in Christ, they conclude, we should all worship and pray and celebrate the Lord's Supper the same way. Early missionaries not only worked to evangelize indigenous cultures; they also tried to "Westernize" their dress, their church services, and their music. Revelation 7 shows us that God celebrates the amazing variety of human expression and style. God takes what is best in each culture and transforms it into an instrument of his praise and glory. It may go a long way toward getting us ready for heaven if we start to learn now to appreciate the contribution Christians from other cultures can make to the great chorus of adoration to God.

of this verse). These are people who believed in Jesus after the rapture and who must then face the consequences of that decision. Some most likely died in the judgments that swept the world; many more died under persecution. They "have come out of the great tribulation" and "have washed their robes and made them white in the blood of the Lamb." Making a robe white by washing it in blood seems absurd, but the picture is of lives washed from sin and defilement and guilt by the saving death of Jesus on the cross. These Tribulation believers were saved by God's grace and cleansed by Christ's sacrifice, and now they are safe in heaven.

The list of blessings in heaven makes us long to be there:

- God spreads his tent over them. The presence of God shelters them from harm.
- No more hunger or thirst or scorching heat, which may describe how some of these believers had died, but they would never suffer like that again.
- The Lamb will be their Shepherd. Psalm 23 is perfectly fulfilled. Jesus leads us in this life to quiet waters; he leads his people in heaven to springs of living water.

☑ In spite of global disasters and intense persecution, God will protect a special group during the Tribulation — 144,000 Jewish believers.

☑ God isn't finished with the people of Israel. He will preserve a faithful remnant of believers, even in the worst time in human history.

☑ The 144,000 will carry the message of Jesus to the nations of the world, and great revival will spring from their preaching.

☑ Millions will believe — and millions will be killed for their faith. But those believers who die will find themselves safe in heaven.

• God will wipe away every tear. The tears of the past will be over. We may still remember some things about our lives on earth — even some bad things, as these Tribulation believers remembered their murders on earth (Revelation 6:10–11). But we will see the events of earth with a new perspective — God's perspective — and the tears will end.

CHAPTER 8

Let the Trumpets Sound

Let the Trumpets Sound

- ▶ The last seal on the scroll is broken.
- ▶ Heaven falls silent!
- ▶ Seven angels prepare to sound their trumpets of judgment.
- ▶ A screaming eagle warns the world of disaster to come.

MR. BLOCKHEAD
HEADS UP

Access Codes

Key Codes: Level 8

→ **Censer:** A shovel-like object used in the temple to carry hot coals from the sacrifice altar to the small altar of incense inside the temple

→ **Incense:** Wood chips soaked in an aromatic oil such as frankincense or spikenard

→ **Wormwood:** A bitter-tasting plant

→ **Midair:** The highest point the sun reaches in the sky; the place visible to everyone

→ **Woe:** Call of despair and warning

The Calm Before the Storm (Revelation 8:1–6)

When he opened the seventh seal, there was silence in heaven for about half an hour.

And I saw the seven angels who stand before God, and seven trumpets were given to them.

Another angel, who had a golden censer, came and stood at the altar. He was given much incense to offer, with the prayers of all God's people, on the golden altar before the throne. The smoke of the incense, together with the prayers of God's people, went up before God from the angel's hand. Then the angel took the censer, filled it with fire from the altar, and hurled it on the earth; and there came peals of thunder, rumblings, flashes of lightning and an earthquake.

Then the seven angels who had the seven trumpets prepared to sound them.

The interlude is over. John gave us a rest in chapter 7—time to let our heart rates return to normal after watching six judgments pound the earth. You can only take so many earthquakes and meteors and moon-turning-to-blood episodes before you need a break. But now in chapter 8 John picks up the action right where he left off.

Jesus breaks the last seal on the scroll, and the rest of God's program is laid out for everyone to see. John and the inhabitants of heaven are stunned into silence for half an hour. Have you been keeping track of how noisy heaven has been? We've heard loud voices, rumblings of thunder, multitudes singing, angels shouting, martyrs praying. But suddenly silence falls over heaven like a giant hand shutting everyone's mouth. When we see the awesome judgments of God ready to be unleashed on humanity, we will stand in sober silence.

In the silence, eight angels make their way onto center stage. Seven of them are given trumpets, and each one starts to get ready to play a short solo. The eighth angel has a censer in his hand—a short shovel or pan filled with red-hot coals. He puts the coals on the golden altar, the altar of incense in the heavenly tabernacle—the same altar under which the souls of those killed during the Tribulation were calling out to God back in chapter 6 (verses 9–11). Then the angel receives incense—wood chips soaked in aromatic oil. When the wood chips are sprinkled over

NAMING THE ANGELS

Only a few angels are named in Scripture:

- Gabriel (Luke 1:19, 26)
- Michael (Daniel 12:1; Revelation 12:7)
- Lucifer, or morning star, also known as Satan (Isaiah 14:12 KJV; Job 1:6)
- Perhaps some demons named

Legion (Mark 5:9) and Abaddon, in Hebrew, or Apollyon, in Greek (Revelation 9:11)

It's likely that all the angels have names, but only these are given in the Bible. The Jewish book of 1 Enoch lists the names of seven "watchers," or the seven archangels, as Uriel, Raphael, Raguel, Michael, Saraquel, Gabriel, and Remiel (1 Enoch 20:1–8).

the hot coals on the altar, a cloud of fragrant smoke rises from the altar. That cloud of incense pictures the prayers of believers, which rise up before the Lord.

The Christians who first read this book must have experienced a wave of emotion at this point. God was not insensitive to their suffering or inattentive to their prayers. He never is. Our prayers to God are like a sweet fragrance to him, and somehow angels assist in lifting those prayers to God's attention.

In response to those prayers, God begins to move in judgment on the wicked inhabitants of the earth. Something goes up in John's vision (the smoke and the prayers), and something comes down (fire and judgment).

The angel who offered the incense now takes a shovelful of burning coals from the altar and throws them to the earth—a taste of the judgments about to fall. The silence of heaven is shattered with the sounds of thunder, and the earth shudders in anticipation of the disasters to come.

First Trumpet (Revelation 8:7)

> The first angel sounded his trumpet, and there came hail and fire mixed with blood, and it was hurled down upon the earth. A third of

Most of us are uncomfortable with silence. We have televisions to fill our family rooms with sound, CD players and radios to fill our cars, and iPods to fill our ears at the gym or while riding a mountain bike. Restaurants and doctors' offices fill the quiet with music or the chatter of televisions. Silence, however, is a wonderful tool for expressing our awe. Several years ago, my wife, Karen, and I visited the Holocaust Museum in Washington, D.C. As we were packed into an elevator and transported to the top floor of the museum to begin our tour, a hush spread through the group. The quiet in the display areas was broken only by an occasional sigh or murmured word or sob. We stood surrounded by reminders of events too powerful for meaningless chatter. Silence gives us the opportunity to pray—and the opportunity to listen for God's whispering voice. Try five minutes of quiet sometime today. Pray. Listen. Be overcome with awe in the presence of God.

the earth was burned up, a third of the trees were burned up, and all the green grass was burned up.

As each angel blows his trumpet, judgment sweeps down over the earth. The first three trumpet judgments are directed toward the created world, the sin-shrouded earth; the last four are directed against the world of mankind, the unrepentant inhabitants of the earth.

As the sound of the first trumpet rings through heaven, hail and fire are hurled to the earth. This "fire" could be lightning or some other form of fire, such as the burning sulfur that destroyed Sodom and Gomorrah (Genesis 19:24). The blood mixed with the hail and fire could be a reference to the blood of people struck or even killed by the hail, or the sky might turn red from the fire falling on the earth and the enormous forest fires that result.

One-third of the vegetation of the earth burns. Imagine the Amazon rain forest, the central African rain forest, and the magnificent forests of Yellowstone and Yosemite National Parks all burning at once. The results would be devastating—air pollution, soil erosion, water contamination. The remaining vegetation could not consume the carbon dioxide and other hothouse gases produced by modern civilization and industry. The world's already stressed ecological system would begin to collapse.

While the first trumpet judgment brings terrible devastation, it is not complete devastation. God still leaves room for humanity to repent and turn to him for mercy, but no repentance is heard.

Trumpet Two (Revelation 8:8–9)

The second angel sounded his trumpet, and something like a huge mountain, all ablaze, was thrown into the sea. A third of the sea turned into blood, a third of the living creatures in the sea died, and a third of the ships were destroyed.

In Other Words

Incense was symbolic of worship and prayer and a reminder that intercession to the Lord has the character of sweet incense.

John Walvoord, in *The Revelation of Jesus Christ* (1966; rev. ed., Chicago: Moody, 1989), 152.

As the second angel sends a blast from his trumpet, something like a huge burning mountain hurtles into the sea. The "sea" may refer to the Mediterranean Sea that surrounded John's prison island or to one of the world's oceans, but John certainly means a large body of saltwater. This could be a meteor or a comet that collides with the earth, or perhaps a burning mountain of the earth (a volcano) falls into the ocean and spreads destruction through the water.

One-third of the ocean becomes bloody red and contaminated to the point that the fish and sea life die. The tsunamis created by the mountain falling into the sea destroy one-third of the ships and bring untold destruction on the seacoasts. One enormous area of the world's surface (think the Pacific Ocean and the entire Pacific Rim) is devastated. It's not complete destruction—God is still leaving room for mercy—but the world will stagger under the shock.

Trumpet Three (Revelation 8:10 – 11)

> The third angel sounded his trumpet, and a great star, blazing like a torch, fell from the sky on a third of the rivers and on the springs of water—the name of the star is Wormwood. A third of the waters turned bitter, and many people died from the waters that had become bitter.

The third trumpet blast calls out a blazing star—a meteor or comet—that falls to the earth and apparently breaks apart in the atmosphere so that pieces of it land in freshwater sources.

BLOW THAT TRUMPET

Trumpets appear often in the Bible and are usually used to announce big events. In the Old Testament, trumpets assembled Israelites for war or even celebrations. The judge Gideon defeated an enemy army with three hundred men armed only with jugs, torches, and trumpets (Judges 7:15–25). The prophet Joel said that trumpets would warn of the coming day of the Lord (Joel 2:1). Among the names the prophet Zephaniah gives to Tribulation, the last is "a day of trumpet and battle cry" (Zephaniah 1:16). Trumpets sounded when the temple was dedicated (2 Chronicles 5:12) and when a new king was crowned (1 Kings 1:34, 39). In Israel's worship there were at least twenty-one blasts of the trumpet in the temple every day; on feast days there could be as many as forty-eight.

Think of the Great Lakes or all of the rivers of Europe polluted at the same time. Groundwater and public water supplies would be compromised almost instantly. Massive water shortages would result, creating panic as human beings scramble for limited supplies.

The star is called "Wormwood," a class of bitter-tasting plants, not poisonous but difficult, if not impossible, to eat. In the Old Testament, God used bitter water to judge the Egyptians (Exodus 7:21) and to test the people of Israel when they rebelled in the wilderness (Exodus 15:23–25). In this future judgment, one-third of the world's freshwater supply is made unfit to drink.

Those who die from the waters may die in the chaos and health crisis that a severe water shortage produces. Another possibility is that the fragments of the blazing star turn the water bitter and poisonous, and those who drink in desperation die. Listen to what Jeremiah said to the rebellious people of Israel: "This is what the LORD Almighty, the God of Israel, says: 'See, I will make this people eat bitter food and drink poisoned water'" (Jeremiah 9:15).

Trumpet Quattro (Revelation 8:12)

The fourth angel sounded his trumpet, and a third of the sun was struck, a third of the moon, and a third of the stars, so that a third

In Other Words

The devastation that [the seven trumpets] predict was unknown and unfathomable in the ancient world. These destructions are certainly beyond anything known to the people of John's day, which makes the Apocalypse all the more fascinating. There is no way John could have merely imagined these great catastrophes had he not seen them by divine permission in these visions.

Ed Hindson, in *The Book of Revelation: Unlocking the Future* (Chattanooga, Tenn.: AMG, 2002), 101.

When the Mediterranean island of Thera, an island near Patmos, exploded in approximately 1440 BC, the sea became red as blood.

Mal Couch, in *The Popular Encyclopedia of Bible Prophecy*, eds. Tim LaHaye and Ed Hindson (Eugene, Ore.: Harvest House, 2004), 393.

Alternative Views of the Seven Trumpets

Not everyone believes that the seven trumpet judgments are calamities that fall on the earth in a future Tribulation. The *preterist* position (the view that Revelation is a largely symbolic description of the Roman conquest of Judea from AD 66 to 70) holds that the trumpet judgments correspond to disasters inflicted by the Romans on the Jews. The third trumpet, for example, pictures the pollution of the water in the Sea of Galilee caused by the decaying corpses of Jewish defenders killed during the Roman conquest of Galilee.

The *idealist* position (the view that Revelation pictures the conflict between God and Satan in every age of the church) advocates that the seven trumpet judgments describe natural catastrophes that have fallen on the earth many times in human history. These catastrophes should have turned humanity's heart toward God, but men and women simply absorb the injuries in defiance and deliberately harden their hearts toward God. The third trumpet reminds us of how often rivers have flooded or epidemics have originated from waterborne organisms. These judg-ments express God's displeasure, but human beings refuse to cry out for God's mercy.

An older view of Revelation, called the *historicist* view, claims that Revelation mapped out the entire future from John's day until the return of Christ. According to advocates of this position, the trumpet judgments prefigure the invasions of the Roman Empire by various outside enemies. The "great star" of the third trumpet judgment, for example, is Attila the Hun, "the scourge of God," and the pollution of the water came from Attila's massacre of Roman soldiers in the rivers of the Italian Alps. Matthew Henry believed that the great star was the heretic Pelagius, who polluted the rivers of truth with his false teaching.

Some who hold to a *futurist* approach to Revelation (the view that most of the book describes a Tribulation that is future to us) prefer to interpret the language of the trumpet judgments figuratively. Ray Stedman explains that the sea is a symbol for the nations of the world. In his mind, the burning mountain falling into the sea of the second trumpet judgment pictures the government of the Antichrist falling on the nations of the world in bloody conquest.

MOUNTAIN-SIZED METEORS

In July 1994, the comet Shoemaker–Levy 9 broke apart and sent nearly two dozen mountain-sized fragments slamming into Jupiter. The impact created a two-thousand-mile-high fireball and dark debris on the planet's clouds visible from earth by telescopes.

of them turned dark. A third of the day was without light, and also a third of the night.

The fourth trumpet judgment touches the objects in space that most affect the earth—the sun, the moon, and the visible stars. God strikes the sun so that its light is reduced by one-third. Some students of Revelation believe that pollution or a partial eclipse will reduce the light by a third. Others think John's words mean that, instead of twelve hours of daylight, each portion of the earth will receive only eight hours of daylight. One-third of the day will be dark, and one-third of the night will be dark.

God touches the planetary heavens for several reasons. Since mankind's earliest civilizations, pagan worshipers have revered the sun and the moon. Astrologers and fortune-tellers rely on the planets and stars to predict the future. In one swift blow, God demonstrates his absolute superiority and his sovereignty over his creation.

The reduced heat and light on the earth will produce staggering results. Crop development, world temperature, wind and storm systems, human health, commerce, and navigation will

Try, Try Again

Signs of the Times

Christians have always concluded (correctly) that they are living in the last days and that conditions exist in the world that point to Christ's soon return. In AD 250 Cyprian, the bishop of Carthage, wrote, "Who cannot see that the world is already in decline, and no longer has the strength and vigor of former times?" The Reformer Martin Luther preached that the conditions in early sixteenth-century Germany matched precisely Jesus' description of the end times. He concluded that "the day of judgment is not far off." In 1756 Massachusetts pastor Jonathon Mayhew preached a series of messages on signs of the end and said, "There has probably been no age or period of the world wherein events have more nearly corresponded to this prophetic description than the present."

The quotations are from Paul Boyer, *When Time Shall Be No More: Prophecy Belief in Modern American Culture* (Cambridge: Harvard University Press, 1992), 239–40.

Bible Networking

Isaiah 13:9-10

> See the day of the LORD is coming
>   —a cruel day, with wrath and fierce anger—
> to make the land desolate
>   and destroy the sinners within it.
> The stars of heaven and their constellations
>   will not show their light.
> The rising sun will be darkened
>   and the moon will not give its light.

The Old Testament prophets repeatedly indicated that darkness would be an element in the future day of the Lord.

Isaiah's prophecy is quoted by Jesus in Mark 13:24. Other passages to check out are Amos 5:18; Joel 2:1–2; and Zephaniah 1:14–15.

Help File

PARALLEL PLAGUES

Four of the trumpet judgments echo the plagues that God brought on Egypt in the time of Moses. When Pharaoh refused to let God's people, Israel, go free, God pounded away at Pharaoh's hard heart with a series of judgments.

- The first trumpet judgment of Revelation echoes the seventh plague against Egypt of thunder, hail, and lightning (Exodus 9:23–24).
- The second trumpet parallels the first plague of water being turned to blood (Exodus 7:19–20).
- The fourth trumpet corresponds to the ninth plague of darkness (Exodus 10:21–23).
- The fifth trumpet echoes the eighth plague of locusts invading the land (Exodus 10:12).

The Old Testament prophets announced that the miracles associated with Israel's escape from Egypt would be repeated in the future. Micah wrote: "As in the days when you came out of Egypt, I will show them my wonders" (Micah 7:15; see also Isaiah 30:30 and Ezekiel 38:22).

Points to Remember

- ✓ Silence fills heaven for half an hour when the seventh seal is broken.

- ✓ The prayers of God's people for vengeance on the earth are answered in seven trumpet judgments.

- ✓ The first four trumpet judgments are directed at the created universe. Everything that was created as a blessing to mankind becomes a source of trouble for those who hate God.

all be dramatically affected. Beyond all this, darkness will spread a sense of dread and fear over the earth that the brightest artificial lights will not dispel.

The Worst Is Yet to Come (Revelation 8:13)

As I watched, I heard an eagle that was flying in midair call out in a loud voice: "Woe! Woe! Woe to the inhabitants of the earth, because of the trumpet blasts about to be sounded by the other three angels!"

John has been standing transfixed on the edge of heaven, watching the earth as God sends wave after wave of judgment crashing over it. Suddenly John's attention is caught by something above him—an eagle flying at the peak of the sun's journey across the sky, at the place where everyone can see it. John must have been startled to hear the eagle speak, but the eagle's cry would have sent shivers down his back.

"Woe, woe, woe" refers to the three trumpet judgments yet to come. Doubling a word in Scripture puts special emphasis on it (like when Jesus said, "Truly, truly I say to you") but tripling a word raises it one

A WORD TO THE WISE

Some translations of Revelation 8:13 (the King James Version, for example) read that an *angel* flew through heaven and made this announcement of woe. This is one of the few places in Scripture where there is serious question about what John originally wrote. Most early copies of the Greek New Testament have the word "eagle" instead of the word "angel." So most modern translations say "eagle." Either way the emphasis is on the message, not on the messenger. Whether John saw an eagle or an angel doesn't change the stunning impact of the message.

notch higher. The eagle brought disastrous news. The worst of God's judgment was yet to come. God had previously touched mankind indirectly by sending judgment on the environment (earth, sea, freshwater). Now judgment will touch those on the earth directly.

CHAPTER 9

Hell on Earth

Hell on Earth

- Angels continue to sound their trumpets and judgments continue to fall.
- A horrific plague of "locusts" is released from hell.
- More people die, but those still standing refuse to repent.

Key Codes: Level 9

→ Abyss: A place where demons are confined
→ Locusts: Devouring insects
→ Scorpion: An eight-legged insect with a painful stinger in its tail
→ Abbadon, Apollyon: Hebrew and Greek for "destroyer"
→ Breastplate: Armor across the chest
→ Golden altar: The small altar of incense in the heavenly tabernacle
→ Euphrates: A river located in modern Iraq
→ Demons: Evil angels who follow Satan

Trumpet Five — Don't Open That Pit! (Revelation 9:1–12)

The fifth angel sounded his trumpet, and I saw a star that had fallen from the sky to the earth. The star was given the key to the shaft of the Abyss. When he opened the Abyss, smoke rose from it like the smoke from a gigantic furnace. The sun and sky were darkened by the smoke from the Abyss. And out of the smoke locusts came down on the earth and were given power like that of scorpions of the earth. They were told not to harm the grass of the earth or any plant or tree, but only those people who did not have the seal of God on their foreheads. They were not allowed to kill them but only to torture them for five months. And the agony they suffered was like that of the sting of a

WORST-CASE SCENARIO: HOW TO SURVIVE A SCORPION STING

SYMPTOMS

- The victim experiences a painful burning sensation at the site of the sting.
- More severe reactions ripple throughout the body: numbness, difficulty swallowing, a thick tongue, blurred vision, nausea, diarrhea, seizures, uncontrolled drooling, and difficulty breathing. (Are we having fun yet?) One medical website adds this note: "Death may occur."
- The correct term for a scorpion sting is "envenomation" (venom is injected into your body—you get the picture).

TREATMENT

- Remain calm (right!).
- Limit the pain at the sting site by applying ice cubes (I'm not kidding).
- Seek medical help for antivenom therapy and morphine-based painkillers.

WEIRDNESS

World magazine reported in September 2004 that a young Malaysian woman, Ms. Nur Malena Hassan, of Kuantan, Malaysia, was attempting to set a new world record for the longest stay in a room full of poisonous arachnids. Her plan was to spend thirty-six days in a locked glass box with six thousand scorpions. She had set a previous record in 2001 of thirty days with 2,700 scorpions, during which time she was stung ("envenomated") seven times and fell unconscious. The whole spectacle took place at a local shopping mall. Later reports confirm that she succeeded in setting the new record and was only stung seventeen times!

scorpion when it strikes. During those days people will seek death but will not find it; they will long to die, but death will elude them.

The locusts looked like horses prepared for battle. On their heads they wore something like crowns of gold, and their faces resembled human faces. Their hair was like women's hair, and their teeth were like lions' teeth. They had breastplates like breastplates of iron, and the sound of their wings was like the thundering of many horses and chariots rushing into battle. They had tails with stingers, like scorpions, and in their tails they had power to torment people for five months. They had as king over them the angel of the Abyss, whose name in Hebrew is Abaddon, and in Greek, Apollyon.

The first woe is past; two other woes are yet to come.

As the fifth angel blows his trumpet, John the apostle sees a star that falls from heaven to earth. But when is a star not a star? We took the word literally in chapter 6 and chapter 8, so why not here? John makes it clear that this is more than just another cosmic body. John first says a key is given to the star. Then he adds that "he" (the star) unlocks a pit. I think we are safe to conclude that the "star" in Revelation 9 is an angel to whom God entrusts an important access key.

Some scholars think that this angel is Satan—a being who has "fallen" morally and spiritually from a prominent place in heaven to the level of the sinful god of this world. If that view is correct, God allows Satan to open this pit and to afflict the world with a swarm of demons.

Other interpreters believe that this angel is a powerful godly angel who has come down from heaven to fulfill God's purpose and who unleashes demonic judgment on the world. I side with this group because, when we get to chapter 20, a strong angel still possesses the key to the Abyss. In that chapter he captures and confines Satan. It makes sense that the same angel opens the Abyss in both chapters.

The Abyss (or "bottomless pit," as some Bible translations put it) is a prison for demons—for evil angels who do Satan's bidding. In Luke 8:31, some demons beg Jesus not to send them to the Abyss. It's a dreadful place. In 2 Peter 2:4, Peter speaks of God consigning certain evil angels to gloomy dungeons, putting them in "chains of darkness" to wait for the day of God's judgment. Satan himself will be confined in the Abyss for the one thousand years of Jesus' reign on earth (Revelation 20:2–3).

The demons who make up this "army from hell" may have been confined gradually over time as God sent various sinful angels to the Abyss, or they may have been confined all at once at the time of their original rebellion against God. Whenever they were locked up, someday they will be set free—at least for a short time. An angel will open this pit of evil and release hordes of demons on humanity.

In Other Words

In this chapter there are more occurrences of the words "as" and "like" than in any other chapter of the Bible, which shows how difficult it was for John to describe the scene.

Charles Ryrie, in *Revelation* (Chicago: Moody, 1968), 61.

Destroyer Demons

The smoke belching from the Abyss will darken the sun. As the smoke spreads and thins, creatures emerge from it—locusts with the power to sting like scorpions. Locusts are associated with severe judgment and destruction in the Old Testament (Exodus 10:12–20; Joel 1:4–7; Deuteronomy 28:38, 42; 1 Kings 8:37). They will come with one goal in mind—devastation.

But are these creatures that John sees just some kind of mutant insects, some weird science project gone horribly bad? What seems clear is that the locusts are the embodiment of evil spirits—demons who set out to bring pain and misery to people on earth. Several factors make it clear that these are more than just insects:

- The locusts are told what they can and cannot do. Normal insects aren't like that.
- These demon locusts have the ability to select their targets. They can't touch human beings who have the seal of God on their foreheads (verse 4). That fact alone reveals intelligence far beyond a bug.
- These locusts have the ability to sting like scorpions—something actual locusts do not have.
- The locust creatures are commanded not to eat any green plant—which is what insect locusts must eat to survive.
- They come up from the Abyss, which other Scripture passages indicate is a place where evil angels are confined.

Help File

HELICOPTERS IN AN ANCIENT BOOK?

Some people have read John's description of these locusts and have seen modern helicopter gunships in John's imagery—breastplates of iron, the sound of their wings like thundering hoofbeats, tails that sting like scorpions. Should we believe that John saw twenty-first-century weapons in his vision and then tried to explain what he saw in images he was familiar with? Or did John see exactly what he described?

It's probably best to conclude that John saw locusts, not helicopters. But John's vision depicts a deeper reality. John is picturing an evil, destructive force moving through human society to bring pain and suffering. These demons carry out God's judgment, but at the direction of Satan, their cruel master. The complete understanding of what this vision involves will probably remain unknown until its actual fulfillment.

Soldiers or Spirits?

Futurist interpreters of Revelation take one of two views on the nature of this army from the east in Revelation 9. I will give you the main arguments for both views, and then you can decide where you stand:

The Army Is Demonic

The first view is that the massive army is an army of evil angels, led by the four "general" angels released from their confinement near the Euphrates River. Support for this position:

- The sheer number of soldiers almost requires that they are demons, not humans. Just gathering and supplying an army of two hundred million human beings would disrupt the economic and social balance of the entire world.
- The Bible portrays God's angels as a supernatural army (2 Kings 6:13–17; Revelation 19:14). Why not a demonic army?
- The weapons of this army are the weapons of hell—fire, smoke, and sulfur (verse 17).
- In John's account the horses are given more prominence than the riders. Their lionlike heads and snakelike tails are characteristic of supernatural creatures, not normal horses.

The Armies Are Human

The alternate view is that this is an army (or group of armies) from the east that move to-ward the final battle at Armageddon. Points that support this view:

- The number in the army is enormous but not unreasonable. They destroy and plunder their way across the Middle East, finally reaching the land of Israel.
- The description of the army's "horses" is a figurative picture of modern war machines—tanks and missile launchers—that pour out fire and smoke and death in the path of the army.
- In Revelation 16 the water in the Euphrates River is diverted to let this army pass. Demonic armies would not find water a barrier. Only a human army would need such obstacles removed.

Some interpreters just can't decide between these two views. Charles Ryrie says, "This army might be composed of human beings and it might equally well be an army of demons" (quoted in Steve Gregg, ed., *Revelation: Four Views* [Nashville: Nelson, 1997], 19). Hal Lindsey is not so reluctant. "I believe these 200 million troops are Red Chinese soldiers accompanied by other Eastern allies.... For the first time in history there will be a full invasion of the West by the Orient" (*There's a New World Coming* [1973; rev. ed., Eugene, Ore.: Harvest House, 1984], 140).

- The locust demons have a leader—an evil, destructive angel named "Destroyer" (Abaddon is the Hebrew form of that word; Apollyon is the Greek form).

The ability to understand and obey commands and to follow a leader's direction implies that these creatures have intelligence, decision-making ability, and the power of choice. Our conclusion has to be that these locusts are not insects; they are a well-disciplined, obedient army of demonic invaders.

Trying to Die

The demon locusts are given a very detailed set of limitations, but their main objective is clear—they torment human beings with physical pain and most likely spiritual agony. The only people protected from their attack are those with the seal of God on their foreheads. This may refer only to the 144,000 who were sealed back in chapter 7, or it may refer to all those who have chosen to follow Christ during the Tribulation. Unbelieving humanity suffers during five months of unrelenting attack.

Human beings will be in so much pain that they will want to die but won't be able to. Men and women will choose death over repentance, but they will not succeed. The demons will have such a grip on them that they won't even be free to take their own lives.

In Other Words

Never since Noah has such a substantial proportion of earth's population come under God's righteous judgment. It may be that the army here described continues to fight until the time of the second coming of Christ, and the number slain is the total number involved in the conflict.

John Walvoord, in *The Revelation of Jesus Christ* (1966; rev. ed., Chicago: Moody, 1989), 167.

Here we see a great reversal. In Luke 10:19 Jesus gave the disciples "authority to trample on snakes and scorpions" while in the fifth and sixth trumpets God gives the scorpions and snakes "authority to harm the earth-dwellers."

Grant Osborne, in *Revelation* (Grand Rapids: Baker, 2002), 384.

The demons can't kill anyone either. God prohibits them from taking human life. Scorpion stings are incredibly painful, but they are rarely fatal. Unbelievers will get a taste of what it is really like to follow the demonic forces of the world instead of following Christ. Satan's evil power will be turned against his own followers.

The mention of "five months" in verse 10 gives us some hint about how long these judgments will afflict humanity. For example, when the daylight is reduced by one-third during the fourth trumpet judg-

In Other Words

All quotations are taken from *Revelation: Four Views*, ed. Steve Gregg (Nashville: Nelson, 1997), 194–95.

Futurist Position: Revelation predicts future events

Whether these are symbols or the best description John can give of modern warfare, this is an awesome picture of an almost irresistible military force destroying all that opposes it.

John Walvoord

Idealist Position: Revelation pictures spiritual conditions throughout the entire church age

The general meaning of these trumpets is clear. Throughout the entire period, extending from the first to the second coming, our exalted Lord Jesus Christ ... will again and again punish the persecutors of the Church by inflicting upon them disasters in every sphere of life.

William Hendriksen

Preterist Position: Revelation is primarily a prophecy of Jerusalem's destruction by the Romans

The Jewish rebellion in reaction to the "locust plague" of Gessius Florus during the summer of 66 provoked Cestius's invasion of Palestine in the fall, with large numbers of mounted troops from the region near the Euphrates.... After ravaging the countryside, his forces arrived at the gates of Jerusalem in the month of Teshri — the month that begins with the Day of Trumpets. The army surrounded the city.

David Chilton

ment (8:12), that judgment may last only a few months and then the cosmic order will return to its normal pattern. These locust demons do not afflict human beings throughout the rest of the Tribulation. God demonstrates his mercy by limiting the time of their activity. At the end of the five months, they most likely are forced to return to the confinement of the Abyss.

Extreme Makeover

John's description of the locusts begins at their heads and moves to their tails. The images convey the power of these demonic beings—power that Christians need to understand and respect in our ongoing spiritual warfare with Satan. We are not to fear demons, because the Holy Spirit in us is far greater than any or all demonic power. But neither should we underestimate Satan's strength to oppose and oppress us. We rebuke Satan and his minions in the awesome name and power of the Lord.

The demons' crowns are "like crowns of gold" (verse 7). The twenty-four elders in Revelation 4 have gold crowns, and Jesus is pictured in Revelation 14 with a gold crown (verse 14). The demonic locusts claim an authority they do not have. They are given temporary victory over human beings by divine permission, but they don't have full authority. Satan is "the god of this world" for a time (2 Corinthians 4:4 KJV) but certainly not forever.

Human beings will have no weapon against the locusts. No physical weapon will destroy spiritual (but real) beings. Not even Raid will bring these creatures down! They are indestructible.

Their faces resembling human faces suggest that these are intelligent beings, not simply insects. Their humanlike features are enhanced by long windblown hair, streaming behind them as they plunge into battle. Lions' teeth picture their vicious nature and their ability to devour people spiritually. Their main weapon, however, is not their teeth but the stinger in their tail.

Fierce warlike demon creatures will attack their own human followers. This is a shocking display of Satan's true objective. God seeks to build up his followers to be like Jesus in holiness and purity. Satan turns on his own children and tortures them. It is Satan's nature to destroy.

The king of these demons from the Abyss is called "Destroyer." Some students of Revelation believe this is another name for Satan himself. John, however, simply calls him an "angel" (verse 11). Satan will make a far more dramatic entrance in chapter 12, and there is no mistaking his identity then. So this angel is most likely the highest-ranking demon of all those confined in the Abyss—one of Satan's wicked generals. If that is the case, he is one of the few angels named in Scripture. This "name" is more a nickname or description of his depraved nature—the Destroyer.

John breathes a short sigh of relief in verse 12—"the first woe is past." The last three trumpet judgments are three "woes" announced against the inhabitants of the earth (8:13). The first woe, as dreadful as it will be, has now passed in John's vision. The reprieve is very short, however, because "two other woes are yet to come."

Trumpet Six: An Army from the East (Revelation 9:13 – 19)

> The sixth angel sounded his trumpet, and I heard a voice coming from the four horns of the golden altar that is before God. It said to the sixth angel who had the trumpet, "Release the four angels who are bound at the great river Euphrates." And the four angels who had been kept ready for this very hour and day and month and year were released to kill a third of the world's people. The number of the mounted troops was two hundred million. I heard their number.
>
> The horses and riders I saw in my vision looked like this: Their breastplates were fiery red, dark blue, and yellow as sulfur. The heads of the horses resembled the heads of lions, and out of their mouths came fire, smoke and sulfur. A third of the people were killed by the three plagues of fire, smoke and sulfur that came out of their mouths. The power of the horses was in their mouths and in their tails; for their tails were like snakes, having heads with which they inflict injury.

Human beings find it impossible to die during the five months of demonic attack, but that all changes when the sixth trumpet-playing angel steps onto center stage. The angel's trumpet blast is answered by a

In Other Words

Past the point of no return, [sinful humanity] responds to greater punishment with increased rebellion. Such is sinful nature untouched and unmoved by the mercies of God.

Robert Mounce, in *The Book of Revelation* (Grand Rapids: Eerdmans, 1977), 193.

voice. John not only sees the book of Revelation unfold; he also hears its startling sounds. We are reminded again that this book is not some literary creation from John's imagination. It's a record of what John saw and heard and smelled and tasted (he eats a scroll in chapter 10).

The voice focuses our attention again on the golden altar in heaven — the place where John saw the souls of those who had been slain, the same altar where the fragrant incense of the prayers of believers had risen up before the Lord. The source of the voice is never identified, but it is probably God's voice. The sixth trumpeting angel is told to release four angels who are confined somewhere near the Euphrates River. The Euphrates River today runs through Iraq, right through the capital city of Baghdad.

We've met clusters of four angels before in Revelation. Four living creatures, magnificent holy angels, stand around God's throne (4:6–8). Four angels held back God's judgment for a time in chapter 7. Both of those angel quartets were made up of holy angels. Here in Revelation 9 are four evil angels — destroying angels who unleash an army that kills millions of people. These four angels are bound right now somewhere

The assault of this future demonic army will bring incredible pain and torment to the world — but evil powers are active even today. The apostle Paul urges every believer to be armed and protected by the spiritual equipment that God provides because "our struggle is not against flesh and blood, but against the rulers, against the authorities, against the powers of this dark world and against the spiritual forces of evil in the heavenly realms" (Ephesians 6:12). Spiritual forces of evil are arrayed against us, and without God's protection we are vulnerable. Satan and the spirits under his control look us over very carefully and plan their strategy to inflict maximum damage. They want to deceive us, defeat us, discourage us, and neutralize our impact. In the Tribulation, the inhabitants of the world will have no defense against the demonic army. Christians today have a full range of protection against enemy attack. The armor is available, but we must put it on.

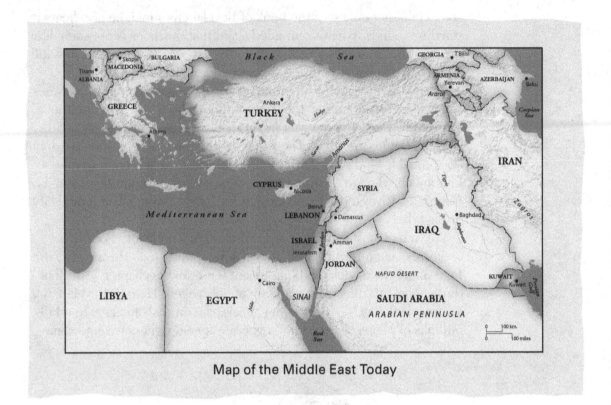

Map of the Middle East Today

near the Euphrates in a realm inhabited by demons and holy angels. They are being held for a very specific moment in God's eternal plan.

Armies from the East

In John's mind, the Euphrates River was the eastern boundary of the Roman Empire. Beyond the Euphrates was the Orient, the East, a shadowy land filled with unknown people. The Euphrates will also mark the boundary of the Antichrist's empire. His power center is the West, in the nations connected to the old Roman Empire—in Europe and the Western Hemisphere.

The nations outside the Antichrist's direct control, even at the height of his power, will be the nations of the East, the vast populations of India and China and southeast Asia. Later in the Tribulation (in Revelation 16), the Euphrates will be dried up to prepare the way for the kings and armies of the East to make their way toward a confrontation with the Antichrist (verses 12–14).

Bible Networking

Ephesians 4:17 – 19

So I tell you this, and insist on it in the Lord, that you must no longer live as the Gentiles do, in the futility of their thinking. They are darkened in their understanding and separated from the life of God because of the ignorance that is in them due to the hardening of their hearts. Having lost all sensitivity, they have given themselves over to sensuality so as to indulge in every kind of impurity, and they are full of greed.

1 Timothy 4:1

The Spirit clearly says that in later times some will abandon the faith and follow deceiving spirits and things taught by demons.

John just gives us a few pieces of the puzzle at this point, but as best as I can piece these passages together, events seem to unfold like this:

- As the sixth trumpet is blown (9:13), four powerful demonic angels spread a lust for war into the regions of the East.
- A massive army begins to gather—two hundred million strong.
- This army in its initial infighting for control of the nations of Asia spreads death to millions of people, a third of the remaining population of the world.
- Apparently only unbelievers die as a consequence of the release of these angels and the onslaught of the army. Verse 20 reads, "The rest of the people who were not killed by these plagues still did not repent"—implying that those who died were also unrepentant.

Since the beginning of John's vision of the Tribulation, the world's population has been reduced by half. One-fourth of the world died under the fourth seal judgment (6:7–8), and many more died as martyrs for their faith in Christ (6:10). Now one-third of the remaining population is killed.

If after the rapture the earth's population is around six billion, three billion will die in the first three and a half years of the Tribulation. No wonder Daniel said, and Jesus confirmed, that the Tribulation would be "a time of distress such as has not happened from the beginning of nations until then" (Daniel 12:1; Matthew 24:21–22).

BREAKING NEWS

In 2005 the world's two most populous nations, India and China, announced a major new political and economic agreement. These two nations had been engaged in a border war in 1962 but now were allies. What stunned students of Bible prophecy was a statement from India's prime minister, who said, "India and China can together reshape the world order." In light of the future scenario of the Tribulation, his words are more prophetic than he realizes.

Based on an Associated Press report in *The Detroit News*, April 12, 2005.

They Would Not Repent (Revelation 9:20 – 21)

> The rest of the people who were not killed by these plagues still did not repent of the work of their hands; they did not stop worshiping demons, and idols of gold, silver, bronze, stone and wood — idols that cannot see or hear or walk. Nor did they repent of their murders, their magic arts, their sexual immorality or their thefts.

In spite of incredible devastation and loss of life, those who live on the earth will not repent or turn to God. They will be like Pharaoh in the days of Moses as the plagues pounded Egypt. Pharaoh wasn't softened by God's judgment; he stubbornly hardened his heart. Men and women will see God's judgment and will refuse to flee to him for mercy. They will simply embrace their wickedness more tightly.

John points out several aspects of evil that will mark the Tribulation period:

- Idolatry and the worship of demons (Deuteronomy 32:17; 1 Corinthians 10:20). Demons bring suffering, pain, and death to human beings, and yet those same human beings continue to worship false gods, which are nothing more than masks for demonic influence and power. Mankind worships the very forces that bring about its destruction. Sin produces unbelievable blindness.
- Murder
- Sorcery and occult practices. The word John uses for "magic arts" is the Greek word *pharmakon*, from which our word *pharmacy* emerges. The use of narcotic drugs will be rampant in the Tribulation.

Points to Remember

☑ The fifth trumpet judgment unleashes demonic attack on the unbelieving world for five months.

☑ The sixth trumpet judgment produces unbelievable devastation from war—a third of the world's population dies.

☑ Human beings will not embrace God's grace, even in the face of God's wrath.

- Sexual immorality, including pornography and homosexual sin
- Theft

You would think that the terrors of God's judgment would bring sinful human beings to their knees in repentance, but that is not the case. They simply push God further away and push themselves further into God's judgment.

CHAPTER 10

A Big Angel and a Little Scroll

A Big Angel and a Little Scroll

- ▶ Another strong angel takes his stand.
- ▶ For the first time John becomes more than an observer. He's part of the action.
- ▶ John eats a book! Would you like fries with that?

Access Codes

Key Codes: Level 10

- → Clouds: Associated in Scripture with God's presence (Exodus 19:9–11) and divine justice (Matthew 24:30; Revelation 14:14–16)
- → Rainbow: A reminder of God's mercy even in a time of judgment; given as a promise to Noah after the flood (Genesis 9:11–16)
- → Little scroll: Not the seven-sealed scroll of chapter 5 but a smaller scroll (or book) representing God's message of judgment and grace
- → Mystery: Something previously hidden but now revealed

Second Intermission

The apostle John has been busy writing down all that he sees and hears, breathlessly recording the trumpet judgments that hammer the earth during the future Tribulation. John knows we need a rest. There's only so much judgment and suffering we can endure to watch. So chapter 10 begins a long interlude. For six chapters John puts the action on pause and explains to us a few things in greater detail.

Back in chapter 7 we had the first intermission. Jesus had broken six wax seals on a scroll given to him by God the Father. As each seal was broken, a new wave of judgment swept over the world. John paused the action back then to tell us about 144,000 Jews who would be saved by God's grace and protectively sealed through the Tribulation. Then John told us about a vast multitude of people who would believe in Jesus and pay the ultimate price for their faith. In the middle of judgment, John gave us a glimpse of God's grace and mercy.

The same thing happens here in chapter 10. Seven angels received seven trumpets back in chapter 8, and at this point six angels have played their solos. Each blast unleashed a new judgment. It's been an exhausting experience to watch—and we aren't the only ones exhausted. John has reached a point of discouragement too.

So chapter 10 focuses on him. God stops his whole program to care for his prophet and to strengthen him for the rest of the journey. In the middle of awesome worldwide catastrophe, we see God's compassion and concern for one man who finds himself discouraged. God recommissions John to finish the work of recording God's final plan.

John's first readers had to be encouraged by this chapter. They were under intense persecution and probably wondered what would eventually happen to them. God wanted to assure them that victory was already guaranteed. Don't lose heart as you face loss and difficulty and discouraging days! God is right on schedule in our world and in your life.

Scene 1: A Strong Angel (Revelation 10:1)

> Then I saw another mighty angel coming down from heaven. He was robed in a cloud, with a rainbow above his head; his face was like the sun, and his legs were like fiery pillars.

Help File

ANGELS AROUND US

Holy angels appear sixty-six times in the book of Revelation—one-quarter of all the references in the Bible. If you add John's references to demons, Satan, and defiant evil angels, the number goes much higher. We aren't surprised by so many angels. It's what we would expect from a book that scans heaven, earth, and hell.

God's angels in Revelation fall into four categories:

- *Commissioned angels*: These are angels sent out from God with special assignments or messages.

- *Judgment angels*: Seven angels blow trumpets of judgment; seven others pour out bowls of wrath on the earth. Other angels throw fire on the earth and release demons from confinement.

- *Warring angels*: The archangel Michael and his angels fight with Satan and his angels to exclude Satan from heaven.

- *Adoring angels*: Some angels simply stand attentively in God's presence and give him praise and honor.

Bible Networking

Psalm 29:3 - 5, 7 - 8

The voice of the LORD is over the waters;
   the God of glory thunders,
   the LORD thunders over the mighty waters.
The voice of the LORD is powerful;
   the voice of the LORD is majestic.
The voice of the LORD breaks the cedars; . . .
The voice of the LORD strikes
   with flashes of lightning.
The voice of the LORD shakes the desert.

The big question we need to answer first is, Who is this angel? Some Bible teachers believe that the angel is Jesus, that Jesus is the only being capable of displaying such glory and majesty. I think we should just take John at his word and conclude that it is an angel. It's true that Jesus is called the "angel of the LORD" in the Old Testament (a reference to his role as the deliverer of God's message), but he is never called an angel in the New Testament. There is no indication anywhere in Scripture that Jesus will stand on the earth in the middle of the Tribulation — and just because this angel is glorious doesn't mean he has to be Christ. Angels are majestic, glorious, powerful beings.

John sees this strong angel come out of heaven clothed with a cloud, crowned with a rainbow. His face glows like the sun, and his feet are like pillars of fire. The angel stands with one foot on dry land and one foot on the sea and lays claim to the earth as God's messenger. This is a foretaste of God's eventual reclamation of his creation. Satan may rule temporarily as the god of this world, but someday soon, God will take back what belongs to him.

Scene 2: A Startling Act (Revelation 10:2 - 4)

He was holding a little scroll, which lay open in his hand. He planted his right foot on the sea and his left foot on the land, and he gave a loud shout like the roar of a lion. When he shouted, the voices of the seven thunders spoke. And when the seven thunders spoke, I was about to write; but I heard a voice from heaven say, "Seal up what the seven thunders have said and do not write it down."

In the language of the Bible, putting your feet on something is a sign of ownership. The angel establishes God's ownership of our planet, and he shouts toward heaven. We aren't told what he says, but heaven echoes back with seven rumbles of thunder—and then a voice. The thunder apparently contained a message that John heard and was about to write down, but another voice, God's voice most likely, told him not to do it. "Seal up what the seven thunders have said," the voice commanded, "and do not write it down."

It's not unusual for God to tell a prophet to seal up words of prophecy. The Old Testament prophet Daniel was told to "seal up the vision" he had seen, "for it concerns the distant future" (Daniel 8:26). Later God tells Daniel to "close up and seal" the words of his entire prophecy "until the time of the end" (Daniel 12:4, 9). Daniel's words would need the light of more truth—truth that came through the writings of the New Testament and particularly the book of Revelation—before they could be understood.

Seven Peals of Thunder Unmasked

In the past some interpreters of Revelation believed that John was laying out the entire history of the church age in a biblical code. The problem was that the interpreters had a hard time agreeing on which historical event corresponded with each biblical symbol. The seven peals of thunder here in chapter 10 have been viewed by different interpreters as:

- the seven Crusades
- the seven wars between the time of the Reformation and the French Revolution
- the seven kingdoms that embraced the teaching of the Reformation
- the seven decrees issued by the pope condemning the teaching of the Reformers (Those who hold this particular view say that John is forbidden to record the words because they are invalid and are therefore unworthy of being recorded in Scripture.)

As I write a book about the Bible's view of the future (and as I listen to prophecy preachers), I have to keep the "seven peals of thunder" incident clearly in mind. The hidden things belong to God alone, and he has chosen not to reveal all the details about every question to us. God has put some boundaries on what he has decided to tell us. We can speculate and suggest how events might work themselves out in God's plan, but we can't be dogmatic about our suggestions. God rules the future, and we know that he has every detail under control—but he has not filled in all the blanks. Some of the Bible's prophecies may be fulfilled in ways we can't even imagine at this point in history. We certainly are to seek to know and believe all that God has revealed, but all of us can hold that truth with a little more humility.

WHAT NO ONE KNEW UNTIL GOD TOLD US

The New Testament writers identify several "mysteries." Remember, a mystery in Scripture is not something spooky or unknowable. It's an event or fact that God kept hidden for a while but has now revealed to his people. Here are a few of the Bible's "secrets" to think about:

- the mystery of the rapture— 1 Corinthians 15:51
- the mystery of Israel's spiritual blindness—Romans 11:25
- the mystery of God's wisdom and human foolishness— 1 Corinthians 2:6–7

- the mystery of Christ and his marriage to the church—Ephesians 5:31–32
- the mystery of Christ in us— Colossians 1:26–27
- the mystery of the kingdom of heaven—Matthew 13
- the mystery of godliness and Christ's coming as a human being—1 Timothy 3:16
- the mystery of the Antichrist— 2 Thessalonians 2:7

No explanation is given to John about why he is not to write down what the voices of thunder spoke. God had said some things that John was allowed to hear, but he was not allowed to pass them on to us. What that tells us is that God has not revealed in Scripture everything that will take place during the Tribulation. Some judgments will be unveiled only at the time. That doesn't satisfy our curiosity, but it certainly emphasizes God's mercy. He spares us from knowing more than we can bear.

Scene 3: A Stirring Announcement (Revelation 10:5 – 7)

> Then the angel I had seen standing on the sea and on the land raised his right hand to heaven. And he swore by him who lives for ever and ever, who created the heavens and all that is in them, the earth and all that is in it, and the sea and all that is in it, and said, "There will be no more delay! But in the days when the seventh angel is about to sound his trumpet, the mystery of God will be accomplished, just as he announced to his servants the prophets."

God's words are sealed, but not the angel's words. He makes an oath in God's name and says, "There will be no more delay!" God will now begin the completion of his plan. The seventh angel will blow the seventh trumpet, and the mystery of God will be accomplished.

The word *mystery* in the Bible does not mean something mysterious. It means something previously hidden but now revealed. *Secret* might be a better word. God's plan for reclaiming his creation and for judging wicked human beings had been hidden in the past. But now as John writes, the secret is being revealed. The Old Testament said very little about the details of the Tribulation. God's plan for judgment was still a mystery. It was a mystery until God began to reveal it to John. John was a privileged apostle. God revealed things to him that had been revealed to no other biblical writer. The angel's announcement is, "There will be no more delay!"

In Other Words

Now nothing stands in the way of the final dramatic period of human history. From this point forward, God will not intervene to give man further opportunity to repent.

Robert Mounce, in *The Book of Revelation* (Grand Rapids: Eerdmans, 1977), 211.

We are still living in a time of delay. God is holding off the final sweep of judgment until the church age is over. It seems sometimes that evil has the upper hand. Men and women can mock God, crucify Jesus, torture or ridicule Christians, but somewhere in heaven is an angel ready to blow the seventh trumpet someday. On that day this sinful world system will begin to crumble. God's mystery of the past will become dreadful reality for those living on the earth.

I'm sure that this fact encouraged John as he walked the paths of the prison island of Patmos. I'm sure that God's promise of victory strengthened those early Christians chained in cells, waiting to be crucified or fed to the lions. God's repeated assurance that he will triumph over Satan and sin should encourage us as we walk through days of doubt and times of trouble. God has a plan to bring evil days to an end.

Scene 4: A Strange Assignment (Revelation 10:8–11)

Then the voice that I had heard from heaven spoke to me once more: "Go, take the scroll that lies open in the hand of the angel who is standing on the sea and on the land."

So I went to the angel and asked him to give me the little scroll. He said to me, "Take it and eat it. It will turn your stomach sour, but 'in your mouth it will be as sweet as honey.'" I took the little scroll from the angel's hand and ate it. It tasted as sweet as honey in my mouth, but when I had eaten it, my stomach turned sour. Then I was told, "You must prophesy again about many peoples, nations, languages and kings."

THE COLOSSUS

Those who first heard or read John's description of this immense angel standing with one foot on the land and one foot on the sea would probably have thought of the Colossus of Rhodes, one of the seven wonders of the ancient world. This towering bronze statue of Chelios, the patron deity of Rhodes, stood overlooking the city's harbor. A popular myth in the ancient world was that the statue's legs spanned the entrance to the harbor and that ships sailed in and out underneath the god's shadow. The reality was less dramatic. The statue stood on the shore and looked out to sea with hand-shaded eyes. The Colossus was still impressive. It stood as tall as the Statue of Liberty, but on a shorter base than the "modern Colossus" in New York Harbor. The statue in Rhodes was completed in 282 BC but broke at the knee and fell when an earthquake struck the city fifty-six years later. In the days of the New Testament, the statue still rested on the ground in Rhodes. In AD 654, Arab Muslims conquered the island, broke the ruins to pieces, and sold it as scrap metal.

What encouraged John most of all, I think, is what God tells him to do next. In the angel's hand is a scroll, or book. It isn't sealed like the scroll in chapter 5 is; it's open in the angel's hand. The scroll isn't big and filled with words; it's little—a mini-scroll. We aren't told what is on the scroll, but it certainly represents God's plan for the recapture of his world. The scroll is God's message, which is being entrusted to John.

John is told to take the scroll and eat it! I've never had a desire to take a bite out of my Bible, but there have been times when I've hungered in my heart to make the Bible a deeper part of my life. Eating the scroll symbolized taking God's Word into John's deepest being, making God's message part of who he is. Being a prophet was to be more than just a career for John. God's call would define who John is.

John wasn't the only biblical prophet who was commanded to eat a book. Jeremiah wrote:

> When your words came, I ate them;
> > they were my joy and my heart's delight,
> for I bear your name,
> > LORD God Almighty.
>
> Jeremiah 15:16

Here's what God told the prophet Ezekiel:

> "Son of man, listen to what I say to you. Do not rebel like that rebellious house; open your mouth and eat what I give you...."
> "Son of man, eat this scroll I am giving you and fill your stomach with it." So I ate it, and it tasted as sweet as honey in my mouth.
> > Ezekiel 2:8; 3:3

The Stamp Act

As the American Revolution against British rule drew closer, American preachers began to cast the revolutionary spirit in prophetic imagery. One pamphleteer described the Stamp Act imposed on America as the first step in the rise of the Antichrist. He advised his readers to avoid all documents bearing the hated stamp, "lest by touching any paper with this impression, you receive the mark of the beast." King George of England was portrayed as the biblical Antichrist and someone calculated that in both Greek and Hebrew the words "Royal Supremacy in Great Britain" had the numerical value of 666.

In Other Words

The true preacher of God's word will faithfully proclaim the denunciations of the wicked it contains. But he does not do this with fierce glee. The more his heart is filled with the love of God, the more certain it is that the telling forth of "woes" will be a bitter experience.

Leon Morris, *The Revelation of St. John* (Grand Rapids: Eerdmans, 1969), 143.

John takes the scroll and does what the angel asks—he eats it! (Wait until someone comes out with the all-scroll diet—two paperbacks for lunch, all the magazines you care to eat.) In his mouth the scroll tastes like honey, but in his stomach it turns sour. That seems to be the character of the book of Revelation. At first, the words of judgment and God's triumph sound sweet. But then, as we think about what God's wrath will produce and as we realize that people we know and love could face that wrath, we get a knot in our stomachs.

Both the sweetness and the bitterness of God's message motivate us to speak God's words. The eaten scroll motivated John too! He is told, "You *must* prophesy again." God tells John that he can't quit. God's Word is in him, part of him, and his ministry has to continue. I don't know what was going on in John's mind. Maybe he was discouraged. Maybe he felt as though his ministry was going nowhere. After all, he was on a prison island with no guarantee that he would ever get off. But God told John that it wasn't the end. He had to keep at it. God will keep his promises!

Points to Remember

☑ A mighty angel lays claim to the earth as God's representative.

☑ No delays from this point on! God's plan will soon be brought to completion.

☑ John eats the little scroll—and is recommissioned to keep proclaiming God's message.

☑ Some people avoid the book of Revelation because it fills them with dread and fear; other people "eat it up" because they see God's triumph over evil and injustice.

CHAPTER 11

Jehovah's True Witnesses

Jehovah's True Witnesses

▶ John measures the temple with a yardstick.
▶ Two witnesses announce God's judgment.
▶ The Antichrist kills the witnesses, but God brings them back to life!
▶ The seventh angel blows the seventh trumpet.

Key Codes: Level 11

→ Temple of God: The place where Israel worshiped the Lord during the time of the Bible
→ Gentiles: People of the world; non-Jews
→ The holy city: Jerusalem
→ Sackcloth: Black cloth made of goats' hair and worn as a sign of sorrow and repentance
→ The beast that comes up from the Abyss: The Antichrist, the evil world ruler of the last days
→ Sodom: A city destroyed by God in the Old Testament
→ Ark of the covenant: Small gold-covered box that was placed in the innermost room of God's temple; the visible presence of God, like a shining cloud, rested above the ark

Measuring Up (Revelation 11:1 – 2)

I was given a reed like a measuring rod and was told, "Go and measure the temple of God and the altar, with its worshipers. But exclude the outer court; do not measure it, because it has been given to the Gentiles. They will trample on the holy city for 42 months.

In chapter 11 of Revelation, John continues the interlude that began back in chapter 10. He is cruising along in chapters 8 and 9, describing the seven trumpet judgments, when he pauses the action to explain some important facts in greater depth. In chapter 10 an angel lays claim in God's name to the earth and then hands John a scroll to eat. Now after enjoying a tender fillet of scroll, John is given another assignment: he's given a reed cut to a standard length (think "yardstick"), and he's told to measure the temple of God.

The limits are clearly defined. John is to measure the temple and the altar and count the worshipers. The outer courtyard is excluded because that area has been given over to Gentiles (non-Jewish unbelievers). Measuring is a sign of ownership. When we buy a piece of property, we have it surveyed (measured) so we know exactly how big the property is and where the boundaries are. God is measuring what belongs to him.

A prophet might also be called to measure something in preparation for judgment. God told Isaiah, "I will make justice the measuring line and righteousness the plumb line" (Isaiah 28:17). God told the prophet Amos that he was setting a plumb line among his people, Israel: "I will spare them no longer" (Amos 7:7–9). I think here in Revelation 11 John

In Other Words

Those who believe the Word of God should not be surprised if a movement begins among the Jews to rebuild their temple. So far there have only been unconfirmed rumors about such a movement, but ultimately it will come. Perhaps it will be in the present age, even before the rapture. If so, it will be but one more evidence that God's Word is forever true, and that the return of the Lord Jesus Christ is drawing near.

Thomas McCall, in "Problems in Rebuilding the Tribulation Temple," *Bibliotheca Sacra* 129 (January–March 1972): 80.

The temple here will be constructed so that orthodox Jews can offer sacrifices according to the Mosaic Law in the period of the first half of the seven-year period known as Daniel's 70th week. At the beginning of the 42-month Great Tribulation, however, the sacrifices will stop and the temple will be desecrated and become a shrine for the world leader of the Great Tribulation who will put an idol in it and proclaim himself to be God.

John Walvoord, in *The Bible Knowledge Commentary: New Testament* (Colorado Springs: Victor, 1983), 955.

A temple in Jerusalem?

The toughest problem in these first two verses of Revelation 11 is deciding which temple John is told to measure. Lots of opinions have been offered, but three views predominate:

Option #1: The temple is Herod's temple

Those who believe that the book of Revelation describes God's judgment on Israel when the Roman armies destroyed Jerusalem in AD 70 take this temple to be Herod's temple—the same temple Jesus and Paul visited (see the four gospels and the book of Acts). Since that temple was doomed to be burned and torn apart by the Romans, John measures the temple as a prelude to judgment.

Option #2: The temple is a symbol of the church

Other interpreters of Revelation believe that the "temple" is symbolic of the faithful church during a time of persecution. Jesus measures the temple, not in preparation for judgment, but as a sign of God's favor for and protection over his people.

Option #3: The temple is a future temple in Israel

Those who hold this view say that the temple John measures could not be Herod's temple since the evidence is that Revelation was written *after* AD 70, and, therefore, Herod's temple had already been destroyed. Furthermore, they believe that the temple is a literal building, not a symbol for the faithful church. Those who hold to this third position believe that John measures a temple that will be rebuilt in Jerusalem during or just before the Tribulation period. The Tribulation temple is the place where the Antichrist will set up his own image and will declare himself to be "God" (2 Thessalonians 2:4). The temple is rebuilt, and God is worshiped for a while, but then the place of worship is defiled by the image of the Antichrist for the last three and a half years (forty-two months) of the Tribulation. This view seems to be the one that fits best into a normal reading of the text.

is asked to measure the part of the temple where God is worshiped as preparation for judgment that is about to come.

Two Witnesses (Revelation 11:3 – 14)

"And I will appoint my two witnesses, and they will prophesy for 1,260 days, clothed in sackcloth." They are "the two olive trees" and the two lampstands, and "they stand before the Lord of the earth." If anyone tries to harm them, fire comes from their mouths and devours their enemies. This is how anyone who wants to harm them must die. They have power to shut up the sky so that it will not rain during the time they are prophesying; and they have power to turn the waters into blood and to strike the earth with every kind of plague as often as they want.

Now when they have finished their testimony, the beast that comes up from the Abyss will attack them, and overpower and kill them.

Their bodies will lie in the public square of the great city, which is figuratively called Sodom and Egypt, where also their Lord was crucified. For three and a half days many from every people, tribe, language and nation will gaze on their bodies and refuse them burial. The inhabitants of the earth will gloat over them and will celebrate by sending each other gifts, because these two prophets had tormented those who live on the earth.

But after the three and a half days the breath of life from God entered them, and they stood on their feet, and terror struck those

Help File

ISLAM AND THE TEMPLE MOUNT

The original area on which Solomon's temple and Herod's temple stood is now occupied by a site revered by Muslims. The Dome of the Rock and the Al-Aqsa Mosque stand on the old Temple Mount. When the expanding Muslim empire conquered old Judea, the temple area was not much more than a place where people dumped their trash. Muslims honor the site as sacred because they believe that the prophet Muhammad ascended on a heavenly journey from that spot.

The Muslim possession of the Temple Mount presents a major obstacle for the rebuilding of the Jewish temple. God selected that site alone as the place where sacrifices could be offered. Until that impasse is resolved, no temple will be constructed. Perhaps it will be the strong treaty signed by Israel and the future Antichrist that will finally give Israel access to their temple site.

Interesting fact: the Dome of the Rock in Jerusalem was destroyed by an earthquake in 1546—and was quickly rebuilt by Muslim faithful.

who saw them. Then they heard a loud voice from heaven saying to them, "Come up here." And they went up to heaven in a cloud, while their enemies looked on.

At that very hour there was a severe earthquake and a tenth of the city collapsed. Seven thousand people were killed in the earthquake, and the survivors were terrified and gave glory to the God of heaven.

The second woe has passed; the third woe is coming soon.

God told John in chapter 10 that his final plan for human history would unfold without delay. Now—suddenly—two witnesses appear on the horizon of the Tribulation. This is a difficult section of Revelation to fit into the puzzle. What these witnesses do and what happens to them are very clear; who they are and when they preach are issues that no one has fully unraveled.

Here's what we know from just reading the passage:

- Two witnesses are given power by God to preach for 1,260 days (about three and a half years).
- These witnesses have miraculous powers that enable them to protect themselves from their enemies.
- When the time of their witnessing is over, God allows them to be killed.
- Miraculously, three and a half days later, they are revived to life and taken to heaven.

Now the more difficult stuff:

Who?

The first thing I want to know is who these witnesses are. John calls them "witnesses" in verse 3 and "prophets" in verse 10. Opinions and

In Other Words

"Fire comes from their mouths" [11:5]: since this seems to be similar to the power of Elijah (2 Kings 1:10 – 14), and since Elijah spoke the word and the fire came down out of heaven, it probably means that fire does not literally come out of the witnesses' mouths, but that they speak and it happens.

Michael Smith, from unpublished notes on Revelation.

interpretations abound as to who or what the witnesses represent. Here's a list:

Some see the two witnesses as symbolic. They are not actual human beings but represent:

- the Law and the Prophets
- the Old and the New Testaments
- the Word of God and the blood of Christ
- two volcanoes

The question is, How can the Old and New Testaments (or any of these other objects) be killed and lie dead in the streets for three and a half days?

Another view is that the two witnesses represent larger groups (like the twenty-four elders in chapter 4 represent the whole church). Their suggestions cover a wide range of possibilities:

- the church
- martyrs who give their lives for Christ
- the Eastern and Western divisions of the church
- Israel and the church
- Arabs and Israelites (two nations descended from Abraham)

But again we have the problem of how these groups are killed and lie dead in the streets and then are revived to life. The passage doesn't make much sense if the two witnesses represent entire groups of people.

If you just read the passage normally, you have to conclude that these are the two human beings who are chosen by God to speak his word during the Tribulation. They speak, they have power to kill, they have bodies, they wear sackcloth—all indicators of real human beings. More opinions arise when interpreters try to identify the witnesses. Here are some suggestions, plus reasons why these specific individuals are nominated:

- *Elijah and Moses*: These Old Testament prophets performed the same kinds of miracles as the future witnesses:
  - Elijah called down fire (1 Kings 18) and caused a drought (1 Kings 17:1).
  - Moses turned water into blood and called down plagues on Egypt (Exodus 7:17, 19; 8–11).

- Both of them appeared on the Mount of Transfiguration with Jesus (Mark 9:2–8).

- *Enoch and Elijah*: These two men went to heaven without dying (Genesis 5:24; Hebrews 11:5; 2 Kings 2:11–12). Since Hebrews 9:27 says that every person is appointed to die once, these men will come back to earth as witnesses and experience death in the Tribulation.
- *Elijah and an unnamed prophet*: Malachi 4:5 says that Elijah will return before the Messiah comes. Jesus, however, indicated that John the Baptist fulfilled that prophecy (Matthew 11:4). It was not Elijah in person who was to come, but a person with the spirit of Elijah.
- *Peter and Paul*—Christian leaders killed by Nero in AD 54.
- *Jeremiah and Elijah*
- *Jesus' half-brother James and the apostle John*
- *Two prophets whom God will raise up in the future*: The best suggestion, I think, is that the two witnesses are two prophets yet to come, who will be empowered with abilities like those of Moses and Elijah. They simply are not named. If they were well-known prophets like Moses and Elijah, it seems likely that John would have identified them.

1260 Was a Very Good Year

Doomsday predictions and prophetic speculation flourished in Europe during the Middle Ages. One group of monks calling themselves "the Spiritual Franciscans" criticized the worldliness of the papacy and claimed to be the model community for a new world, for a millennial "Age of the Spirit." They were fascinated by the fact that Matthew's gospel records forty-two generations from Abraham to Jesus. They then concluded that the present age would also last forty-two generations. Taking thirty years as the length of a generation, the Spiritual Franciscans calculated that the new age would begin in 1260. They found further support for their view in Revelation 13:5, where John refers to forty-two months. If you figure thirty days per month and one day equal to one year, you come out with 1,260 years. The year 1260 seems to have passed pretty quietly, even for the Spiritual Franciscans.

When?

The second big issue with these witnesses is when they appear. John says that they prophesy for 1,260 days (about three and a half years), but is that the first half of the seven-year Tribulation, or the second half—or some time that overlaps both sections?

An argument can be made for placing their ministry in the second half of the Tribulation. Unbelievers control Israel and the temple for the last three and a half years, and these prophets are a testimony against the Antichrist. Finally just before the end, the Antichrist kills them. That's a possible scenario, and several students of Bible prophecy hold that view.

I am persuaded that the two witnesses preach during the *first* three and a half years of the Tribulation. This is the way I see the scenario unfolding:

- After the rapture, God calls and empowers two witnesses to preach the message of Jesus and his soon return to earth. The witnesses focus on Jerusalem. They may be Jews themselves, but they begin to speak to the people of Israel.
- Through their testimony, the 144,000 (12,000 from each of the 12 tribes or extended families in Israel) are saved. John introduced the 144,000 back in chapter 7. They are sealed and protected by God throughout the Tribulation because they bring the message of Jesus to the world. Thousands are saved through the preaching of the 144,000. But how do all those Jews come to believe in Jesus in the first place? I think that it is through the testimony of the two witnesses.
- In the first half of the Tribulation, the Antichrist opposes the message of the two witnesses, but there isn't a lot he can do about it. He has made a treaty (a covenant) with Israel and can't interfere with Israel's internal affairs.

In Other Words

These two witnesses have a combination of the greatest powers ever given prophets on earth, and this accounts for their ability to withstand their enemies for the entire period of 1,260 days.

John Walvoord, in *The Revelation of Jesus Christ* (1966; rev. ed., Chicago: Moody, 1989), 180.

- In the middle of the Tribulation, the Antichrist breaks the treaty and finds an excuse to invade Israel (more on this when we get to chapter 13). At that point, he kills the two witnesses, and the 144,000 scatter to the ends of the earth, preaching the gospel.
- The witnesses are killed at the end of their three and a half years of ministry, so it seems likely that they preached in Israel during the first half of the Tribulation.
- The witnesses had plenty of enemies, even without the Antichrist. God gives them the power to hold off their enemies with miraculous signs until their testimony is complete.

What?

So the purpose of the two witnesses is to prophesy, to speak God's message to Israel, during the relative peace of the first half of the Tribulation. John sees these two prophets as uniquely empowered by and filled with the Holy Spirit. They are olive trees and lampstands—two pictures from the Old Testament book of Zechariah of leaders filled with the oil of the Holy Spirit. They burn brightly as a light to Israel and to the nations in the dark days of the Tribulation.

One hundred forty-four thousand Israelites might accept the message of the witnesses, but most of the world despises what they have to say. It's possible that the two witnesses will predict some of the judgments that

Help File

ENTER THE BEAST

John's mention of "the beast" in verse 7 is the first of thirty-six references in Revelation. The Old Testament prophet Daniel used fierce wild beasts to portray future world empires that opposed and oppressed God's people (see Daniel 7:2–3, 17–18). John uses the word "beast" to describe future world leaders who will hate God and God's people. Usually the word refers to the Antichrist, but it can also refer to a false religious leader called "the false prophet." Since John has not formally introduced the Antichrist into the narrative of Revelation (that happens in chapter 13), he simply refers to him here in chapter 11 as "the beast that comes up from the Abyss" (verse 7).

Some interpreters believe that John is talking about Satan, not the Antichrist, since the Abyss is a place where some of Satan's evil angels (also called demons) are confined. (We had a biblical tour of the Abyss back in chapter 9.) Satan, however, is usually identified by John as "the dragon," while the Antichrist is almost always called "the beast." The fact that the beast comes from the Abyss describes the Antichrist's satanic, evil character— he's the beast from hell.

God gives supernatural power to these two witnesses, but when the time comes, God does not spare them from a violent death. The moment we become fully committed followers of Jesus, we give up the right to hold on to our lives. His call is to take up the cross (an instrument of death) daily and follow him. The message of the two witnesses to us is that God may ask us at some point to give up our lives for our faith in Christ. The book of Revelation calls us to be a martyr church, ready to sacrifice all that we hold dear if the Master so requires it.

fall on humanity during the first years of the Tribulation. The witnesses will need supernatural power to keep their enemies from killing them. But finally, when their work is completed, God allows the "beast," the Antichrist, to kill them. As the world views their dead bodies flashed on the screens of their televisions or on computer monitors, a global party breaks out. An unbelieving world will gloat over the witnesses and will celebrate by sending each other gifts, because these two prophets "had tormented those who live on the earth" (11:10). This will be an "anti-Christmas" gift-giving and partying because God's messengers are dead.

But then, with television cameras still focused on their unburied bodies, God will breathe life back into his prophets, and they will stand on their feet. A voice from heaven will say, "Come up here," and the prophets will be taken up in a cloud while their enemies stare with mouths wide open. God throws some serious cold water on their global party.

Where?

All this takes place in "the great city" (verse 8). I think it's clear that John is referring to Jerusalem because he says it is the place "where also their Lord was crucified." Another widely held view is that this city is Rome. The argument for seeing Rome in this verse goes like this: Jesus was crucified under Roman law and by order of a Roman official, and John uses the phrase to refer to Rome in code. John is already under arrest; he doesn't want any more trouble from Roman authorities, so he writes in this cryptic style.

Bible Networking

Zechariah 4:1 - 6

Then the angel who talked with me returned and wakened me, as one is wakened from sleep. He asked me, "What do you see?"

I answered, "I see a solid gold lampstand with a bowl at the top and seven lamps on it, with seven channels to the lamps. Also there are two olive trees by it, one on the right of the bowl and the other on its left."

I asked the angel who talked with me, "What are these, my lord?"

He answered, "Do you not know what these are?"

"No, my lord," I replied.

So he said to me, "This is the word of the LORD to Zerubbabel [the governor of Jerusalem at the time]: 'Not by might nor by power, but by my Spirit,' says the LORD Almighty."

I think it's better to see the city as Jerusalem. If the Antichrist takes over Israel in the middle of the Tribulation and uses that as his opportunity to rid the world of these two witnesses, then Jerusalem is a much better choice for the great city. It's the same city called "the holy city" in verse 2—the place where the temple will stand.

Figuratively, the city is called "Sodom and Egypt" (verse 8). Sodom refers back to the Old Testament city that was destroyed by God because of moral degradation. (Check out Genesis 19:4–11.) Several prophets apply the name Sodom to the land of Judah in the worst days of the nation's idolatry (Isaiah 1:9; Ezekiel 16:46).

Egypt was a symbol of oppression and slavery. Both Egypt and Sodom were marked by hatred of God and God's people. Certainly at this point in the Tribulation, under the Antichrist's direct dominance, Jerusalem will be a city set against God and against the prophets. People of every nation will flock to see the bodies of the dead prophets for themselves.

The party that breaks out when the prophets are dead is the only reference in the Bible to rejoicing on earth during the years of the Tribulation. Earth-dwellers will celebrate because they no longer have to listen to messages from God. Their celebration ends abruptly, however, when God raises the two prophets back to life. These two witnesses had undoubtedly been preaching about Jesus, who had risen from the dead, and now God proves that a resurrection after three days can really happen. The Antichrist doesn't hold the power of life or death; God does!

What Then?

As the two witnesses ascend into heaven, four dramatic events take place in Jerusalem.

1. *A great earthquake shakes the city.* This was not the first earthquake to hit Jerusalem! When Jesus died, "the earth shook, the rocks split" (Matthew 27:51); when he rose from the dead three days later, "a violent earthquake" rocked the city as an angel rolled away the stone from the empty tomb (Matthew 28:2). Here John tells how God shakes the city again as his witnesses are raptured away.

2. *A tenth of the city falls.* A tenth of the buildings in Jerusalem collapse from the force of the earthquake.

3. *Seven thousand dead bodies are dragged from the rubble.*

4. *The rest of the people are terrified.*

Those in Jerusalem who survive the devastation of the earthquake are stunned by God's power. Amazingly, they give "glory to the God of heaven" (verse 13). We've seen unbelievers repeatedly refusing to repent, but on this occasion they give glory to God. This may not be an indication of true faith, however. They acknowledge God's hand in what has happened and God's power to raise the dead, but it certainly stops short of wholehearted commitment to Jesus as Lord and Savior.

John brings this interlude to an end by drawing us back to the unfolding sequence of the seven trumpet judgments. The last three trumpets were three "woes" pronounced on the inhabitants of the earth. John reminds us in verse 14 that the second woe (the sixth trumpet and its resulting events) is now past and the final woe is coming quickly.

The Seventh Trumpet Sounds (Revelation 11:15 – 19)

The seventh angel sounded his trumpet, and there were loud voices in heaven, which said:

> "The kingdom of the world has become
> the kingdom of our Lord and of his Messiah,
> and he will reign for ever and ever."

The Last Trumpet

Christians who believe in a mid-tribulation or pre-wrath rapture argue that this is the point in the Tribulation when Jesus returns in the air for his church. They believe that genuine Christians will go through the first part of the Tribulation on earth but not the last part, which they call "the time of God's wrath." One of the biblical passages they use to support this view is 1 Corinthians 15:51–52, where Paul writes that the rapture will occur "at the last trumpet." Since the seventh trumpet in Revelation 11 is the last of the seven trumpets, this must be (in their view) where the rapture occurs. They believe that the song of praise recorded in Revelation 11:17–18 is the song of the newly raptured church.

Pre-tribulation rapturists do not agree. Paul's reference in 1 Corinthians to "the last trumpet" means the last trumpet for us, not the final trumpet of the judgments. Paul in 1 Thessalonians 4:16 says that the rapture will be signaled by "the trumpet call of God."

Genuine Christians will hear that "last trumpet" and be taken out before the seven-year Tribulation begins. Furthermore, the entire span of the Tribulation, not just the last half, is called the time of God's wrath. The song sung in Revelation 11:17–18 is sung by the raptured church, but only after they have been in heaven for at least three and a half years. We sing in anticipation of Christ's full and final victory over a rebellious world.

And the twenty-four elders, who were seated on their thrones before God, fell on their faces and worshiped God, saying:

"We give thanks to you, Lord God Almighty,
  the One who is and who was,
because you have taken your great power
  and have begun to reign.
The nations were angry,
  and your wrath has come.
The time has come for judging the dead,
  and for rewarding your servants the prophets
and your people who revere your name,
  both great and small—
and for destroying those who destroy the earth."

In Other Words

This is not the last trumpet of 1 Corinthians 15:52 because that trumpet signals rapture and resurrection while this one signals judgment.

Stanley Toussaint, in "The Revelation of John," unpublished class notes (Dallas Theological Seminary, 1970).

The wrath of men is impotent; the wrath of God is omnipotent; the wrath of men is wicked; the wrath of God is holy. That which was anticipated in Revelation 6:16 – 17 as well as in Psalm 2:4 is here being fulfilled.

John Walvoord, in *The Revelation of Jesus Christ* (1966; rev. ed., Chicago: Moody, 1989), 185.

Help File

THE LOST ARK

The last biblical reference to the ark of the covenant is in 2 Chronicles 35:3. King Josiah orders the ark restored to the inner room of the temple in Jerusalem—the Holy of Holies.

After that, the ark disappears from Israelite history. Most scholars believe it was taken to Babylon when Nebuchadnezzar's army burned the temple in 586 BC. There was no ark in the second temple, nor does the original ark appear in the future Tribulation temple.

Jewish tradition claims that the ark was hidden in a mountain by the prophet Jeremiah and will only be restored to Israel when the Messiah comes.

"This place [the hiding place] shall remain unknown," [Jeremiah] said, "until God finally gathers his people together and shows mercy to them. Then the Lord will bring these things to light again, and the glory of the Lord will appear with the cloud, as it was seen both in the time of Moses and when Solomon prayed."

2 Maccabees 2:7 – 8

Psalm 2:2-6

> The kings of the earth rise up
>   and the rulers band together
>   against the LORD and against his anointed, saying,
> "Let us break their chains,
>   and throw off their shackles."
> The One enthroned in heaven laughs;
>   the Lord scoffs at them.
> He rebukes them in his anger
>   and terrifies them in his wrath, saying,
> "I have installed my king
>   on Zion, my holy mountain."

Daniel 2:44

In the time of those kings, the God of heaven will set up a kingdom that will never be destroyed, nor will it be left to another people. It will crush all those kingdoms and bring them to an end, but it will itself endure forever.

Zechariah 14:9

The LORD will be king over the whole earth. On that day there will be one LORD, and his name the only name.

> Then God's temple in heaven was opened, and within his temple
> was seen the ark of his covenant. And there came flashes of lightning,
> rumblings, peals of thunder, an earthquake and a great hailstorm.

The seventh trumpet is the last and it opens the way for the seven bowl judgments that crash on the earth at the end of the Tribulation. Even though John says that the final woe will come quickly, the next series of judgments will not begin until chapter 16 opens. John gives us an extended interlude from chapter 12 through chapter 15.

Before he launches into the details of that interlude, however, John records the song of worship that the inhabitants of heaven sing in anticipation of Christ's victory and his coming kingdom. God the Father and God the Son step forward to begin their reign over a reclaimed earth. Christ's triumph is so certain that believers in heaven speak as though it has already happened.

In contrast to the silence that followed the opening of the seventh seal judgment (Revelation 8:1), the seventh trumpet elicits loud voices. If you hear Handel's "Hallelujah Chorus" in verse 15 it's because the musician borrowed his words from John: "The kingdom of the world has become the kingdom of our Lord and of his Messiah, and he will reign for ever and ever." The long-anticipated reign of God's anointed King over the earth is about to begin.

Chapter 11 closes with a scene of God's temple in heaven. The chapter opened with God's temple on earth (a rebuilt Tribulation temple) being measured and its courts being trampled for forty-two months. The original earthly tabernacle (constructed by Moses) and the first temple (constructed by Solomon) were copies of the temple in heaven, according to Hebrews 9:23. Now John sees the heavenly temple open, and the ark of the covenant is visible to all. The heavy veil above the ark that kept worshipers separated from the visible presence of God has been removed by Christ's sacrifice on the cross. We are now invited into God's immediate presence. John's vision of the temple and the ark suggests that God will be faithful to the promises made to Israel—and in the very next chapter Israel begins to experience God's protection in a time of national crisis.

Points to Remember

☑ John measures the earthly temple, preparing it for three and a half years of contamination by unbelievers and judgment from God. God's heavenly temple, however, still reflects the majesty and holy character of God.

☑ Two witnesses faithfully proclaim God's message and are finally killed by the Antichrist.

☑ After three and a half days, the witnesses are raised back to life and taken to heaven. The world is stunned by this display of God's power.

☑ The seventh angel blows the seventh trumpet, and heaven explodes in praise as they see God's long-awaited kingdom approaching.

CHAPTER 12

Watch Out for That Dragon!

Watch Out for That Dragon!

- ▶ John sees an awesome light show in the sky.
- ▶ Satan shows up.
- ▶ Angels battle in heaven.
- ▶ Refugees flee on wings of an eagle.

Key Codes: Level 12

- → Sign: A supernatural event that illustrates what God is doing
- → Iron scepter: Symbol of a ruler's power
- → Michael: One of God's highest, most powerful angels
- → The serpent: A reference in this chapter to Satan; he took on the form of a serpent in the garden of Eden (Genesis 3:1)

A Spectacular Sign (Revelation 12:1 – 2)

> A great and wondrous sign appeared in heaven: a woman clothed with the sun, with the moon under her feet and a crown of twelve stars on her head. She was pregnant and cried out in pain as she was about to give birth.

Throughout the book of Revelation, the apostle John sees the unfolding of the future from the perspective of heaven. Sometimes he is focused on what is going on around God's throne as angels blow trumpets or as millions of redeemed people shout God's praises. At other times John's attention is focused on the earth. It's as if he stands at the edge of heaven and looks down as judgment unfolds or as revival breaks out.

As chapter 12 opens, John's attention is drawn to the sky, the huge expanse of space between heaven and earth. A "great and wondrous sign" appears.

John is going to use the next three chapters (12–14) to introduce events and people that are extremely important at this particular point in the Tribulation. John is not very concerned with the passage of time in these chapters. He is showing us what is going on behind the scenes. The middle of the Tribulation is a crucial time in the unfolding of God's plan. John wants to make sure that we have a depth of knowledge about the major players and key events that take place. What we learn in these chapters influences how we interpret the rest of the book of Revelation.

Seven key figures appear in Revelation 12 and 13:

- a women clothed with the sun (12:1–2)
- the red dragon with seven heads and ten horns (12:3–4)
- the woman's male child (12:5–6)
- the archangel Michael (12:7–12)
- the rest of the offspring of the woman, persecuted by the dragon (12:13–17)
- the beast who comes out of the sea (13:1–10)
- another beast who comes out of the earth (13:11–18)

SIGN SEEING

John sees these people and the events they set in motion as a series of signs, or pictures. The word *sign* refers to a wonder or a miraculous event that points to some deeper significance or meaning. Revelation is not the only New Testament book that talks about signs. In addition to the book of Revelation, the apostle John also wrote the gospel of John (the fourth book of the New Testament). In his gospel account of Jesus' life, John selected just seven miracles (out of the hundreds that Jesus did) and called them "signs." These miracles, such as changing water into wine and raising dead Lazarus from the grave, had a deeper significance than just helping people in need. The miracles pointed to the fact that Jesus was God in human flesh. The miraculous signs called attention to another reality that might at first escape our notice.

John uses the same word in the same way here in the book of Revelation. This is not just a light-and-laser show in the sky for our entertainment. When John says he saw a "sign" in heaven, he wants us to realize that there is a deeper meaning than just images in the sky. The images convey a deeper significance. The woman John sees in verse 1 and the enormous dragon who appears in verse 3 both point to another reality that might at first escape our notice.

A Woman Clothed with the Sun

The first remarkable wonder-producing image John sees is a woman standing in front of and surrounded by the sun, with the moon under her feet and twelve stars in a crown on her head. Everyone agrees on what John saw; disagreements emerge about who this woman represents. John will tell us very clearly who the red dragon in verse 3 is, but he does not specifically identify the woman. We are left to work that out from hints in the text.

Roman Catholic interpreters take this woman to be Mary, Jesus' mother. If you've ever seen a picture of Mary with stars over her head or have heard Mary called "the queen of heaven," this is the biblical passage that Roman Catholics base that on. The strongest point in favor of seeing this woman as Mary is that she gives birth to a child who is obviously Jesus. Identifying the woman as Mary gets difficult later on in the passage, however, when the dragon pursues the woman as she flees into the wilderness (verse 13) and then makes war "against the rest of her offspring—those who keep God's commands and hold fast their testimony about Jesus" (verse 17). Most Roman Catholics explain this by saying that Mary is the spiritual mother of the entire church, and

The Woman Clothed with the Sun

In 1792, a forty-two-year-old domestic servant in Exeter, England, claimed to have visions of the future. Joanna Southcott accurately predicted a poor harvest and the death of a local bishop, and her notoriety grew. In her mind she was a biblical prophet. She called herself "the greatest prophet that ever came into the world" and identified herself as the "woman clothed with the sun" in Revelation 12.

In 1814, at the age of sixty-four, she announced that, like the woman in Revelation 12, she was going to give birth to a child. The son she would bear would be named Shiloh and would be a new Messiah. He would rule the nations with a rod of iron.

Ms. Southcott showed all the signs of pregnancy, and several doctors confirmed that she was pregnant—but no baby appeared. Two months after the expected arrival of the child, Joanna died. Her hard-core followers kept the faith into the mid-1800s, but eventually the group disbanded.

so when the dragon persecutes faithful believers, he is persecuting Mary's spiritual offspring.

Many evangelical students of Revelation believe that the woman represents the people of Israel, the descendants of Abraham, Isaac, and Jacob. The sun, moon, and twelve stars were part of a vision that Joseph (one of Jacob's sons) had in Genesis 37. There the sun and the moon refer to Jacob and Rachel, Joseph's parents, and the stars picture the twelve sons of Jacob who became the fathers of the twelve tribes (think: extended families) that made up the Old Testament nation of Israel. The people of Israel suffered before Jesus came as the promised Messiah.

BIBLICAL PICTURE, OR PAGAN MYTH?

Some interpreters of Revelation have tried to find the background to Revelation 12 in pagan mythology. Here's what one writer says: "The key to the interpretation of this scene comes from ancient mythology. An ancient Greek myth described how the dragon Python desired to kill Apollo, the newborn son of Zeus, but was foiled when his mother, Leto, escaped to an island where Apollo was born. Apollo returned to kill the dragon in its cave. In Egypt, Set the red dragon chased Isis and was killed by her son Horus, offspring of the chief God Osiris" (Charles Chapman, *The Message of the Book of Revelation* [Collegeville, Minn.: Liturgical Press, 1995], 79).

Other interpreters acknowledge the parallels with ancient myths, but they see a greater purpose behind John's imagery. See what you think of this: "The main question is why John would tell the story in mythical form.... The purpose of this is evangelistic, to say that what the Greeks have known only as myth has now been actualized in history.... What the pagans longed for in their myths has now become true in Jesus. Therefore, the form is both deliberate and brilliant, using what has in our time been called a 'redemptive analogy' to present the gospel in such a way as to capture the interest and hearts of the non-Christian reader" (Grant Osborne, *Revelation* [Grand Rapids: Baker, 2002], 454).

Another group of scholars admits that some peripheral parallels with mythology are evident in Revelation 12, but they deny that John deliberately borrowed from paganism. Listen to these words: "That partial parallels can be found in the ancient folklore of many nations cannot be denied.... John probably borrowed some of his imagery from the thought-world of his day, but it is very unlikely that he consciously took over a pagan myth.... Would a writer who elsewhere in the book displays such a definite antagonism toward paganism draw extensively at this point upon its mythology? As always, John is a creative apocalyptist who, although gathering his imagery from many sources, nevertheless constructs a scenario distinctly his own" (Robert Mounce, *The Book of Revelation* [Grand Rapids: Eerdmans, 1977], 235).

Joseph's dream
Genesis 37:9–11

Then he had another dream, and he told it to his brothers. "Listen," he said, "I had another dream, and this time the sun and moon and eleven stars were bowing down to me."

When he told his father as well as his brothers, his father rebuked him and said, "What is this dream you had? Will your mother and I and your brothers actually come and bow down to the ground before you?" His brothers were jealous of him, but his father kept the matter in mind.

A prophetic statement about Israel's future glory
Isaiah 60:1–3, 20

Arise, shine, for your light has come,
   and the glory of the LORD rises upon you.
See, darkness covers the earth
   and thick darkness is over the peoples,
but the LORD rises upon you
   and his glory appears over you.
Nations will come to your light,
   and kings to the brightness of your dawn....
Your sun will never set again,
   and your moon will wane no more;
the LORD will be your everlasting light,
   and your days of sorrow will end.

Israel pictured as a woman in labor
Isaiah 26:17

As a pregnant woman about to give birth
   writhes and cries out in her pain,
   so were we in your presence, LORD.

Jesus' bloodline through Mary stretched back to David and Abraham and Adam. I think it is best to see the woman as Israel, the source and the matrix from which Jesus the Messiah emerges.

Another Sign in Heaven (Revelation 12:3 – 6)

> Then another sign appeared in heaven: an enormous red dragon with seven heads and ten horns and seven crowns on its heads. Its tail swept a third of the stars out of the sky and flung them to the earth. The dragon stood in front of the woman who was about to give birth, so that it might devour her child the moment he was born. She gave birth to a son, a male child, who "will rule all the nations with an iron scepter." And her child was snatched up to God and to his throne. The woman fled into the wilderness to a place prepared for her by God, where she might be taken care of for 1,260 days.

As John watches in astonishment, another sign appears in the heavens — an enormous red dragon. Dragons are creatures of myths and fairy tales, but in this case the dragon points to another reality that John doesn't want us to miss. The dragon represents a fierce evil being who stands opposed to God and who seeks to destroy God's plan for the redemption of humanity. Unlike the woman who is never clearly identified, John identifies the dragon in verse 9 — "that ancient serpent called the devil, or Satan, who leads the whole world astray." Robert Mounce sums it up like this: "The dragon of John's vision would immediately be understood as the archenemy of God and his people" (*The Book of Revelation* [Grand Rapids: Eerdmans, 1977], 237).

John describes the dragon/Satan in startling terms:

- *He is enormous, great, large* (think: powerful).
- *He is flame-colored, red* — the perfect color for his murderous, bloodred intentions to kill the offspring of the woman. This does *not* mean that we should envision Satan as a little red imp with horns, a tail, and a pitchfork. John is describing the dragon he sees in the heavens. Satan can appear as an attractive, sophisticated angel of light if it furthers his goal of leading people away from God's truth (2 Corinthians 11:13 – 15).
- *He has seven heads, seven crowns, and ten horns.* The heads, horns, and crowns clearly link the dragon (Satan) with the final human earthly kingdom. Daniel in the Old Testament and John

later in Revelation will portray the Antichrist in the same way—with seven heads and ten horns (Daniel 7:7–8; Revelation 13:1; 17:3). The dragon is the power behind the earthly power of the Antichrist.

- *He is crowned with authority.* The crowns on the dragon's heads are crowns of royal authority—diadems, or kingly crowns. When Jesus returns to earth in awesome power in Revelation 19, he will be crowned with many diadems (19:12, 16). The dragon seems to have sovereign power for a while, but the one who holds true sovereign authority, the King over all kings and the Lord over all lords, will defeat him.

- *He has great power.* Satan is not an enemy to be taken lightly. Jesus called him "the prince [or ruler] of this world" (John 12:31; 14:30; 16:11). Paul said Satan is the "ruler of the kingdom of the air" (Ephesians 2:2) and "the god of this age" (2 Corinthians 4:4). Satan certainly is not greater than God or more powerful than the Holy Spirit, who indwells the Christian (1 John 4:4), but Satan's power is not to be dismissed either. We resist him in the Lord's name, not in our own authority.

In Other Words

God's children have often been in flight. The nation Israel was born in the Exodus (Deuteronomy 8:2 ff). Elijah fled into hiding by the brook Cherith and was nourished there by the ravens (1 Kings 17:2 ff). Joseph and Mary fled to Egypt to save the life of the Christ-child (Matthew 2:13 ff). The intent of the verse [Revelation 12:6], however, is not so much the flight of the church as the provision of God for her sustenance. To the Jewish people the wilderness spoke of divine provision and intimate fellowship. It was in the wilderness that God rained down bread from heaven (Exodus 16:4 ff) and nourished his people for forty years. Of Israel God said, "I will allure her, and bring her into the wilderness, and speak tenderly to her" (Hosea 2:14; cf. 1 Kings 17:2 – 3; 19:3 – 4). For John's readers the wilderness would not connote a desert waste inhabited by evil spirits and unclean beasts, but a place of spiritual refuge.

Robert Mounce, in *The Book of Revelation* (Grand Rapids: Eerdmans, 1977), 239.

Sweeping Stars from Heaven

The enormous dragon in John's vision sweeps his tail across the sky, and one-third of the stars are cast to the earth—but what is the deeper reality behind this scene? Some interpreters think that the dragon literally causes stars to fall in a gigantic meteor shower on the earth. Others think that the stars represent believers on earth during the Tribulation who are martyred for their faith.

Another possibility (and the one that I think fits best in this vision) is that the stars represent angelic beings. Believers are never represented by stars in the book of Revelation, but several times stars represent angels (1:20; 2:1; 3:1; 9:1). If that is the case, Satan sweeps one-third of the angels into his rebellion against God.

A more difficult question is, *When* does this occur? Most Bible teachers think that this is a flashback to Satan's original rebellion against God in the earliest days after creation. When Satan was puffed up with pride and fell into sinful rebellion against God, he put all the other angels to a test. Would they follow Satan in rebellion and become part of Satan's kingdom, or would they remain true to God? One-third of the millions of created angels followed Satan in his defiance of God.

The problem with this view is that John sees this event in the *future*, in the middle of the Tribulation. Part of the vision certainly relates to the past—Jesus, the woman's child, is born in the past, for example, and some of the angels followed Satan in rebellion in the past and were judged by God for it (Jude 6; 2 Peter 2:4). But I don't think we have to place the entire rebellion of the angels in the past. There is nothing in Scripture that says an angel can't follow Satan in rebellion even today or at some time in the future. What we can say with some certainty is that by the middle of the Tribulation, one-third of the angels will have chosen to side with Satan in his sinful rebellion against God. The dragon/Satan pulls those forces together into the earthly realm in preparation for the war with the archangel Michael and with God's angels, which is about to erupt (Revelation 12:7–9). That war did not take place in the long ago past but is yet to take place in the middle of the future Tribulation.

Kill the Child!

Before that angelic war in heaven begins, the dragon/Satan places himself before the woman and prepares to destroy the child who is about to be born. Satan's primary animosity is against the child, not the woman. But when the child is snatched from his murderous jaws, Satan's anger will focus on the woman/Israel.

Satan has tried from the beginning to destroy the child who would rule the nations with an iron scepter and with sovereign, irresistible power. The child is clearly a reference to Jesus, the promised Messiah of Israel, the Redeemer, the King and Lord of all. Here is just a partial list of Satan's attempts throughout history to prevent the Messiah from being born or to kill or corrupt him once he had been born:

- Satan tried to thwart God's plan for humanity by enticing Adam and Eve to join him in sinful disobedience to God (Genesis 3).
- Satan tried to destroy or corrupt the godly line from which the Messiah would be born

    ← by prompting Cain to murder Abel (Genesis 4:8);

    ← by corrupting the line of godly Seth (Genesis 4:3; 6:5, 11–12);

    ← by plotting the potential rapes of Sarah (Genesis 12:10–20; 20:1–18) and Rebekah (Genesis 16:1–18);

    ← by inciting the Egyptians to kill all the male Israelite children (Exodus 1:15–22);

    ← by inciting Saul to try to murder David (1 Samuel 18:10–11), evil queen Athaliah to kill all the living descendants of David (2 Chronicles 22:10), and wicked Haman to slaughter all the Jews in the days of Esther (Esther 3:8–9).

Help File

DO YOU REALLY BELIEVE IN SATAN?

Some people have a hard time believing in a personal being called Satan. They recognize the presence of evil in the world, but they look at Satan and demons as part of the ancient prescientific explanation of why bad things happen. The Bible, however, never backs down from identifying Satan as a real being. Jesus repeatedly referred to Satan's existence and power and even had a few face-to-face confrontations with Satan during his earthly ministry (check out Matthew 4:1–11, for example).

Satan was originally created as a beautiful, powerful angel of God, but he allowed pride to fill his heart with jealousy. He wanted to be like God and be a ruler of a kingdom like God is. Satan's pride led him to fall from his high place of privilege, and he set out on a path of rebellion and opposition to God that only intensifies as God's plan for human history begins to come to an end.

In Other Words

Those who already know the gospel story realize that the dragon did indeed kill Jesus. But what looked for all the world like Jesus' defeat turned out to be his victory because God raised him from the dead and gave him a place at the heavenly throne. His death was in fact the very event that qualified him to open the scroll and so begin the implementation of God's plan for establishing his kingdom. Here again Revelation drives home the point that victory comes through what seems to be defeat.

Paul Spilsbury, in *The Throne, the Lamb and the Dragon: A Reader's Guide to the Book of Revelation* (Downers Grove, Ill.: InterVarsity, 2002), 91.

Future FAQs

What are the key steps on the way out?

John outlines very clearly in Revelation how Satan will be defeated and destroyed by God:

- In the middle of the Tribulation, Satan is confined to the earth (12:7–9).
- At the end of the Tribulation, Satan is confined for a thousand years to the Abyss, the prison house for demons (20:1–3).
- After being released for a short time at the end of Jesus' thousand-year kingdom, Satan will bow his knee and confess that Jesus alone is Lord (Philippians 2:9–11).
- Then Satan will be cast into the lake of fire forever (20:10). Don't ever think of Satan as the king of hell. He hates hell and doesn't want to go there. God is the king over hell and Satan.

Satan's defeat was secured when Jesus died on the cross (John 12:31; 16:11). Satan is still alive and angry, but his final end has already been determined.

- Satan's most direct attacks on Jesus came from Herod, who had his soldiers kill all the male children in Bethlehem who were two years old or younger (Matthew 2:16), from the residents of Nazareth who intended to push Jesus from a cliff to his death (Luke 4:28–30), and from the Jews who picked up stones to kill Jesus because he claimed to be equal with God (John 10:30–31).
- Satan even tried to tempt Jesus to join him in disobedience and rebellion against God (Matthew 4:1–11).
- Satan found an ally in Judas Iscariot (Luke 22:3–6) and may have thought he had finally defeated God's plan when Jesus was cruci-

---

Help File

NAME BELOW ALL NAMES

God's enemy is given five names or titles in Revelation 12:9. Just as God's names in Scripture reveal the holy nature of the Lord, Satan's names reveal the depravity of this evil being.

The great dragon

The title used throughout Revelation emphasizes the cruelty and power of Satan.

The ancient serpent

This title refers back to Satan's deception of Adam and Eve in the garden of Eden (Genesis 3:1) and points out his goal of deceiving people by leading them to doubt God's Word (2 Corinthians 11:3).

The devil

This title is based on a word meaning to slander or separate; Satan wants to separate human beings from God.

Satan

Originally a title meaning "adversary," it gradually became the evil one's name; the word appears eighteeen times in the Old Testament, sixteen times in the Gospels, twice in Acts, ten times in Paul's letters, and eight times in Revelation.

The one who leads the whole world astray

This title signals Satan's main job; his cunning is to lure people to ruin and then to accuse them when they fall.

Other names or titles given to Satan in Scripture are:

- the accuser of our brothers and sisters (Revelation 12:10)
- the evil one (John 17:15; 1 John 5:18–19)
- the tempter (1 Thessalonians 3:5)
- the prince of this world (John 12:31)
- the god of this age (2 Corinthians 4:4)
- the ruler of the kingdom of the air (Ephesians 2:2)
- the spirit who is now at work in those who are disobedient (Ephesians 2:2)
- the prince of demons (Luke 11:15)
- morning star [Lucifer in the KJV] (Isaiah 14:12)

fied. Satan hadn't expected a miraculous, powerful resurrection, even though Jesus had repeatedly predicted that he would rise from the dead.

If any of those events had been successful, Jesus would not have been born or he would not have completed God's redemptive plan. If Jesus had died as an infant or if Jesus' body were still in the grave, Satan would have won. But Satan is not the supreme power in the universe. There is only one sovereign Lord, and God will not share his authority with any angel. God ruled and overruled every attempt by Satan to corrupt or destroy or derail his plan. The child was snatched out of Satan's power and was taken up to God's throne.

Destroy the Woman!

With Jesus out of reach, the dragon turns to other enemies. In every century of the church age, Satan has accused believers before God's throne day and night. If he can't get at Jesus, he will attack God's people. In the future Tribulation, Satan will make one more desperate attempt to thwart God's plan. He will seek to destroy the people of Israel. God has made an unconditional promise of an earthly kingdom to Abraham's descendants. That promise has not yet been fulfilled. But God has determined that a godly remnant of Israel will survive the Tribulation and will inherit the Messiah's kingdom on earth. All Satan has to do to derail God's plan is to destroy the remaining people

Satan's time and power are limited. That's important to remember when it seems as though evil has the upper hand. God has given Satan a certain amount of time for the exercise of his power and influence, but in God's time, that permission will come to a quick and decisive end. God has left no doubt about Satan's final defeat. The enemy may seem sometimes to be the one in control, but he's not. When sin and evil have run their course, God will intervene to bring the evil one down.

of Israel. Satan tries his best, but God has already made provision for a remnant of Israel to survive.

The woman/Israel will flee into the wilderness and will be preserved by God for 1,260 days—the last three and a half years of the Tribulation. We don't learn why Israel flees until later in Revelation but, whatever Satan can dish out, God can handle. You would think Satan would have learned by now that he can't succeed against God. Just look at Satan's dismal record over the centuries!

But he is someone who is motivated by his failure. In defeat he tries even harder—and his master plan has yet to be unveiled.

War in Heaven (Revelation 12:7 – 9)

> And there was war in heaven. Michael and his angels fought against the dragon, and the dragon and his angels fought back. But he was not strong enough, and they lost their place in heaven. The great dragon was hurled down—that ancient serpent called the devil, or Satan, who leads the whole world astray. He was hurled to the earth, and his angels with him.

The dragon's attention suddenly shifts from his earthly pursuit of the woman to a war cry in heaven. John will explain why the dragon/Satan is so angry in persecuting Israel. The passage makes better sense if we try to answer a few simple questions.

RÉSUMÉ OF AN ARCHANGEL

- Name: Michael (meaning "who is like God?")
- Origin: Created angelic being
- Current Position: Protector of Israel (Daniel 12:1); one of the chief angels, an archangel
- Past Experience: Disputed with Satan over who had authority over the body of Moses (Jude 9). Assisted another holy angel in overpower-ing the resistance of the evil angel, "the prince of the Persian kingdom" (Daniel 10:13, 21)
- Future Challenges: Protects the people of Israel during the future "time of distress" in the great Tribulation (Daniel 12:1). Casts Satan out of heaven and confines him to the earth (Revelation 12:7–9)

Bible Networking

I Peter 5:8 – 9

Your enemy the devil [Satan] prowls around like a roaring lion looking for someone to devour. Resist him, standing firm in the faith.

John 16:11

The prince of this world [Satan] now stands condemned.

John 12:31 – 32

Now is the time for judgment on this world; now the prince of this world [Satan] will be driven out. And I, when I am lifted up from the earth, will draw all people to myself.

Who?

The war in heaven is between Michael and his angels on one side and Satan and his angels on the other side. Michael is usually pictured in Scripture as the military angel, the protector of Israel. He gathers the holy angels under his command and wages war with Satan and the evil angels who have linked themselves to God's enemy.

When?

Some students of Revelation think that this war in heaven took place long ago at the beginning of earth's history or at the time of Satan's initial sin of rebellion against God. Others believe that Satan was cast out of heaven when Jesus died on the cross. I think we are on safer ground to see this war as in the future. In the middle of the Tribulation, Satan and his angels are denied further access to heaven and are confined to the earth. Here's why I think the battle is still in the future:

- It is true that early in earth's history Satan "fell" from his exalted position as one of God's highest angels (Isaiah 14:12). The Bible makes it clear, however, that Satan still has access to the presence of God. In the book of Job, all the angels, including Satan, are called in to report on their activities (Job 1:6; 2:1–2). In Zechariah

3:1–2 Satan accuses Israel's high priest before God. Even here in Revelation 12:10 we are told that Satan continues to accuse believers "before our God day and night."

- So Satan today has access to God and accuses us before God continually. Satan is not a permanent occupant of heaven but a tolerated intruder. Satan's temporary realm of authority is the earth and the earth's atmosphere (Job 1:7; Ephesians 2:2), but he spends a lot of time in heaven accusing us before God.
- In the future, at the midpoint of the Tribulation, Satan and his angels will be blocked and expelled from heaven. Once confined to the earth, Satan's rage will explode against God's people and against the nation of Israel.

In response to the victory of his disciples over demons, Jesus said in Luke 10:18, "I saw Satan fall like lightning from heaven." He was "seeing" into the future to this day in the Tribulation when Satan's final defeat would begin. The disciple's authority over demons was just a preview of Satan's ultimate destruction in the end-times.

IS AMERICA IN BIBLICAL PROPHECY?

America is never mentioned by name in the Bible—but other modern nations aren't either! Some students of prophecy, however, believe that the Bible indirectly identifies the United States in three passages.

The first is Ezekiel 38:13: "Sheba and Dedan and the merchants of Tarshish and all her villages will say to you [that is, to an army invading Israel in the Tribulation], 'Have you come to plunder? Have you gathered your hordes to loot?'" Tarshish was the farthest western point in the ancient world (modern Spain today). Some interpreters see this as a veiled reference to nations to the far west of Israel, including the United States.

A second passage is Revelation 12:14. When the Antichrist takes control of the temple in Jerusalem, people from Israel (pictured as a woman in the passage) flee into the desert: "The woman was given the two wings of a great eagle, so that she might fly to the place prepared for her in the wilderness."

"The two wings of a great eagle" have been taken by some to mean a rescue airlift by the United States Air Force! It's true that in the modern world the eagle is the symbol of the United States (and to think that Benjamin Franklin wanted the wild turkey to be our national bird!), but I can't imagine that John had the United States in mind when he wrote this. John

Satan is Grounded (Revelation 12:10 – 12)

Then I heard a loud voice in heaven say:

"Now have come the salvation and the power
and the kingdom of our God,
and the authority of his Messiah.
For the accuser of our brothers and sisters,
who accuses them before our God day and night,
has been hurled down.
They triumphed over him
by the blood of the Lamb
and by the word of their testimony;
they did not love their lives so much
as to shrink from death.
Therefore rejoice, you heavens
and you who dwell in them!
But woe to the earth and the sea,
because the devil has gone down to you!
He is filled with fury,
because he knows that his time is short."

IS AMERICA IN BIBLICAL PROPHECY? (CONTINUED)

used the wings of a great eagle to picture the swiftness and silence of their escape into the wilderness.

The third passage is Revelation 17 – 18, where the destruction of a great commercial center is described. Some interpreters believe the future "Babylon" will be New York City. After the terrorist attack on the twin towers of the World Trade Center in September of 2001, many prophecy buffs were quoting these eerie, descriptive words:

Therefore in one day her plagues will
overtake her:
death, mourning and famine.
She will be consumed by fire,
for mighty is the Lord God who
judges her.

When the kings of the earth who committed adultery with her and shared her luxury see the smoke of her burning, they will weep and mourn over her. Terrified at her torment, they will stand far off and cry:

"Woe! Woe to you, great city,
you mighty city of Babylon!
In one hour your doom has come!"
Revelation 18:8 – 10

My own opinion is that none of these passages refer directly to America. I think that the United States will be part of the Antichrist's alliance. His base of power will be the old Roman Empire (western Europe) *and* those nations that trace their cultural and historical roots primarily to western Europe.

When Satan is expelled from heaven, spontaneous praise explodes from heaven's inhabitants. Finally, this deceiving accuser's end has begun. God has tolerated his presence long enough. The hymn of celebration in verses 10–12 helps us see the significance of what God has done. This victory over Satan is one more step in the establishment of God's kingdom on earth.

Satan's defeat and expulsion from heaven don't come just at the hands of Michael and his angels. Satan is also overcome by believers who are faithful to God, even to the point of death. Those who come to believe in Jesus during the Tribulation have been praying for Satan's defeat. They have given their lives in faithfulness to Christ, and that loyalty played a part in Satan's destruction. God moves in power in response to the prayers of his people.

Heaven can rejoice over Satan's expulsion, but earth is a different story. The earth-dwellers are in for the worst time in human history. Satan's confinement to the earth sends him into a rage, and he takes it out on everyone. Satan knows now that the time to accomplish his goals is short. He puts maximum effort into his two main objectives—destroying God's people and unveiling his final world leader. Persecution intensifies in the last part of chapter 12; the Antichrist is unveiled in chapter 13.

The Woman Flees (Revelation 12:13–17)

> When the dragon saw that he had been hurled to the earth, he pursued the woman who had given birth to the male child. The woman was given the two wings of a great eagle, so that she might fly to the place prepared for her in the wilderness, where she would be taken care of for a time, times and half a time, out of the serpent's reach. Then from his mouth the serpent spewed water like a river, to overtake the woman and sweep her away with the torrent. But the earth helped the woman by opening its mouth and swallowing the river that the dragon had spewed out of his mouth. Then the dragon was enraged at the woman and went off to make war against the rest of her offspring—those who keep God's commandments and hold fast their testimony about Jesus.

Satan's opportunity to accuse believers is gone. That gives him full time to persecute believers. His attention turns to the woman (the remnant of the nation of Israel), those who flee from the dragon's fury. The Jews who heed Jesus' warning to flee from the Antichrist's betrayal of

Bible Networking

Jesus in Matthew 24:15 – 21

"So when you see standing in the holy place 'the abomination that causes desolation,' spoken of through the prophet Daniel—let the reader understand—then let those who are in Judea flee to the mountains. Let no one on the housetop go down to take anything out of the house. Let no one in the field go back to get their cloak. How dreadful it will be in those days for pregnant women and nursing mothers! Pray that your flight will not take place in winter or on the Sabbath. For then there will be great distress, unequaled from the beginning of the world until now—and never to be equaled again."

Moses in Deuteronomy 32:9 – 11

> For the LORD's portion is his people,
>   Jacob his allotted inheritance.
> In a desert land he found him,
>   in a barren and howling waste.
> He shielded him and cared for him;
>   he guarded him as the apple of his eye,
> like an eagle that stirs up its nest
>   and hovers over its young,
> that spreads it wings to catch them
>   and carries them aloft.

In Other Words

[Satan's] task is to arraign men before the bar of divine justice. When not actively doing this, he roams the earth, collecting evidence for his next prosecution.

Robert Thomas, in *Revelation 8–22*
(Chicago: Moody, 1995), 131.

Israel will be helped by God to escape swiftly (on "two wings of a great eagle") to a place of protection in the desert.

The hiding place is not identified. Some scholars have suggested that the Jews will flee to Petra, the ancient city of the Nabateans in the area south of the Dead Sea. Some Bible scholars believe that the 144,000 Jews who were sealed by God in chapter 7 will already be in Petra. Wherever the place of protection is located, a remnant, a small piece, of Israel's population will find refuge from the persecution of Satan.

A relatively few people from Israel will be preserved and provided for by God during the last half of the Tribulation — "for a time, times and half a time" (12:14) or a year plus two years plus half a year, the same three and a half years referred to earlier as 1,260 days (12:6). We will learn in chapter 13 that no one will be able to buy or sell during this time without the beast's mark on their hand or forehead, so it will require supernatural provision to keep these people alive. That kind of supply is not something new for God:

- God provided manna to keep two million Israelites alive in the wilderness for forty years after their escape from slavery in Egypt (Exodus 16:35).

- God provided meat and bread to Elijah for a year by sending
  ravens twice a day (1 Kings 17:3–6).
- Elijah and a widow and her son were kept alive by God's provision
  of a jar of flour and a jug of oil that would not be used up or run
  dry (1 Kings 17:14–16).
- Jesus multiplied five small loaves of bread and two small fish so
  that more than five thousand people were fed (John 6:8–11).

No matter how God chooses to provide for those Israelites in the future,
they will have all they need to survive.

In his desperation to destroy the remnant of Israel, Satan sends a
flood after the fleeing people. It's possible that this is a literal flood of
water. The fact that John sees it coming out of the serpent's mouth, however, suggests that this will be a flood of oppression or pursuit. Satan
sends his forces out with one objective—to destroy the woman/Israel.
The earth itself helps Israel either by providing countless places of refuge or by destroying the enemy. God uses both natural and supernatural means of protecting and providing for a remnant of Israel through
the dark days of the great Tribulation.

Watch Out for that Dragon!

At each step in God's plan, Satan becomes more enraged for these reasons:

- The male child, Jesus, escapes from his clutches.
- His access to heaven is cut off.
- He is confined to earth.
- He knows that his time is short.
- The woman/Israel is rescued by God from his attempts
  to destroy her.

In Other Words

**The Antichrist, indwelt by Satan, is going to be furious that the believers have escaped his
grasp, so he will send his henchmen after them like a flood.**

David Jeremiah, in *Escape the Coming Night* (Dallas:
Word, 1997), 156.

- ☑ John sees several signs in the heavens that introduce key people or explain important events.

- ☑ The woman/Israel, the dragon/Satan, and the child/Jesus reenact God's redemptive plan.

- ☑ Satan is cast out of heaven and confined to the earth.

- ☑ A remnant of the people of Israel escape to the wilderness, where they are protected for the last three and a half years of the Tribulation.

When every other avenue closes, the dragon turns finally to persecute "the rest of [the woman's] offspring" (12:17). Several ideas have been proposed about the identity of the offspring. The best proposal, I think, and the one most consistent with my interpretation so far, is to see the offspring as the 144,000 Jews who were selected and sealed back in chapter 7. With the remnant of Israel protected in the wilderness, Satan seeks to hunt down the 144,000 Jewish believers who are now going out into the world with the message of the gospel.

The dragon won't succeed in destroying these Jewish evangelists because God will protect them, but the dragon can pick off and kill those who come to believe in Jesus through their witness.

Satan's main offensive against the people of Israel, against the 144,000 witnessing believers, and against followers of Christ worldwide will take shape in the rise and empowerment of a world leader. That's where Satan turns his attention next—to unveiling the centerpiece of his evil plan.

The Antichrist is revealed!

CHAPTER 13

Bring Out the Beasts

Bring Out the Beasts

- ▶ Enter "the beast"—the evil world ruler called the Antichrist!
- ▶ Find out what Adolf Hitler, John Kennedy, and Bill Gates have in common.
- ▶ A religious leader appears to give life to an image.
- ▶ "666" on the bar code of your new DVD player—coincidence, or Satanic sign?

Key Codes: Level 13

- → Dragon: Satan
- → Beast: A fierce wild animal; a description of a person's character
- → Blasphemy: To speak lies and slander against God
- → Saints: All true believers in Jesus, not just the superpious ones
- → Book of Life: A record in heaven of those who believed in Jesus as Savior
- → Another beast: The "false prophet" mentioned later in Revelation
- → An image: A statue or visible representation
- → Mark: A brand; a sign of ownership

Satan's Final Solution

Chapter 13 of Revelation leads us into the heart of Satan's ultimate attack against God and against God's people. Under Satan's direction, two beastlike leaders appear on the world stage and rule with ruthless power. For a moment it appears that God's enemies will succeed. But as dark as that future day seems as we read this chapter, we also see a sovereign God standing in the shadows. He allows sin and Satan to run their course, but only so far. In his time, God will bring even Satan's greatest scheme to a crashing end.

The events of chapter 13 happen in the middle of the Tribulation. The Antichrist has been on the scene for at least three and a half years and has risen to power fairly peacefully. War has marked the first half of the Tribulation, but the Antichrist (as the rider on the white horse introduced in chapter 6) has gained power with a bow but no arrows. The threat of military action has been enough to bring the Antichrist to power over an expansive Western empire. The heart of his empire is a revived Roman Empire in Europe, centered most likely in Rome. But his authority extends beyond Europe to include Africa, North America, South America, and perhaps even Japan. Most of the Westernized world is under his direct or indirect control.

Something happens in the middle of the Tribulation that pushes the Antichrist into absolute control of his empire. He declares himself to be a god and demands the worship of the world. In addition, he suffers a fatal wound but survives or revives—in an astonishing miracle. One more factor leads to the Antichrist's dominance—he is fully empowered by Satan himself.

A Beast from the Sea (Revelation 13:1 – 2)

The dragon stood on the shore of the sea. And I saw a beast coming out of the sea. It had ten horns and seven heads, with ten crowns on its horns, and on each head a blasphemous name. The beast I saw

Bible Networking

Isaiah 27:1

In that day,
the LORD will punish with his sword—
    his fierce, great and powerful sword—
Leviathan the gliding serpent,
    Leviathan the coiling serpent;
he will slay the monster of the sea.

resembled a leopard, but had feet like those of a bear and a mouth like that of a lion. The dragon gave the beast his power and his throne and great authority.

At this point in the Tribulation, Satan has been excluded from heaven and is confined to the earth (Revelation 12:8). He has been thwarted in his attack on the woman/Israel, and he knows that his time is short. In his rage, Satan now sets in motion his master plan to deceive humanity and to derail the purposes of God. In John's vision, the dragon/Satan stands on the shore of a great sea and calls forth a terrifying beast.

The "sea" may represent the nations of the world, the swirling mass of humanity—an image used several times in Scripture. The prophet Daniel saw four beasts emerge from the sea (Daniel 7:2–3), each one representing a Gentile (non-Jewish) world power. If the sea represents the nations, this is a clear indication that the future Antichrist will be a Gentile, not a Jew. Many students of Bible prophecy think that the

ROME REVIVED

In Daniel's prophecy, the Babylonian king, Nebuchadnezzar, has a dream that only God can properly interpret. God's prophet Daniel tells the king that his vision represents successive kingdoms that will rule over God's people, Israel. The giant statue of a man, which Nebuchadnezzar saw, was made of different metals—each part of the body and each new metal represented a new empire. Nebuchadnezzar's Babylon (head of gold) was followed by the Persian Empire (arms of silver), the Greek Empire (abdomen of bronze), and the Roman Empire (legs of iron). The feet and toes of the statue were a mixture of iron and brittle chunks of dried clay. Daniel made it clear that Jesus, the Messiah, would usher in his kingdom in the days of the ten-nation

confederacy represented by the toes.

Many prophecy students believe that this ten-nation form of the Roman Empire will emerge just before or during the Tribulation. The Antichrist will eventually gain control of that revived Roman Empire, and it will be the center of his power. The Antichrist's influence will spread then to other nations linked by culture or language to the European center of influence. (For more insight, read Daniel 2:1–45 and Revelation 17:3–18.)

In a later prophecy, Daniel saw four beasts (which represented the same four empires) and ten horns on the fourth beast (Rome), which represent the ten-nation revived empire and the reign of the Antichrist (see Daniel 7:2–10, 23–27).

Antichrist will be a counterfeit Messiah and therefore must be a Jew. I think that he will be welcomed (at first) by Israel as a political protector, but that he will be a non-Jew, a Gentile. The Antichrist will not be so much a counterfeit Christ as a man who stands *against* Christ ("anti-Christ").

Other interpreters take "the sea" in this passage to be a reference to evil and ultimately to the Abyss, the place where evil angels are confined until the day of judgment. Later in Revelation, John describes the Antichrist as the beast coming up out of the Abyss (17:8), but this "Abyss" experience seems to be related to the Antichrist's recovery or resurrection from the fatal wound rather than his origin. Another interpretation of "the sea" is that it refers to the Mediterranean Sea. The point is that the Antichrist will come from that area of the world.

Actually all three views could be correct. Satan will elevate the Antichrist from the evil nations that are in rebellion against God. Because the Antichrist rules over a revived Roman Empire, he will most likely be European. The key issue for John is not so much the Antichrist's human origin as it is that the Antichrist emerges at Satan's direction and is under Satan's control.

NAMES OF THE ANTICHRIST

The Bible uses several names and titles to describe the future Antichrist. I've listed them in the reverse order in which they appear in the Bible because the later names are the clearest.

Revelation 13:1	the beast
1 John 2:18	the Antichrist
2 Thessalonians 2:8	the lawless one
2 Thessalonians 2:3	the man doomed to destruction
2 Thessalonians 2:3	the man of lawlessness
Zechariah 11:15–17	the foolish shepherd/the worthless shepherd
Daniel 11:36	the king
Daniel 11:21	a contemptible person
Daniel 9:26	the ruler who will come
Daniel 7:8	a little horn

Antichrist: Alternate Views

Christians who hold to a *preterist* view of the book of Revelation believe that the prophecies were fulfilled during the attack of Rome against Israel and Jerusalem in AD 70. Those who take this approach believe that the Antichrist was the Roman emperor Nero or the Roman Empire itself—a horrible beast bent on crushing the Christian church.

Other Christians come to Revelation with an *idealistic* view. They believe that Revelation describes the ongoing conflict between good and evil in every age. The beast in Revelation 13 in their view represents political authority that can rise up at any time against the church. Several "Antichrists" have arisen in opposition to Christians down through history.

I take a *futurist* view in this book. Those who hold this view believe that the events of Revelation will unfold in the future. The beast of Revelation 13 is an evil future world ruler who will rise to power in the seven-year Tribulation.

Here are some quotes about the Antichrist representatives of each view:

Nero is at least a prima facie candidate for the role of the beast. As described by ancient historians, Nero is a singularly cruel and unrestrained man of evil.

R. C. Sproul, in *The Last Days According to Jesus* (Grand Rapids: Baker, 2000), 186–87 (preterist ["past"] position).

The Rising

The political leader who ultimately is revealed as the Antichrist may be on the world scene years before the rapture. We won't recognize him as the Antichrist, but he could even now be in a place of political leadership in Europe or in the Westernized empire over which the Antichrist will ultimately rule. After the rapture, after Jesus removes true believers from the earth, the Antichrist moves quickly to consolidate his power over a ten-nation empire. Early in the Tribulation, John saw a powerful political leader ride out on a white horse, conquering the territory around him (Revelation 6:2).

At first, the Antichrist will be welcomed. World problems will be so complex and persistent that people will gladly give up freedom for more security. The Antichrist will have solutions (or at least *promised* solutions) for the staggering problems of hunger and energy and world

Antichrist: Alternate Views (Continued)

I understand the beast to portray the Roman Empire (kingdom) generally and Emperor Nero Caesar (king) specifically.

Kenneth Gentry, quoted in *Revelation: Four Views*, ed. Steve Gregg (Nashville: Nelson, 1997), 68 (preterist ["past"] position).

For John, [the beast] meant, of course, the Roman Empire; but every succeeding generation of Christian people knows some equivalent of it.... The beast from the sea represents "the powers that be," ... in a word, the State.

Michael Wilcock, in *I Saw Heaven Opened* (Downers Grove, Ill.: InterVarsity, 1975), 124 (idealist position).

The beast has always been the deification of secular authority.

Robert Mounce, in *The Book of Revelation* (Grand Rapids: Eerdmans, 1977), 251 (idealist position).

The Antichrist is presented in Scripture as a literal person who will be revealed to this world scene immediately after the rapture of the church.

Walter K. Price, in *The Coming Antichrist* (Chicago: Moody, 1974), 172 (futurist position).

economic growth. One of the first things the Antichrist will do—and the event that starts the clock ticking on the seven years of the Tribulation—is to make a treaty with the nation of Israel. He will guarantee Israel's security in the Middle East. The covenant with Israel is based on a verse in Daniel 9: "He [the Antichrist] will confirm a covenant with many for one 'seven' [one period of seven years]" (verse 27).

The Antichrist's promise of protection will bring a temporary sense of peace to Israel and will allow the people of Israel to turn their attention and resources to issues other than national security. Perhaps they will focus on rebuilding a temple in Jerusalem as a national place of worship. The people of Israel have not offered the sacrifices required by the Old Testament law since the Romans destroyed the temple back in AD 70. A rebuilt temple would be a source of national and ethnic pride for the Jews.

I believe that near the middle of the Tribulation, Israel will be invaded by a coalition of nations, including Russia and many of the

1 John 2:18

Dear children, this is the last hour; and as you have heard that the antichrist is coming, even now many antichrists have come. This is how we know it is the last hour.

2 Thessalonians 2:7 – 8

The secret power of lawlessness is already at work; but the one who now holds it back will continue to do so till he is taken out of the way. And then the lawless one will be revealed, whom the Lord Jesus will overthrow with the breath of his mouth and destroy by the splendor of his coming.

Arab or Islamic nations around Israel—Iran, Syria, Egypt. The Antichrist will honor his covenant with Israel by coming to her aid and defeating the enemies gathered against the nation. (This war is described, I believe, in Daniel 11. No time frame is given for when it occurs, but I think it fits best at the midpoint of the seven-year Tribulation.)

At first Israel hails the Antichrist as a great deliverer, but things quickly turn ugly. The Antichrist uses his presence in Israel to stage his own takeover. He claims Israel's temple as his own and puts an end to the sacrifices being offered to Israel's God. Daniel says it this way: "In the middle of the 'seven' he will put an end to sacrifice and offering" (Daniel 9:27). In Daniel 11, the prophet adds this: "His armed forces will rise up to desecrate the temple fortress and will abolish the daily sacrifice" (verse 31). The apostle Paul in the New Testament adds another crucial detail:

> He [the man of lawlessness, the Antichrist] will oppose and will exalt himself over everything that is called God or is worshiped, so that he sets himself up in God's temple, proclaiming himself to be God.
>
> 2 Thessalonians 2:4

The Antichrist will invade Israel as a deliverer but will then turn against Israel and take over the temple as a worship center for himself. He will proclaim himself to be God. All other worship will be outlawed. The choice for the world will be very clear: worship the Antichrist, or die.

Israel will be shocked by the Antichrist's betrayal. We've already learned that thousands of Jews will flee to the wilderness and will be protected by God from the Antichrist's pursuit (Revelation 12:14–16). The people of Israel will not yet turn to Jesus as their Messiah. That will happen when he returns in majesty at the end of the Tribulation. But the Jews will recognize their betrayal at the hands of the Antichrist and will run from his murderous threats.

Beastly Character

The Antichrist is called a "beast" because that is exactly what he is in God's eyes—a ruthless, thoroughly evil dictator. Outwardly, of course, the Antichrist will be persuasive and convincingly attractive. Inwardly, in his true nature, he will be ravenous and cruel.

The beast John sees has ten horns and seven heads with one crown on each horn. The dragon/Satan was described in 12:3 as having seven heads and ten horns with a crown on each head. The parallel description points out that the beast is united with Satan but has a unique role to play. The ten horns are symbols of power and represent the ten

In Other Words

When you find the Antichrist, look for a big mouth!

Stanley Toussaint, in "The Revelation of John,"
unpublished class notes (Dallas Theological
Seminary, 1970).

The Antichrist will be shown all the kingdoms of the world from a different vantage point, from beneath, which is the demonic perspective. Jesus refused to bow down to Satan. The Antichrist will not refuse, but will worship him. He will then come forth from the abyss (Revelation 11:7), his death stroke healed, as it were, to conquer the world spiritually in the great tribulation, as he has already conquered it politically during the first three and one-half years of his tribulation reign.

Walter K. Price, in *The Coming Antichrist* (Chicago:
Moody, 1974), 147.

nations at the heart of the Antichrist's empire. The seven heads are the leaders of the remaining seven nations after the Antichrist takes direct control of three of the nations (Daniel 7:8).

The beast in Revelation 13 has the characteristics of three animals—a leopard, a bear, and a lion. The prophet Daniel saw these same beasts in a vision recorded in Daniel 7. The beasts represented world empires. This beast and his empire that John sees combine all the elements of all the human empires that have gone before. The Antichrist is the fullest expression of humanity apart from God. He embodies all the evil forces that oppose and hate God.

A Fatal Wound (Revelation 13:3 – 4)

> One of the heads of the beast seemed to have had a fatal wound, but the fatal wound had been healed. The whole world was filled with wonder and followed the beast. People worshiped the dragon because he had given authority to the beast, and they also worshiped the beast and asked, "Who is like the beast? Who can make war against it?"

The beast represents both the empire of the Antichrist and the man who rules the empire. The empire is centered on a ten-nation coalition (ten horns) ruled by seven leaders (seven heads), but one of those leaders is the dominant ruler. He rules the beast and he *is* the beast. His authority and power come from the dragon—from Satan himself. The Antichrist all along has been under Satan's control, but something happens at this point that brings the beast under Satan's absolute domination. John sees that one of the heads—the head representing the Antichrist has suffered a fatal wound.

The fatal wound may be a political defeat or military setback from which the Antichrist recovers and goes on to gain worldwide power. I think it's more likely that the Antichrist suffers an actual fatal wound. He may encounter an assassination attempt or be wounded in a military battle. The wound is serious; it may even be fatal. John says he "seemed to have had a fatal wound." It's certainly possible that the Antichrist dies, but then the fatal wound is healed. Satan by his own power is able to revive the dead or dying Antichrist. The apostle Paul said that Satan "will use all sorts of displays of power through signs and wonders" to deceive people about the Antichrist (2 Thessalonians 2:9). Satan can perform miracles for his own purposes, and his goal with the Antichrist is to startle the world with a spectacular healing.

Bible Networking

Daniel 7:23-24

He gave me this explanation: "The fourth beast is a fourth kingdom that will appear on earth. It will be different from all the other kingdoms and will devour the whole earth, trampling it down and crushing it. The ten horns are ten kings who will come from this kingdom. After them another king will arise, different from the earlier ones; he will subdue three kings."

Daniel 2:42

As the toes were partly iron and partly clay, so this kingdom will be partly strong and partly brittle.

The Antichrist's fatal wound is nothing more than Satan's attempt to counterfeit the death and resurrection of Jesus. Jesus suffered a fatal wound on the cross and three days later burst from the tomb alive to take the supreme position of authority in God's kingdom. Satan mimics God's work by bringing the Antichrist to death or the point of death and then healing him in an incredible miracle. That miracle propels the Antichrist to a new level of authority in Satan's kingdom. He now has absolute power. The Antichrist is like God.

The Antichrist's fatal head wound has led prophecy buffs to identify several possible candidates for the role of the Antichrist. Any leader who has suffered a violent death would qualify—Roman emperor Nero, Judas Iscariot, Adolf Hitler, Benito Mussolini (Italy's World War II leader), former United States president John Kennedy. Ronald Reagan and Pope John Paul II narrowly escaped assassination attempts. Even Mikhail Gorbachev's prominent birthmark on his forehead created speculation that he was the Antichrist.

When the Antichrist dies (or comes near death), he descends into the Abyss. In Revelation 11:7 the Antichrist is described as "the beast that comes up from the Abyss." The Abyss is the compartment of hell where evil angels are confined. The Antichrist apparently goes to the Abyss and comes under Satan's complete domination. When the Antichrist

Bible Networking

The world's question "Who is like the beast?" (Revelation 13:4) is a mockery of the worship that belongs only to God.

Exodus 15:11

> Who among the gods
>   is like you, LORD?
> Who is like you—
>   majestic in holiness,
> awesome in glory,
>   working wonders?

Isaiah 46:5

> "With whom will you compare me or count me equal?
>   To whom will you liken me that we may be compared?"

revives to life, he is Satan's supreme tool to lead the world in rebellion against God.

The world looks on this Satanic miracle with amazement. People follow the beast and worship the dragon. They know that this miracle didn't come from God. They know the power came from Satan, but they are so awed by the Antichrist's recovery or revival to life that they are ready to follow Satan anywhere. The people of the earth keep asking: "Who is like the beast?" If he can die and return to life, who can possibly succeed in war against him? At this point, the Antichrist possesses absolute power. No one can stand against him, and he sets himself on a course of domination unlike anything the world has ever seen.

The Antichrist's supernatural recovery from the mortal wound may be "the lie" that the apostle Paul said the Antichrist would deceive the world into believing (2 Thessalonians 2:11). After such an amazing event, the world will follow the Antichrist anywhere he leads—even to hell.

And the List Goes On

No biblical theme has stirred as much debate over the centuries as the identity of the Antichrist. Hundreds of people have been labeled as the Antichrist. Here are a few of the most notorious and their qualifications for the job:

- *Roman Emperor Nero.* Nero was the first emperor to persecute Christians. When he was overthrown and put into prison, he committed suicide by stabbing himself in the throat. For years after his death, the myth of *Nero redivivus* ("Nero revived") floated around the Roman Empire. The fear was that either Nero had not committed suicide but had escaped or that he would return to life with superhuman power. The story was taken pretty seriously, and between AD 69 and 88, three wannabe emperors claimed to be Nero come back to life. Fortunately, the myth has pretty much faded. Nero's greatest claim to Antichrist fame was that his name added up to the number 666—if you used the title Nero Caesar, and if you translated his Latin name into Hebrew. Christians who believe that Revelation was a prophecy about the first-century destruction of Jerusalem and *not* about a future Tribulation (the preterist view) are fully on board with the "Nero is the Antichrist" view.

The Second Beast

Some interpreters of Revelation believe that the *second* beast is the final Antichrist. They see this person as a counterfeit Messiah. He is a false lamb, and his two horns represent the two roles of the Messiah as priest and king. This view, however, is difficult to defend. The second beast finds his whole purpose in exalting and promoting the first beast, the Antichrist. The second beast definitely plays a secondary role in the unfolding of the end-times.

Christians who hold the view that the book of Revelation predicted events surrounding the fall of Jerusalem in AD 70, not a future Tribulation, have a difficult time identifying a historical figure who fulfills the role of the second beast.

- *The Pope.* It was popular from the time of the Reformation until the nineteenth century to claim that the Antichrist was or would be the pope—any pope.
- *Adolf Hitler.* The leader of Nazi Germany was called the Antichrist many times both before and after his death in 1945. The world was told that he shot himself in the head in his German bunker, but rumors swirled for years that he escaped to Argentina—or that he would revive to even greater power. Plus, if you give numerical value to the letters of the alphabet so that A = 100, B = 101, C = 102 (and so on), the name "Hitler" adds up to 666—in English, of course, not in German.
- *John F. Kennedy.* Lee Harvey Oswald's shot to this United States president's head in 1963 put Kennedy at the very top of some Antichrist candidate lists. When I was a young man, rumors still persisted that Kennedy was being kept alive on life support in a secret wing of a Dallas hospital, waiting for the day when his fatal wound would be healed.
- *Ronald Reagan.* Three names—Ronald Wilson Reagan—six letters each—a composite "666"! Maybe it was that speculation (or Nancy Reagan's psychic powers) that prompted Reagan to insist that the street number of a California mansion given to him by wealthy friends in 1988 be changed from 666 to 668. Plus, in 1981 he survived a gunshot to the chest inflicted by John Hinkley.

Other candidates are as follows:

- Napoleon: His name totals 666—if it is translated into Arabic and two letters are omitted.
- Bill Clinton: "William J. Clinton" adds up to 666 in both Hebrew and Greek.
- Bill Gates: World power through Windows.

In Other Words

The false prophet will be the chief propagandist for the beast, his right-hand man, his closest colleague and companion, and he will lead the world in the false worship of its emperor.

Mark Hitchcock, in *The Complete Book of Bible Prophecy*
(Wheaton, Ill.: Tyndale House, 1999), 134.

Bible Networking

Daniel 7:25 – 26

He will speak against the Most High and oppress his holy people and try to change the set times and the laws. The holy people will be delivered into his hands for a time, times and half a time.

But the court will sit, and his power will be taken away and completely destroyed forever.

Daniel 11:36

The king will do as he pleases. He will exalt and magnify himself above every god and will say unheard-of things against the God of gods. He will be successful until the time of wrath is completed, for what has been determined must take place.

- Saddam Hussein: Not any more.
- Mikhail Gorbachev: Mikhail had the birthmark on his forehead trademarked to prevent a Russian vodka company from using it on their label.
- Henry Kissinger: Needs to work on his public speaking.
- Both sides and both presidents in the Civil War. Right!

And the list keeps growing! Remember all these names when someone comes out with a new prediction. Change the channel, don't buy the book, block the website!

On the other hand, we shouldn't be surprised that often in world history a man of great evil surfaces who *could* become the Antichrist. Satan does not know the time of Christ's return! He has to have a potential Antichrist ready in each generation just in case the rapture and the events of the Tribulation begin to unfold.

Power, Lies, and Deception (Revelation 13:5 – 10)

The beast was given a mouth to utter proud words and blasphemies and to exercise its authority for forty-two months. It opened its mouth to blaspheme God, and to slander his name and his dwelling place and those who live in heaven. It was given power to make war against God's people and to conquer them. And it was given authority over

Bible Networking

Matthew 7:15

Watch out for false prophets. They come to you in sheep's clothing, but inwardly they are ferocious wolves.

Matthew 24:24 – 25

For false messiahs and false prophets will appear and perform great signs and wonders to deceive, if possible, even the elect. See, I have told you ahead of time.

---

every tribe, people, language and nation. All inhabitants of the earth will worship the beast—all whose names have not been written in the Lamb's book of life, the Lamb who was slain from the creation of the world.

Whoever has ears, let them hear.

"If anyone is to go into captivity,
    into captivity they will go.
If anyone is to be killed with the sword,
    with the sword they will be killed."

This calls for patient endurance and faithfulness on the part of God's people.

After describing the character of the beast, John turns next to the activities of the beast. The Antichrist's career can be summarized as blasphemy and hatred toward God, persecution of believers, and deception of the world.

You might get the impression from just these verses that the Antichrist is a bigger enemy than God can handle, but nothing is further from the truth. John makes it clear that all of the beast's power to act "was given" to him. That is a code word throughout Revelation to point out the fact that God is *allowing* Satan and evil to strengthen for a while, but in the end, God will triumph. Yes, God gives the Antichrist great power for three and a half years ("forty-two months," verse 5), but his doom is certain. It's already recorded in God's Word. The followers of Jesus in the Tribulation who are called to endure the Antichrist's

NOT THE ONLY FALSE PROPHET

Some other false prophets and prophetesses you will meet in the Bible:

- Balaam (Numbers 22–24; 2 Peter 2:14–17)
- Hananiah (Jeremiah 28:1–17)
- Shemaiah (Jeremiah 29:24–32)
- Ahab (Jeremiah 29:21)
- Noadiah (Nehemiah 6:14)
- A group of false prophets and prophetesses in Ezekiel's day (Ezekiel 13:1–23)
- Elymas (Acts 13:6–8)
- A string of false prophets in the last days (Matthew 24:24)

onslaughts will find wonderful comfort in the assurance that God *will* succeed in the end.

God allows the beast, first of all, to speak proud words and blasphemies and to act in authority for forty-two months (Daniel 7:25). Blasphemy is to speak against the character and work of God. To know that God is holy but to call him unholy is to blaspheme God. To see God do a good work but call it an evil work is blasphemy. The enemies of Jesus when he was on earth never questioned the *reality* of his miracles; they questioned the *source* of his miracles. They said he performed miracles by Satan's power, not by God's power. Jesus called that "blasphemy."

The Antichrist's pride in himself and his hatred of God will mark his entire career, but after the fatal wound and his journey into the Abyss, the Antichrist's blasphemies will intensify. He will slander God's character (God's "name" in verse 6) and God's dwelling place in heaven. He will speak against the angels who dwell in heaven. The Antichrist will share Satan's hatred of the angels who succeeded in throwing him out of heaven and confining him to earth (Revelation 12:7–12).

The beast is given authority to act for a very limited time—the three and a half years of the last half of the Tribulation. God draws the line ahead of time! Several factors combine to intensify the Antichrist's activity:

- Satan is enraged because he knows that the time before God's judgment is short (Revelation 12:12).
- The Antichrist recovers from a fatal wound and receives the wonder and adoration of the world (Revelation 13:4).

- The Antichrist's presence in Israel allows him to seize the temple area and proclaim himself to be God (2 Thessalonians 2:4).
- The chaos created by the upheaval of war and the judgments from God will make the people of the world ready to follow anyone who will promise some level of security.

War against God's Holy People

The Antichrist's hateful words are followed by hateful actions. He makes war against God's people. God even allows the Antichrist to conquer them and kill them. Throughout the beast's empire, followers of Christ will be hunted down, arrested, and executed. The beast's ultimatum will be simple: worship the Antichrist as God, or die. Those who reject Christ will worship the beast; those who believe in Christ

Help File

THE BOOK OF LIFE

The "book of life" appears several times in Revelation and interpreters have wrestled with how a person's name gets in the book and whether a person's name can be erased from the book. The best explanation (I think) is this:

- Every person's name originally was written in the book of life.
- When a person rejects Christ and his salvation gift and dies in unbelief, that person's name is removed from the book of life.
- Jesus' death was adequate to pay for the sins of the whole world, but his death is *applied* only to those who believe in him for salvation.
- Jesus promises the faithful Christians at Sardis that their names will not be blotted out, or erased, from the book of life (Revelation

3:5), implying that some names *have* been erased—the names of those who have refused to believe.

- A person's name is also removed when that person commits an act of disobedience so final it demonstrates that he or she will never believe in Jesus. Those who worship the Antichrist or who receive his mark are so hardened against Christ that they will never believe, and so their names are removed (Revelation 13:8). Their names no longer stand written in the book of life (Revelation 17:8).
- At the final judgment of unbelievers, the book of life will be opened; they will then see that their names no longer appear there (Revelation 20:12, 15).

Bible Networking

Matthew 7:21 – 23

"Not everyone who says to me, 'Lord, Lord,' will enter the kingdom of heaven, but only those who do the will of my Father who is in heaven. Many will say to me on that day, 'Lord, Lord, did we not prophesy in your name and in your name drive out demons and in your name perform many miracles?' Then I will tell them plainly, 'I never knew you. Away from me, you evildoers!'"

Exodus 7:20, 22

Moses and Aaron did just as the LORD had commanded. He raised his staff in the presence of Pharaoh and his officials and struck the water of the Nile, and all the water was changed into blood....

But the Egyptian magicians did the same things by their secret arts, and Pharaoh's heart became hard.

will refuse to worship the beast and so will immediately be singled out for death.

Satan and the Antichrist will believe that they have conquered the saints of God. The reality is (as we were told in Revelation 12:11) that the followers of Christ are the conquerors. They triumph over Satan and the power of the Antichrist by the blood of the Lamb and by the word of their testimony. The believers give up their lives, but they gain the approval of God for their faithfulness. Satan doesn't win; God does. The Antichrist appears to conquer temporarily, but in the end he is crushed. God allows the beast to succeed for a time, but that time is short.

The same thing happened when Jesus died on the cross. Satan thought he had finally put an end to Jesus. He even had a willing human instrument that he used to get Jesus arrested—Judas Iscariot. But when Satan plotted Jesus' death, he was sealing his own doom. He appeared to conquer Christ but was in fact conquered by Christ.

John is clear that by this time in the unfolding of the end-times, the Antichrist will have virtual control over the whole world. He will have "authority over every tribe, people, language and nation" (verse 7). "All inhabitants of the earth" will be required to worship the beast (verse 8).

The dream of past dictators will finally come to pass. A single ruler, a single world government, will finally come to power. It won't result in a peace-filled utopia, however. It will be a reign of terror and oppression, dominated by a ruthless beast of a ruler. These world-embracing statements eliminate any past king or kingdom. Nero or Napoleon or Hitler—none of them ever had this kind of authority. This monster has yet to emerge on the world scene.

The only earth-dwellers who will not worship the beast are those whose names are written in the "Lamb's book of life" (verse 8), true believers in Jesus. John adds that the Tribulation believers should be prepared to suffer at the hands of the beast. God is allowing the Antichrist to succeed for a while, and believers will have to endure patiently through this time of persecution. As long as their names are written in the Lamb's book, the worst the Antichrist can do is take their life. Their eternity is secure with the Lord.

The Second Beast (Revelation 13:11 – 15)

> Then I saw another beast, coming out of the earth. It had two horns like a lamb, but it spoke like a dragon. It exercised all the authority of the first beast on its behalf, and made the earth and its inhabitants worship the first beast, whose fatal wound had been healed. And it performed great signs, even causing fire to come down from heaven to the earth in full view of everyone. Because of the signs it was given power to do on behalf of the first beast, it deceived the inhabitants of the earth. It ordered them to set up an image in honor of the beast who was wounded by the sword and yet lived. It was given power to give breath to the image of the first beast, so that it could speak and cause all who refused to worship the image to be killed.

Revelation 13 introduces us to two powerful leaders who will rise up in the future Tribulation. One will be a political leader—the Antichrist. The second will be a religious leader—a "false prophet" who will exalt the Antichrist as the world's new god. Both leaders will operate under the power and authority of Satan.

In God's eyes, both of these men are beasts—wild, cruel, ruthless leaders who set out on a path of rebellion and hatred against God. The first beast, the Antichrist, rose from the sea of lost humanity to a place of influence in the world and then a place of dominance. The second beast rises in John's vision "out of the earth"—or perhaps it should be translated "out of the land," meaning the land of Israel. The evidence is pretty clear that the Antichrist is a Gentile, a non-Jew; the second beast, the false prophet, may be a Jew. Since this religious leader functions so freely in the Jewish temple, perhaps he is a priest or high priest in Israel, another "worthless shepherd" that the prophet Zechariah predicted would come against God's people (Zechariah 11:17).

When the Antichrist invades Israel in the middle of the Tribulation, he will seize control of Israel's temple. He will cause the sacrifices to cease and will declare that he is God—worthy of the world's worship. He will be aided in that religious domination by the false prophet. This second beast may originate from the land of Israel or his origin from the earth may point to an obscure or inferior place of origin compared to the Antichrist. Whatever his background, the false prophet steps up to lead the world in worship of the first beast.

Help File

SATAN THE IMITATOR

Revelation 13 is filled with examples of Satan attempting to mimic the character and work of God:

- Satan is a counterfeit for God the Father.
- The first beast is a counterfeit Christ.
- The false prophet is a counterfeit Holy Spirit.
- The Antichrist has a counterfeit resurrection in the form of a fatal wound that is healed. His healing creates astonishment among his followers, just as Jesus' resurrection created wonder among the followers.
- The beast has ten crowns, parallel to Christ's many crowns in Revelation 19:12.
- The dragon gives the beast his power and authority in the same way the Father gives the Son all authority (John 5:22–27).
- The Antichrist claims worldwide allegiance, just as Jesus is Lord over all the nations (Revelation 7:9–10).
- Satan mimics God's creation when he stands on the shore of the sea and calls up a beast in his own image.
- The mark of the beast placed on his followers is a counterfeit to the seal of the Holy Spirit placed on every believer (Ephesians 1:13) and the seal of God on the foreheads of the 144,000 (Revelation 7:3).

The first beast, the Antichrist, will be held in awe by the world for his power and because of the miracle of his survival of a fatal wound. The second beast, in contrast, will be far more approachable and warm-hearted. The beast out of the sea looked terrifying; the beast out of the earth appears in John's vision as a little pet lamb. The Antichrist had ten horns as symbols of power; the false prophet has two horns. But don't be deceived by this guy's cuddly looks. He speaks with the voice of a dragon—with Satan's power and with Satan's evil purposes.

Furthermore, the second beast exercises all the authority of the Antichrist. His goals and the Antichrist's goals are the same. The false prophet listens to the Antichrist, who listens to Satan. Satan loves nothing more than trying to counterfeit God, and in this passage we have the counterfeit trinity—Satan stands in the place of God the Father, the Antichrist stands in the place of God the Son, the false prophet stands in the place of God the Holy Spirit. The beast from the earth exalts the beast from the sea—and they both exalt the dragon.

The second beast's goal will be to bring the entire world to worship the Antichrist. Every other religion will be replaced by the worship of the first beast. Just as the Holy Spirit works to draw men and women to faith in a risen Jesus, the false prophet will urge the world to put their trust in the Antichrist, who survived a fatal wound and now declares himself to be God. The inhabitants of earth who do not worship the Antichrist willingly will be compelled to worship by a variety of methods. Anyone who refuses to worship will be executed as a traitor.

God even allows Satan to empower the false prophet to perform stunning miracles. Every word used of Jesus' miracles or the miracles performed by godly men and women is used here to refer to Satanic miracles. The second beast performs signs and miraculous works, even calling fire down from heaven. The end result of his miracles, however, is not to display the glory of God (as in Jesus' miracles) but to deceive the people of the earth. Those who see these spectacular works of power will believe that the Antichrist really is God. But miracles alone are not proof enough that a man or woman speaks from God. Jesus warned that some people at the final judgment would claim that they had worked great miracles and even mentioned Jesus' name in doing them. His response will be to send them into darkness. Those who claim to speak from God must also demonstrate that they have a personal relationship with Christ—one defined by faith in and love for him—and that they are acting and speaking in obedience to him.

An Image in the Temple

The false prophet's most astonishing miracle centers on an image that he orders to be set up in honor of the Antichrist. Most futurist interpreters of Revelation believe that the image is set up in the temple in Jerusalem. The apostle Paul declares that the Antichrist himself will sit in the temple and receive worship (2 Thessalonians 2:4). The image may take his place when he is absent. The people of the earth may still come to worship, but the worship would be directed to the beast through his image.

Most likely, the image is also the abomination that Daniel and Jesus predicted would someday stand in the temple as a sign that the time of the Great Tribulation had arrived. At the end of his prophecy about the Antichrist in Daniel 9, the prophet Daniel writes this:

> And at the temple he will set up an abomination that causes desolation, until the end that is decreed is poured out on him.
>
> Daniel 9:27

Jesus expands on Daniel's prophecy:

> "So when you see standing in the holy place 'the abomination that causes desolation,' spoken of through the prophet Daniel— let the reader understand—then let those who are in Judea flee to the mountains.... For then there will be great distress, unequaled from the beginning of the world until now—and never to be equaled again."
>
> Matthew 24:15–16, 21

Help File

TRACKING THE BEAST

The "image" of the beast is mentioned six times in Revelation after this chapter:

- Revelation 14:9, 11; 15:2; 16:2; 19:20; 20:4

The "mark" of the beast is mentioned five times:

- Revelation 14:9, 11; 16:2; 19:20; 20:4

The term "false prophet" does not appear in Revelation 13 but is found later in Revelation 16:13; 19:20; and 20:10.

Any image that becomes an object for worship is an abomination, a repulsive sin, before God. A worship image in God's holy temple is especially repulsive. When the Jews see an image of the Antichrist erected in the holy place for worship, they will realize that the Antichrist has not been a deliverer, but a deceiver. Jesus' directive to Jews living in Israel at that time is to flee into the wilderness for protection. We saw back in Revelation 12 that God will protect a remnant of the population of Israel through the Tribulation. The betrayal represented by the image standing in the temple will begin the process of turning the hearts of the people of Israel back to the Lord.

As stunning as the image itself is to the people of Israel and the world, no one will expect what happens next. The false prophet is allowed to give breath to the image so that the image itself speaks (verse 15). It's not clear whether this is actual life or just the appearance of life, but it will be one more display of the second beast's power. The world will see it as evidence of Godlike power. In several places in Scripture a demon speaks through a human being (see Mark 5:1–9; Acts 16:16–18). Perhaps the image speaks by demonic power or even by an elaborate act of ventriloquism. Whatever the mechanism Satan uses, the world is convinced that a genuine miracle has taken place.

The Antichrist is still to be revealed, but the *spirit* of Antichrist and many embodiments of the Antichrist are already at work in the world (1 John 2:18; 4:3; 2 John 7). Political leaders who oppress God's people, spiritual leaders who steer people away from God's truth, economic leaders who are motivated only by greed and materialism, social leaders who ignore God's holy character and who pronounce what is evil to be good—they all drink from the same evil well of rebellion and hatred toward God. They foreshadow in small ways what the Antichrist will seek to impose on the whole world. The power of the spirit of the Antichrist, and even the arrival of the personal Antichrist, is not a reason to throw up our hands in despair. We serve a conquering King. We can take on the world's evil and injustice in Christ's power, knowing that in the end Jesus *will* prevail.

Future FAQs

Is my Social Security Number — or the bar code on my groceries — the mark of the beast?

Christians have jumped to paranoid conclusions several times in history over what they think may be the mark of the beast. I've encountered many Christians who live in fear that someday they will wake up and discover too late that they have taken the mark and didn't know it. A couple of facts from Revelation 13 should calm any of those fears. First, John is clear that the mark will be received for one thing—worshiping the beast. Everyone will know exactly what is going on. No surprise tactics on this issue. Second, receiving the mark will be voluntary. The choice will be clear: refuse the mark, die, go to heaven; or accept the mark, live a while, go to hell forever.

The image speaks and commands that any person who refuses to worship the beast or his image is to be executed. The decree goes out, but, of course, it takes time to make sure that it is carried out. As the worship of the beast is enforced throughout the Antichrist's empire, true believers in Jesus will be confronted with a decision—worship Satan's emissary, or die. Hundreds of thousands of Christians will be executed during the last three and a half years of the Tribulation.

The false prophet doesn't stop, however, with just a command to worship. He also implements an economic plan that makes ferreting out the Christians a lot easier.

The Mark of the Beast (Revelation 13:16 – 18)

> It also forced all people, great and small, rich and poor, free and slave, to receive a mark on their right hands or on their foreheads, so that they could not buy or sell unless they had the mark, which is the name of the beast or the number of its name.
>
> This calls for wisdom. Let those who have insight calculate the number of the beast, for it is the number of a man. That number is 666.

The false prophet initiates a system in which only those who receive a mark on their foreheads or on their right hands will be able to buy or sell or conduct any financial business. Everyone—rich and poor, important and insignificant, upper crust and common citizen—is required to receive a mark, a brand, similar to a tattoo. It will be permanent and visible. It will also be conspicuous. The mark is placed on the right hand or on the forehead.

In the ancient world, slave owners sometimes marked or branded their slaves as a sign of ownership. Those who receive the mark of the beast during the Tribulation will be acknowledging that they are slaves to the Antichrist. Roman soldiers would sometimes brand themselves with the name of their general as a sign of absolute devotion. Those who are devoted to the Antichrist will wear his mark with pride.

The mark will be required to buy and sell. I take that to mean that the mark will be necessary to conduct any kind of personal business. A person won't be hired anywhere without the mark. No access to a bank account, no credit card transactions, no paycheck, no purchases of any kind. Cash won't help because it will be illegal to accept the cash without first confirming that the customer has the mark.

The mark proves that the person has worshiped the beast. Just as citizens of the Roman Empire demonstrated their loyalty to the emperor by offering incense at his altar, Tribulation earth-dwellers will have to prove their loyalty to the Antichrist by worshiping his image and receiving the

BARNEY AND THE BEAST

This humorous "Antichrist Alert" made its way around the Internet a while ago—the "proof" that the cute purple dinosaur Barney is really the beast in disguise!

1. Start with his standard description:

    CUTE PURPLE DINOSAUR

2. Change all U's to V's (which is proper Latin anyway):

    CVTE PVRPLE DINOSAVR

3. Extract all Roman numerals in the phrase:

    C/V/V/L/D/I/V

4. Convert the value of the Roman numerals to Arabic numbers:

    100 / 5 / 5 /50 / 500 / 1 / 5

5. Add all the numbers:

    666

Barney Is the Beast!!

mark. Christians who refuse will be executed. Followers of Jesus will survive only by going "underground" and by pooling their resources or by God's supernatural provision. To appear in any public setting without the mark will be to put yourself at risk of immediate arrest and execution.

"666"

The mark itself, according to John, is the name of the beast or the number of his name. The Antichrist's name, written in letters, has a numerical value of 666. No sentence of Scripture has stirred as much debate or controversy as the last sentence of Revelation 13. It has

Try, Try Again

666

If you punch "666" into the Google search engine on the Internet, more than 20 million hits show up in less than one second. After reading all 20 million links (just kidding), the two most interesting were these:

- the site that came up with a creative way to derive "666" from Abraham Lincoln's name and rank as the sixteenth president (yes, there's a six in there)
- the site that found "666" in three letters "www"—the abbreviation for the worldwide web

Other interesting Internet lore:

- The shock-rock band "Marilyn Manson" released their album *Antichrist Superstar* on June 6, 1996 (the 6th day of the 6th month).
- The first Apple Computer supposedly sold for $666.66.
- The sum of the numbers on a roulette wheel (1–36) total 666.
- The name "Bill Gates III" in the ASCII computer language has the numerical value of 666. "Windows 95" also adds up to 666 (if you count the space as one).
- "666" is the brand name of a cough syrup. (No thanks—I'll stick with coughing.)
- U.S. Highway 666 (called the "Highway of the Beast" by locals) was renumbered in 2003 after a load of complaints about its connection to the Antichrist.

IN THE NEWS: RADIO-FREQUENCY MICROCHIPS

The U.S. Federal Drug Administration has approved radio-frequency microchips that can be implanted under a patient's skin and scanned to instantly reveal a person's medical history, blood type, and allergies. The chip, about the size of a grain of rice, has already been implanted in more than a thousand people in Mexico. Privacy advocates have denounced the chips, claiming that they mark a dangerous step toward a future in which people will be tracked by implants or will be required to have them inserted for identification or surveillance.

One opponent said, "It would obviously be possible to inject one of these in everyone." Mexico's attorney general had the device injected into his arm and those of about 160 employees to control access to high-security offices. Future uses, according to the manufacturer, include enabling stores to verify a customer's identity before accepting a credit card.

Based on an article in *The Dallas Morning News*, October 14, 2004.

COMPUTERS AND CREDIT CARDS

The escalating use of credit cards has been widely regarded by prophecy buffs as the first step toward a universal money card that the Antichrist will use to control all buying and selling. One writer came up with this ingenious proposal: "VI" is the Roman numeral for 6; the number 6 in classical Greek "resembles" the letter S; and "it is possible" that the Babylonian letter for the A sound also had the value of 6. Put it all together, and 6 + 6 + 6 spells— "VISA"! (Talk about a stretch!)

Computers have made more possible the threat of absolute control over income and spending. Jerry Church figured out that if you give A the value of 6, B the value of 12, and so on, you come up with the following:

C = 18
O = 90
M = 78
P = 96
U = 126
T = 120
E = 30
R = 108

C-O-M-P-U-T-E-R adds up to 666! By the way, "Mark of the Beast" and "New York City" also total 666.

Some writers have suggested that the Antichrist will be a computer—an idea that picked up some steam when employees at the European Common Market headquarters in Luxembourg affectionately nicknamed the central computer "The Beast."

Note: These illustrations come from Paul Boyer, *When Time Shall Be No More: Prophecy Belief in Modern American Culture* (Cambridge, Mass.: Belknap/Harvard, 1992), 282–83.

I would suggest that we not waste our time trying to identify a person by this number. Instead, we need to present Jesus Christ so that we might reduce the population of those who have to go through the Great Tribulation period and who will therefore know what the number of the beast is.

J. Vernon McGee, on the radio broadcast, *Thru the Bible Radio*, 1983.

Probably the best interpretation is that the number six is one less than the perfect number seven, and the threefold repetition of the six would indicate that, for all their pretentions to deity, Satan and the two beasts are just creatures and not the Creator.

John Walvoord, in *The Bible Knowledge Commentary: New Testament* (Colorado Springs: Victor, 1983), 963.

provided more fodder for more preachers and prophecy writers than any other verse in the Bible—and the truth is, we still aren't certain what it means.

John warns the reader that understanding this riddle takes divine wisdom and great depth of insight. Furthermore, the reader is to calculate the number. It takes not only insight but information to figure this out. Believers might not have that information until the Antichrist is actually on the scene. Only then will the insightful person be able to calculate the number of the beast's name and to see how it comes out to "666"—"the number of a man."

In the ancient world, the languages of Greek, Latin, and Hebrew did not have access to Arabic numerals—the "numbers" we use all the time. Those languages used letters of the alphabet to represent numbers. In Greek, for example, the first nine letters of the alphabet represented the nine single digits of one through nine. The next nine letters represented 10, 20, 30, 40, and so on. Then came the hundreds.

The Romans devised "Roman numerals." The letter *I* stood for number one. Five was represented by *V*; one hundred by *M*. Large numbers were written as combinations of letters: XL, for example, represents "40"—X (10) subtracted from L (50).

Hundreds of attempts have been made to figure out the Antichrist's name—or to prove that someone was the Antichrist—by translating the name into Greek, Latin, or Hebrew and adding up the numerical equivalent. So far everyone from Barney the purple dinosaur to the VISA credit card to Franklin Roosevelt (and Eleanor Roosevelt) has been calculated to equal "666." In my mind, John is telling us right in the passage that we won't be able to calculate the number until we know the Antichrist's name, and *that* won't be revealed with any certainty until the middle of the Tribulation. The number of his name will simply confirm the identity of the man. So speculation today about who the Antichrist might be may be interesting, but it's only speculation.

Vern Poythress summarizes Satan's character well: "Satan is not a second creator but only a counterfeiter. And he is a poor one at that because all his imitations are hideous. Can anyone in his right mind, with eyes open to the true nature of Satan's imitations, still honestly want to follow him?" ("Counterfeiting in the Book of Revelation as a Perspective on Non-Christian Culture," *Journal of the Evangelical Theological Society 40* [September, 1997]: 412).

Points to Remember

- ☑ The Antichrist will suffer a fatal wound and be miraculously healed by Satan's power.

- ☑ The Antichrist will blaspheme and hate God and seek to kill all the followers of Jesus.

- ☑ A second beast, the false prophet, will emerge as a religious leader. He will lead the world in the worship of the first beast.

- ☑ An image honoring the beast will be set up as an object of worship. The false prophet will miraculously give breath to the image.

- ☑ No one will be able to buy or sell or conduct business of any kind during the last half of the Tribulation without a mark on their hand or forehead indicating that they had worshiped the Antichrist.

- ☑ If someone comes up with the number "666" from a president's name or a pope's birth date, just walk away.

CHAPTER 14

Hang On!
Help Is on the Way!

Hang On! Help Is on the Way!

▶ Tune in to a preview of things to come.
▶ The 144,000 survive the Tribulation.
▶ Proclamations and shouts cascade from heaven.
▶ A sharp blade of judgment sweeps the earth.

Access Codes

Key Codes: Level 14

→ The Lamb: Jesus
→ Mount Zion: The fortified hill where the temple and David's fortress were built in Jerusalem
→ Babylon the Great: The world system under the Antichrist's control
→ Sickle: A long, sharp instrument used to cut grain for harvest
→ Winepress: Large vat for pressing juice from grapes
→ 1,600 stadia: Distance of about 180 miles (300 kilometers)

Seven Signs

In these middle chapters of Revelation, John records seven important signs—awe-inspiring pictures that introduce key people or crucial events into the story of the Tribulation. John is not concerned about advancing the timeline of events; he's more concerned that we understand the significance of the people and places he introduces.

So let's review:

* In chapter 12 we saw the first sign/picture—the woman/Israel, protected and nurtured by God (12:1–6).
* Also in chapter 12 Satan makes his grand entrance on the stage of the book by engaging in a war in heaven with Michael, a powerful angel of God (12:7–12).

- An enraged Satan persecutes the woman/Israel, and she flees into the wilderness (12:13–17).
- Satan then unveils the centerpiece of his plan to thwart God's reconquest of earth. The "beast," the Antichrist, rises to great power over the kingdoms of the world (13:1–10).
- Another beast arrives on the scene to lead the world in worship of the Antichrist. The false prophet performs astonishing miracles (13:11–18).

Now, in chapter 14, John sees two more signs—(1) Jesus standing in victory with the 144,000 (14:1–5), and (2) a spectacular preview of God's judgment on the earth (14:6–20). Every scene in chapter 14 anticipates what is about to happen. None of these events actually occur in the middle of the Tribulation, but they are about to come to pass. It's as if we get to sneak to the last pages in a mystery novel and peek at how the story ends.

The Lamb on Mount Zion (Revelation 14:1–5)

> Then I looked, and there before me was the Lamb, standing on Mount Zion, and with him 144,000 who had his name and his Father's name written on their foreheads. And I heard a sound from heaven like the roar of rushing waters and like a loud peal of thunder. The sound I heard was like that of harpists playing their harps. And they sang a new song before the throne and before the four living creatures and the elders. No one could learn the song except the 144,000 who had been redeemed from the earth. These are those who did not defile themselves with women, for they remained virgins. They follow the Lamb wherever he goes. They were purchased from among the human race and offered as firstfruits to God and the Lamb. No lie was found in their mouths; they are blameless.

You can't read Revelation 13 without being stunned into silence and dread. Two powerful world leaders are about to appear on the stage of human history. They are leaders in league with the devil, and earth-dwellers will be forced to worship and obey them, or die. Some of the Christians who first read Revelation must have felt as though they knew leaders like that. Several of the Roman emperors demanded worship as a god. The penalty for refusal was death in the Coliseum as a gladiator or as prey for lions.

Bible Networking

Joel 2:32

> And everyone who calls
>   on the name of the LORD will be saved;
> for on Mount Zion and in Jerusalem
>   there will be deliverance,
>   as the LORD has said,
> even among the survivors
>   whom the LORD calls.

Psalm 48:1 – 2

> Great is the LORD, and most worthy of praise,
>   in the city of our God, his holy mountain,
> Beautiful in its loftiness,
>   the joy of the whole earth,
> like the heights of Zaphon is Mount Zion,
>   the city of the Great King.

Isaiah 2:2

> In the last days
> the mountain of the LORD's temple will be established
>   as the highest of the mountains;
> it will be exalted above the hills,
>   and all nations will stream to it.

John might have felt discouraged too. He was already paying a heavy price for his commitment to Jesus as Lord. He was confined to a prison island, with very little hope of release. But just as those dark thoughts pressed in, John's eyes were drawn to another vision. In contrast to the dragon standing on the seashore or the mark of the beast branded into people's foreheads, John sees Jesus, the Lamb. Jesus isn't sitting up in heaven, fretting over how everything will turn out. He's standing on Mount Zion.

In the prophetic tradition, Zion came to signify not just the Temple Mount but the location where the Messiah would deliver his people and gather them to himself. As Jerusalem was the capital of Israel, Mount Zion is the capital of the renewed kingdom of God to be established by the Messiah.

Grant Osborne, in *Revelation* (Grand Rapids: Baker, 2002), 525.

Mount Zion is the name of the place in Jerusalem where God's temple was built. John may be referring to the heavenly Mount Zion, the place where God's throne rests, but it makes better sense to see this as the earthly Mount Zion. I say that because standing around Jesus in John's vision are the 144,000 Jews who were sealed by God back in chapter 7. These 144,000 are protected by God throughout the Tribulation. Satan tries to persecute them and the Antichrist tries to kill them, but God sees to it that they survive. If this were the *heavenly* Mount Zion, the 144,000 would have to be dead. Instead, John is allowed to see down to the end of the Tribulation when Jesus returns to earth, and standing with Jesus on a reclaimed Mount Zion are the 144,000 Jewish survivors.

The Song They Sing

John tells us some things here about the 144,000 that he didn't tell us back in chapter 7. These Jewish believers are commissioned to do a great work and are protected by God's power, but they are also called to lives of personal sacrifice. Six factors mark these believers as servants of God:

- *They are sealed with Jesus' name (the Lamb's name) and the Father's name.* In chapter 7 John said that they had God's seal on their foreheads, but here we learn that both the Father and Jesus mark them as their own possession. When I buy a new book or a new power tool, I write my name on it; when God purchases these believers (verse 4), he writes his name on them.
- *They sing a song that no one else can sing.* A cosmic orchestra begins to play—rushing water, rumbling thunder, a chorus of

Bible Networking

Paul — on remaining single
1 Corinthians 7:32 – 34

I would like you to be free from concern. An unmarried man is concerned about the Lord's affairs — how he can please the Lord. But a married man is concerned about the affairs of this world — how he can please his wife — and his interests are divided.

Jesus — on following him
Luke 9:23

Whoever wants to be my disciple must deny themselves and take up their cross daily and follow me.

Paul — on Israel turning to the Lord
Romans 11:26

And in this way all Israel will be saved. As it is written:

> "The deliverer will come from Zion;
>   he will turn godlessness away from Jacob."

Zechariah — on the future repentance of Israel
Zechariah 12:10

And I will pour out on the house of David and the inhabitants of Jerusalem a spirit of grace and supplication. They will look on me, the one they have pierced, and they will mourn for him as one mourns for an only child.

harps — and the 144,000 sing a song to God that only they can learn. Those of us already in heaven only get to listen. We aren't told what the words of the song are, but most likely it's a joy-filled song about the preserving power and grace of God.

- *The 144,000 are sexually celibate and spiritually pure.* The first line of verse 4 has probably stirred up more controversy than any other single line in Revelation (except maybe that "666" line in chapter 13). Some interpreters have claimed that the 144,000 have to be males since it says they did not defile themselves with *women.* But Paul in 2 Corinthians calls the whole church (including males and females) "a pure virgin" who is presented to Christ our husband (11:2). So John could be including males *and* females in the 144,000 and simply mean that they remained sexually celibate. Both Jesus and Paul advocated celibacy for believers who found themselves in a time of persecution and crisis (Matthew 19:12; 1 Corinthians 7:26). John could also be using a figure of speech to talk more generally about the moral purity of the 144,000. In a time of moral chaos, they remain true to Christ, undefiled by the immorality around them.

- *They are fully committed followers of Jesus.* "They follow the Lamb wherever he goes" (verse 4). Considering the time they live in, it would be hard to imagine a stronger commendation. During the darkest days of the Tribulation, they are willing to follow Jesus. To "follow" means to stay true to Jesus' instructions and to vigorously promote his cause. These men and women never waver.

- *The 144,000 are purchased from among mankind as a firstfruits offering to God and to the Lamb.* In the Old Testament, when the barley or wheat harvest began, Israelites would cut a handful of the ripe grain and offer it to the Lord as a firstfruits gift. (Check Leviticus 23:9–14.) They honored God first with their resources

In Other Words

So persecuted will these evangelists be that they will have to depend on their converts to provide for their everyday needs. They'll be unable to buy or sell, they'll be unclothed and hungry, they'll be sick and imprisoned. When Christ judges the people still alive at the end of the Tribulation period, he will assign them to eternal life or eternal death on the basis of their treatment of his 144,000 evangelists, since that will reflect their attitude toward Christ himself (Matthew 25:31 – 46).

Hal Lindsey, in *There's a New World Coming* (Eugene, Ore.: Harvest House, 1984), 197.

In the Great Tribulation, you will either be led by the Lamb or bossed by the beast.

Adrian Rogers, in *Unveiling the End Times in Our Time* (Nashville: Broadman & Holman, 2004), 176.

in anticipation of a larger harvest to follow. The 144,000 may be the first Jews to be saved after the rapture, but they represent a much larger harvest from Israel to follow. Many in Israel will turn to the Lord as the Tribulation comes to an end.

- *The 144,000 speak God's truth during a time when satanic deception will deceive virtually the whole world.* They will stand with Jesus as blameless men and women. John doesn't say *sinless*; he says *blameless*. There's a difference. Blameless means we handle our sin correctly before God, and therefore we have nothing to hide and nothing to fear.

A Bounty of Judgment (Revelation 14:6 – 20)

Then I saw another angel flying in midair, and he had the eternal gospel to proclaim to those who live on the earth—to every nation, tribe, language and people. He said in a loud voice, "Fear God and give him glory, because the hour of his judgment has come. Worship him who made the heavens, the earth, the sea and the springs of water."

A second angel followed and said, "'Fallen! Fallen is Babylon the Great,' which made all the nations drink the maddening wine of her adulteries."

A third angel followed them and said in a loud voice: "If anyone worships the beast and its image and receive its mark on their forehead or on their hand, they, too, will drink of the wine of God's fury, which has been poured full strength into the cup of his wrath. They will be tormented with burning sulfur in the presence of the holy angels and of the Lamb. And the smoke of their torment will rise for ever and ever. There will be no rest day or night for those who worship the beast and

In Other Words

"Babylon" will epitomize ungodliness in the world during the Tribulation, as it has throughout human history since the tower of Babel (Genesis 11:1 – 9). Like "Hollywood" the name represents the world system as well as being the name of a particular city.

Thomas Constable, in "Notes on Revelation," (*www.soniclight.com/constable/notes/pdf/revelation.pdf*), 126–27 (accessed January 23, 2007).

its image, or for anyone who receives the mark of its name." This calls for patient endurance on the part of the people of God who keep his commandments and remain faithful to Jesus.

Then I heard a voice from heaven say, "Write: Blessed are the dead who die in the Lord from now on."

"Yes," says the Spirit, "they will rest from their labor, for their deeds will follow them."

I looked, and there before me was a white cloud, and seated on the cloud was one like a son of man with a crown of gold on his head and a sharp sickle in his hand. Then another angel came out of the temple and called in a loud voice to him who was sitting on the cloud, "Take your sickle and reap, because the time to reap has come, for the harvest of the earth is ripe." So he who was seated on the cloud swung his sickle over the earth, and the earth was harvested.

Another angel came out of the temple in heaven, and he too had a sharp sickle. Still another angel, who had charge of the fire, came from the altar and called in a loud voice to him who had the sharp sickle, "Take your sharp sickle and gather the clusters of grapes from the earth's vine, because its grapes are ripe." The angel swung his sickle on the earth, gathered its grapes and threw them into the great winepress of God's wrath. They were trampled in the winepress outside the city, and blood flowed out of the press, rising as high as the horses' bridles for a distance of 1,600 stadia.

The next sign John sees is a vision of God's judgment. The first part of chapter 14 focuses on believers who will survive the Tribulation; the last part focuses on unbelievers who won't survive. A series of four

In Other Words

Chapter 14 brings to a conclusion the material found in the section of chapters 12 through 14.

Chapter 12 deals with the important characters of the period, chapter 13 with the wicked rulers of the period, and chapter 14 with the ultimate triumph of Christ. All this material is not chronological but prepares the way for the climax which begins in chapter 15. Chapter 14 consists of a series of pronouncements and visions assuring the reader of the ultimate triumph of Christ and the judgment of the wicked. Much of the chapter is prophetic of events that have not yet taken place, but which are now impending.

John Walvoord, in *The Revelation of Jesus Christ* (1966; rev. ed., Chicago: Moody, 1989), 213.

announcements leads us through an incredible scene of harvest and condemnation. God, in his anger against sin, is about to swing a sharp blade over the earth. The announcements will encourage believers who read these words in the future Tribulation to remain faithful to God in the days of the Antichrist's greatest power.

A Preaching Angel

John first sees an angel in mid-heaven, at the place in the sky that is most visible from earth. The angel is doing something that angels rarely do—preaching. Angels announce and angels warn and angels shout, but they almost never preach. In fact, in the present age before the rapture, God has entrusted the proclamation of the message about Jesus to us, to men and women who are already committed to Jesus. We are the ones commanded to go into the whole world with the gospel (Mark 16:15). But here in the middle of the Tribulation, God in his grace and mercy gives mankind one final call by sending an angel to preach.

In Other Words

This [Revelation 14:6–20] is the most horrible picture of eternal punishment in the entirety of Revelation.

Robert Thomas, in *Revelation 8–22*
(Chicago: Moody, 1995), 212.

Normally people added water to wine to dilute it, but God will not weaken his punishment of beast-worshipers.

Thomas Constable, in "Notes on Revelation" (*www. soniclight.com/constable/notes/pdf/revelation.pdf*), 127 (accessed January 23, 2007).

A young atheist chose to consider the claims of Christ immediately rather than deferring the decision because the doctrine of hell made the stakes too high to ignore. Twenty-four years later, that former atheist remains a committed Christian — and is writing this commentary.

Craig Keener, in *Revelation* (NIV Application Commentary; Grand Rapids: Zondervan, 2000), 382.

Matthew 24:30 – 31

At that time the sign of the Son of Man will appear in the sky, and all the peoples of the earth will mourn. They will see the Son of Man coming on the clouds of heaven, with power and great glory. And he will send his angels with a loud trumpet call, and they will gather his elect from the four winds, from one end of the heavens to the other.

Matthew 26:63 – 64

The high priest said to him, "I charge you under oath by the living God: Tell us if you are the Messiah, the Son of God."

"You have said so," Jesus replied. "But I say to all of you: From now on you will see the Son of Man sitting at the right hand of the Mighty One and coming on the clouds of heaven."

The angel doesn't preach a different gospel from the one we preach. Men and women are saved in the Tribulation by believing exactly what we are called to believe today. The angel's message is really pretty simple. He issues three commands to the inhabitants of the earth:

- "Fear God": The gospel message involves a realization and admission that we are accountable to God. We have all sinned; we have all fallen far short of God's demands.
- "Give him glory": After we admit our sin, we receive God's offer of forgiveness. We are made new by God's grace and by faith in God's Son, Jesus. To give God glory means to accept the salvation that God offers. The choices are clear—believe in Jesus, or face God's judgment.
- "Worship him": Genuine worship emerges from a heart and life in right relationship with God. We worship God only when we truly know God, and we know God only through committed faith in his Son, Jesus.

The angel's message may not sound like our presentation of the gospel today. He doesn't say anything specifically about Jesus or his death on the cross or his resurrection, but all the elements of the gospel are part of a complete understanding of the angel's message. The angel is not

Joel 3:11 - 16

Come quickly, all you nations from every side,
    and assemble there.

Bring down your warriors, LORD!

"Let the nations be roused;
    let them advance into the Valley of Jehoshaphat,
for there I will sit
    to judge all the nations on every side.
Swing the sickle,
    for the harvest is ripe.
Come, trample the grapes,
    for the wine press is full
    and the vats overflow—
so great is their wickedness!"

Multitudes, multitudes
    in the valley of decision!
For the day of the LORD is near
    in the valley of decision.
The sun and moon will be darkened,
    and the stars no longer shine.
The LORD will roar from Zion
    and thunder from Jerusalem;
    the earth and the heavens will tremble.
But the LORD will be a refuge for his people,
    a stronghold for the people of Israel.

Zephaniah 3:8b

"I have decided to assemble the nations,
    to gather the Kingdoms
and to pour out my wrath on them—
    all my fierce anger.
The whole world will be consumed
    by the fire of my jealous anger."

Revelation 14 is a chapter of contrasts: the Lamb and the beast, earth and heaven, the harvest of unbelievers and the rescue of believers, eternity with God and eternity in hell. The Bible never offers a third way. There are only two—the *right* way that leads to life, and the *wrong* way that leads to death. Those who die in the Lord are blessed and at rest forever. Those who die under God's wrath never rest and are in torment forever. Wisdom from the Bible's perspective has very little to do with education or a college degree. True wisdom is recognizing God's path and following it. Sadly, only a few find God's path. Most people think that the wide road leading to destruction is the wisest choice.

preaching to people who have some background knowledge about Jesus; he's preaching to people who have been living in spiritual darkness with only a rudimentary sense of who God is. In that light, the angel's message sounds a lot like the message preached by Paul and Barnabas in the pagan city of Lystra: "We are bringing you good news, telling you to turn from these worthless things to the living God, who made heaven and earth and sea and everything in them" (Acts 14:15).

A Predicting Angel

No sooner had the preaching angel left the scene than another angel took his place. This angel looks ahead in time and sees the destruction of Babylon the Great. This is the first occurrence of Babylon in Revelation, although we will get thoroughly acquainted with Babylon in chapters 17 and 18. We will save the long discussion about what Babylon represents until we get to those chapters. For now, I think Babylon represents the entire political, religious, and economic system ruled and directed by the Antichrist. It's the world system that the Antichrist (and Satan) control in the Tribulation. That whole system, this angel says, will soon come crashing down. He's reading the end of the book again. He knows that Jesus will ultimately prevail over the Antichrist and that the kingdoms of this earth will be swept aside by the invading kingdom of God.

Today is a day of grace; but what is true of the Tribulation is also true today, namely that God will ultimately judge all men. Today, however, the invitation is still open to those who trust in Christ and who thereby can avail themselves of the grace of God and be saved from entering this awful period.

John Walvoord, in *The Revelation of Jesus Christ* (1966; rev. ed., Chicago: Moody, 1989), 224.

The Warning Angel

The third angel brings a message of eternal judgment on all who worship the beast or his image or who receive his mark. Refusing the mark of the Antichrist will mean almost certain death; receiving the mark of the Antichrist secures a place in hell. The Bible's teaching on the eternal torment of those who refuse to believe in Jesus is one of the most difficult truths to talk about or even to hear about. But you can't escape the reality of hell, no matter how much you try to talk around it.

Those who receive the beast's mark in the future will be so hardened against the Lord that they won't even care about the heavy price attached to such an act. John wants us, however, to understand the consequences very clearly. Five aspects of God's judgment are emphasized:

- God's wrath will be poured out in full strength. Those who reject God's grace will experience the undiluted anger of a holy God against their sin.
- Judgment will be overseen by holy angels and by Jesus himself. Satan's angels are not in charge of hell; God's angels are in control of what happens in that place.
- The judgment against those who worship the beast is eternal. Lost people are never given any hope that the torment of hell will end.
- People condemned by their own choice to hell will never find rest. The only true rest in this life and in eternity is found in our relationship with Jesus.

- People in hell will be in conscious torment. John uses stunning imagery to drive home the point that people who experience God's wrath in eternity will feel it. They are not annihilated. They don't cease to exist. Instead, they experience torment day and night forever.

God knows how difficult it is for us to think about the judgment of hell, and so he adds words of comfort after this angel's solemn warning. The voice from heaven says, "Blessed are the dead who die in the Lord from now on" (verse 13). In contrast to beast-worshipers who will never find rest, those who are faithful to Jesus will experience an eternal rest. Facing death at the hands of the Antichrist will be a horrific experience, but those who die in the Lord will have the assurance of heaven beyond. Those who receive the mark of the beast will live a few weeks or months longer than the Christians, but their eternity is worse than anything they can imagine.

A Great Harvest

With the encouraging words of the Holy Spirit still ringing in his ears, John's attention is drawn to a man sitting on a cloud. Since John describes him as "like a son of man," most interpreters think that this is Jesus. In his hand is a sharp sickle, a tool with a curved blade used to cut grain or to cut clusters of grapes from a vine. The sickle in Jesus' hand suggests a time of harvest and separation. The good grain is swept into God's protection; the weeds are gathered to be destroyed.

It's not a sign of inferiority for Jesus to be commanded by an angel in verse 15. That simply indicates that the angel will signal the right time for God's judgment, and then Jesus and the angels will harvest

Help File

THE BATTLE HYMN OF THE REPUBLIC

The last verses of Revelation 14 are the backdrop for a familiar poem and patriotic hymn written by Julia Ward Howe in the middle of the American Civil War:

Mine eyes have seen the glory of the coming of the Lord,
He is trampling out the vintage where the grapes of wrath are stored;
He hath loosed the fateful lightning of his terrible swift sword,
His truth is marching on.

A River of Blood

A Preterist View of Revelation 14:20

Those who believe the book of Revelation predicts the destruction of Jerusalem by the Roman armies think that John is describing the carnage of the final Roman conquest. J. Stuart Russell writes: "Where was there ever such a sea of blood as was shed in that exterminating war of Vespasian and Titus?" (quoted in *Revelation: Four Views*, ed. Steve Gregg [Nashville: Nelson, 1997], 338).

An Idealist View of Revelation 14:20

Christians who see Revelation as a spiritual record of the world's attacks against believers in every age take the number 1,600 as symbolic of judgment. Since it is the product of 40 times 40, and the number 40 often pictures God's judgment, God's enemies will be fully trampled in Jesus' final victory.

A Futurist View of Revelation 14:20

Interpreters who believe that the book of Revelation outlines a future time of judgment take the river of blood more literally. As the death toll mounts in the final battle of Armageddon, the blood will flow in streams for the length of the land of Israel.

the earth. John is once again summarizing the rest of Revelation and looking ahead at God's completed plan. Jesus made it clear in Matthew 24 that at the time of his return in glory, at the end of the Tribulation, angels would sweep over the earth at his direction and remove those who are evil and reward those who have remained faithful. The harvest Jesus initiates here in Revelation 14 could be the final harvest of believers as Jesus separates his followers from the rest of humanity.

The flip side of Jesus' gathering of his own is the judgment of those who do not believe in Jesus. Another angel appears (the fifth angel so far in this chapter), and he has a sickle too. But his sickle harvests the rebellious. Unbelieving men and women are thrown into the final chaos of the Tribulation, pictured as a huge vat where ripe grapes are trampled to produce grape juice that eventually becomes wine. At the end of the Tribulation, humanity will be gathered in Israel for a great war, and God will bring astonishing judgment on those who have rejected his mercy and forgiveness.

Points to Remember

- ☑ John is given a preview of God's final triumph.

- ☑ The 144,000 Jews who are protected by God survive the Tribulation and stand with Jesus on Mount Zion.

- ☑ The Antichrist's political, economic, and religious system will collapse, and the Antichrist's followers will face eternal fire.

- ☑ The harvest of the earth will sweep God's people to safety and God's enemies to destruction.

What emerges from the winepress of God's wrath is not grape juice but blood. It covers the length of the land of Israel—1,600 stadia, or about 180 miles. So much blood is shed in that final war that the blood is spattered up to the bridles of the horses. As has happened so often before, the ground of the Holy Land will be soaked with blood.

CHAPTER 15

Seven Angels with Seven Plagues

Seven Angels with Seven Plagues

▶ Look for another set of seven angels, with seven bowls of God's wrath.
▶ Victorious believers sing another song of praise.
▶ The temple of God in heaven becomes the stage for the final judgments against those who dwell on the earth

Key Codes: Level 15

→ Sign: An awesome and miraculous symbol
→ Plagues: Devastating judgments
→ Moses: An Old Testament leader of God's people; he brought the people of Israel out of slavery in Egypt
→ Temple, tabernacle of the covenant law: The place in heaven where believers worship God

Short Stuff

Revelation 15 is the shortest chapter in the book, but it's not a chapter you want to miss. John sees the preparation in heaven for the final wave of judgment on the earth. The end of the Tribulation and the completion of God's judgment are within sight. Jesus is about to return to sweep away the kingdoms of earth and to establish his own kingdom of peace. But first, seven plagues will bring the Antichrist's rule to the verge of collapse.

John sees one more sign, one more awe-inspiring vision. Seven more angels emerge from God's temple in heaven with the last of God's wrath. In our politically correct age, we don't hear much about God's anger against evil and evildoers. We don't sing about it in our songs. We don't preach about it in our churches. The trend today is to emphasize the positive and ignore the negative or difficult aspects of God's truth. The book of Revelation, however, isn't nearly as nervous about God's wrath as we are. John realizes that at times there can be power in negative thinking. Sometimes our lives will change only when we are confronted with the hard, cold truth.

A Victorious Song from a Righteous Throng (Revelation 15:1–4)

I saw in heaven another great and marvelous sign: seven angels with the seven last plagues—last, because with them God's wrath is completed. And I saw what looked like a sea of glass glowing with fire and, standing beside the sea, those who had been victorious over the beast and its image and over the number of its name. They held harps given them by God and sang the song of God's servant Moses and of the Lamb:

> "Great and marvelous are your deeds,
>   Lord God Almighty.
> Just and true are your ways,
>   King of the nations.
> Who will not fear you, Lord,
>   and bring glory to your name?
> For you alone are holy.
> All nations will come
>   and worship before you,
> for your righteous acts have been revealed."

John's attention is focused first on the shimmering expanse of glass or crystal around the throne of God in heaven. Standing beside that "sea" of glass and fire is a group of people who were victorious over the beast. These people had not defeated the Antichrist in battle or destroyed his

TECHNO-SPEAK

The word John uses in verse 1 translated "last" is a form of the Greek word *eschatos*. Bible scholars have used that word to form the term *eschatology*, the branch of Christian theology that deals with "last things." When you hear someone say that they are interested in eschatology, you will know that they are talking about biblical prophecy and the study of God's plan for the future.

The song of Revelation 15 must have blessed the Christians in John's day who were facing arrest and death, just as it has encouraged and strengthened Christians in every age when they have had to stand against the anti-Christian forces opposing them. Satan does not write the last words of history; Jesus does. Believers have nothing to fear from political or spiritual powers lined up against us. Whether it's today or during the Tribulation, Jesus reigns over human affairs. Jesus reigns over the job situation that seems so impossible right now; he reigns over the marriage or the friendship that seems to be beyond hope of repair; he reigns over the habit or addiction that seems to dominate your life. Sing the victory song of Revelation 15, and follow Jesus out of despair and into his freedom and light. He's ready to help.

In Other Words

Many people ask where is God when there is so much sin in the world — wickedness, rape, arson, pillage, child abuse, blasphemy, war. Where is God? He is on his throne! And you can be certain that every sin will be punished. Yours will be punished. Mine will be punished.

The only question is: who will bear that punishment? Every sin will be pardoned by Christ or punished in hell, but it will not be overlooked. Nobody's sin is ever overlooked. All sin is dealt with.

Adrian Rogers, in *Unveiling the End Times in Our Time*
(Nashville: Broadman & Holman, 2004), 185.

Once the time of final judgment has come, none can stay the hand of God. The time for intercession is past. God in his unapproachable majesty and power has declared that the end has come. No longer does he stand knocking; he enters to act in judgment.

Robert Mounce, in *The Book of Revelation*
(Grand Rapids: Eerdmans, 1977), 290.

empire. As John witnesses this scene, the Antichrist is still in power on the earth. These people had, in fact, been killed by the Antichrist, executed for their faith in Jesus and their refusal to accept the beast's mark. But in God's view, they are the victorious ones. Their victory lies in the fact that they remained faithful to God, even to the point of death. Instead of yielding to the beast's demands to worship him and to receive his mark, they endured execution.

Now these Tribulation martyrs stand redeemed in heaven and sing a powerful song of praise and exaltation to God. We look at the execution and martyrdom of a Christian as a great tragedy. Those who actually experience it will refer to their spiritual deliverance as one of God's great and marvelous deeds. They aren't complaining that their deaths were unfair. They are rejoicing that all God's actions are just and true.

The song that these Tribulation believers sing is called "the song of God's servant Moses and of the Lamb" (verse 3). Apparently, two songs are blended together in praise to God. The first song, the song of Moses, emphasizes the faithful character of God and his greatness in defeating the enemies of God's people. Moses certainly knew about God's power over his enemies. Moses was the instrument God used to bring a series of crippling plagues against Egypt when Pharaoh refused to release the Israelites from slavery. Moses saw firsthand the judgment of God

SEVEN PLAGUES

When God made his agreement or covenant with the people of Israel, each side had serious responsibilities. Some of God's covenants with Israel were *unconditional*. They rested on God alone. The covenant of the law was *conditional*. God promised to bless, protect, and provide for Israel *if* (here's the condition) they obeyed God's law. If the people rebelled against God or turned away from worshiping him, God would bring judgment on them. The judg-

ments were part of God's promise too. In Leviticus 26:21, God said to Israel, "If you remain hostile toward me and refuse to listen to me, I will multiply your afflictions seven times over, as your sins deserve." God mentions "seven times over" in that chapter four times (verses 18, 21, 24, 28).

In Revelation 15 and 16, God uses that principle of seven judgments against a world that refuses to accept his grace and mercy.

Exodus 15:1 – 2, 11

I will sing to the LORD,
　for he is highly exalted.
Both horse and driver
　he has hurled into the sea.
The LORD is my strength and my defense;
　he has become my salvation.
He is my God, and I will praise him,
　my father's God, and I will exalt him....
Who among the gods
　is like you, LORD?
Who is like you—
　majestic in holiness,
awesome in glory,
　working wonders?

Deuteronomy 32:3 – 4, 43

I will proclaim the name of the LORD.
　Oh, praise the greatness of our God!
He is the Rock, his works are perfect,
　and all his ways are just.
A faithful God who does no wrong,
　upright and just is he....
Rejoice, you nations, with his people,
　for he will avenge the blood of his servants;
he will take vengeance on his enemies
　and make atonement for his land and people.

BOWLS OF WRATH

The bowls given to the seven angels are most likely sprinkling bowls that were used in tabernacle worship for carrying and sprinkling the blood of certain animal sacrifices. The outpouring of these judgments on an unbelieving world was to be seen as a sacred offering to God.

on Pharaoh's army at the Red Sea. Then, for forty years in the desert, Moses witnessed God's faithful provision for his people.

Some interpreters think that the song of Moses is recorded for us in Exodus 15. Others believe Deuteronomy 32 fits better as the song of Moses. Both passages emphasize the themes of God's faithfulness and his triumph over those who oppose him.

The second emphasis of the song in Revelation 15 comes from "the song ... of the Lamb" (verse 3), which would include the theme of redemption from sin made possible by the sacrifice of Jesus as the Lamb of God. Any believer in any age could sing this song, but the Tribulation believers find it to be a powerful expression of worship and adoration to God. All of God's acts, whether they are acts of redemption or acts of judgment, are great and marvelous and just and right. Even when God allows his servants to be killed and imprisoned for their faith, God is acting in a way that is right and worthy of praise. He is worthy of worship in every circumstance.

Open House in God's Temple (Revelation 15:5–8)

> After this I looked, and I saw in heaven the temple—that is, the tabernacle of the covenant law—and it was opened. Out of the temple came the seven angels with the seven plagues. They were dressed in clean, shining linen and wore golden sashes around their chests. Then one of the four living creatures gave to the seven angels seven golden bowls filled with the wrath of God, who lives for ever and ever. And the temple was filled with smoke from the glory of God and from his power, and no one could enter the temple until the seven plagues of the seven angels were completed.

As the words of this magnificent song fade, John's attention is drawn to the temple in heaven, the place where the worship of God is centered.

In Other Words

People living during the Tribulation will think the Antichrist is overcoming the saints, but in reality he is sending them out into eternity to be with their Lord.

Tim LaHaye, in *Revelation Unveiled* (Grand Rapids: Zondervan, 1999), 245.

Rapture-Ready in 1967

According to Reverend Sun Myung Moon, leader of the Unification Church, the kingdom of heaven was supposed to arrive in 1967. It was to be marked by a great spiritual awakening (to the value of the Unification Church, I'm sure). When 1967 passed uneventfully as far as the whole kingdom of heaven thing was concerned, Reverend Moon said it was because the world was just not ready for spiritual enlightenment.

Evangelical Christians had plenty to crow about with the Six-Day War in Israel in 1967. Israel decisively defeated her enemies, and for the first time since AD 70, the entire city of Jerusalem was back under Jewish control. Those events had Christians sitting on the edge of their pews, waiting for the trumpet call of the rapture.

John also describes it as "the tabernacle of the covenant law," reminding us of the tent constructed under Moses' direction for worship in the wilderness. That tabernacle had an inner room known as the Holy of Holies, or the Most Holy Place.

One piece of furniture stood in the center of that room—the ark of the covenant. The ark was a gold box that contained the stone tablets on which God's law had been written. Above the box two gold angels spread their wings over the solid gold lid. Above the angels a brilliant light rested, the visible glory of God. The Holy of Holies represented God's presence among his people.

Now, in John's vision, that tabernacle in heaven is opened and seven holy angels emerge from the holy room and from the presence of God. Even their clothes shout their purity, righteousness, and glory. Pure white linen and golden sashes let us know that, whatever these angels are set to do, it's perfect before God.

One of the majestic angels who stood at God's throne hands each angel a golden bowl (the older versions of the Bible say "golden vials") filled with the wrath of God. Smoke pours out of the temple as a sign

Points to Remember

☑ Believers who have been executed during the Tribulation praise God for his faithfulness and righteous deeds.

☑ The Antichrist thought he had been victorious over his enemies when he killed them, but God says that they are victorious over the beast.

☑ Seven more angels emerge from God's temple in heaven with the final judgments of the Tribulation.

of God's power and as a means of emphasizing the seriousness of this moment in God's plan. No one can enter the tabernacle until God's judgment is completed. It's as though God is saying, "I'm busy right now bringing my sovereign plan to completion. Whatever you have come for will have to wait." Heaven and earth stop to witness the final blast of God's justice against a wicked, rebellious world.

I Don't Like
What's in Those
Bowls

CHAPTER 16

I Don't Like
What's in Those Bowls

I Don't Like What's in Those Bowls

MR. BLOCKHEAD
HEADS UP

- The end of God's judgment comes as the seven bowls of wrath are poured out.
- The entire universe begins to unravel.
- Blood, fire, pain!
- The armies of the world gather for one final war.

Access Codes

Key Codes: Level 16

→ Wrath: God's consistent attitude toward evil
→ The mark of the beast: Everyone who worships the Antichrist receives this mark; having it is required in order to buy or sell during the last half of the Tribulation
→ Euphrates River: A river in modern-day Iraq; the eastern border of the Roman Empire
→ Babylon the Great: The political, economic, and religious system ruled by the Antichrist

Rapid-Fire Judgment (Revelation 16:1–11)

Then I heard a loud voice from the temple saying to the seven angels, "Go, pour out the seven bowls of God's wrath on the earth."

The first angel went and poured out his bowl on the land, and ugly, festering sores broke out on the people who had the mark of the beast and worshiped its image.

The second angel poured out his bowl on the sea, and it turned into blood like that of a dead person, and every living thing in the sea died.

The third angel poured out his bowl on the rivers and springs of water, and they became blood. Then I heard the angel in charge of the waters say:

"You are just in these judgments,
  you who are and who were, the Holy One,
  because you have so judged;
for they have shed the blood of your people and
  your prophets,
  and you have given them blood to drink as they deserve."

And I heard the altar respond:

"Yes, Lord God Almighty,
  true and just are your judgments."

The fourth angel poured out his bowl on the sun, and the sun was allowed to scorch people with fire. They were seared by the intense heat and they cursed the name of God, who had control over these plagues, but they refused to repent and glorify him.

The fifth angel poured out his bowl on the throne of the beast, and its kingdom was plunged into darkness. People gnawed their tongues in agony and cursed the God of heaven because of their pains and their sores, but they refused to repent of what they had done.

The first two series of Tribulation judgments left room for a display of God's mercy and for the possibility of human repentance. This final

Napoleon

Some interpreters of Revelation believe that the book predicts the unfolding of events in the current church age. Alexander Keith, a nineteenth-century Scottish scholar who accepted this "historicist" perspective, believed the sun in Revelation 16 pointed to the French general and emperor, Napoleon. Here's what he wrote:

> Napoleon performed the miracles of genius. His achievements still dazzle, while they amaze the world. Within the space of eight years he scorched every kingdom in Europe, from Naples to Berlin, and from Lisbon to Moscow. Ancient kingdoms withered before the intense blaze of this power.... Like the sun, there was nothing hid from his great heat.

Quoted in *Revelation: Four Views*, ed. Steve Gregg (Nashville: Nelson, 1997), 368.

Deuteronomy 28:27, 35

The LORD will afflict you with the boils of Egypt and with tumors, festering sores and the itch, from which you cannot be cured....

The LORD will afflict your knees and legs with painful boils that cannot be cured, spreading from the soles of your feet to the top of your head.

Psalm 78:44

He turned their river into blood;
they could not drink from their streams.

series shows that God's mercy has come to an end. During the seal judgments (Revelation 6) and the trumpet judgments (Revelation 8–9), only part of the earth was affected—one-third of the ocean, one-third of the freshwater. Under the bowl judgments, the entire earth suffers. The earlier judgments were spaced out. Five months or more might have passed between judgments. The bowl judgments fall rapidly, one after another, in a relentless pounding that shakes loose the foundations of the universe.

Twenty times in the book of Revelation we hear "loud voices." Here what seems to be the voice of God issues a command to the seven angels: "Pour out the seven bowls of God's wrath on the earth" (verse 1). Each angel in turn walks to the edge of heaven and pours the contents of his bowl onto the earth below.

The first bowl judgment brings painful sores on those who have received the mark of the beast. Back in chapter 13 the Antichrist and the false prophet demanded worship from those living on the earth. Those who worshipped the beast or the image of the beast received a mark on their forehead or on their right hand that identified them as beast-followers. The mark was required to buy food, hold down a job, or get a driver's license. Any person who had not received the mark was condemned to arrest and execution.

Followers of the Antichrist will discover that the mark of the beast brings another consequence: they break out with ugly, festering sores.

We aren't talking about a teenager's embarrassing blemishes. These are open, disfiguring sores that will stun a world obsessed with physical beauty and attractiveness. Most likely these sores are boils—painful, infected sites on the body that make it almost impossible to walk, sit, or even lie down without excruciating pain. Medical supplies will be exhausted in days, but even the best medical care will bring little relief.

The second bowl judgment affects mankind physically and economically. The oceans are turned to blood. At the second *trumpet* judgment earlier in the Tribulation, a meteor crashed into the sea, and one-third of it became like blood. The results of the second *bowl* are more catastrophic—every living creature in the oceans dies. The water doesn't simply turn red; it turns deadly. The water is like the thick, sickening blood of a rotting corpse. The beaches of the earth will be covered with the carcasses of sea animals.

As the third bowl is poured out, the pollution of the water extends to the rivers and springs. The freshwater supply becomes undrinkable. John doesn't say that fish die or that humans die from the corruption of the water, but he may want us to assume that related affliction will result.

What makes the third bowl judgment unusual is that the angel comments about the justice of God's judgment. None of the other angels speak (except the seventh angel, who just says, "It is done!"). The third angel, the angel in charge of the waters, sings a hymn of praise to God and justifies God's works of judgment. God acts as the Holy One. Unbelievers have shed the blood of God's people and God's prophets over the years of the Tribulation, and now they are forced to drink blood to keep themselves alive. The martyrs gathered at the altar, those who died for Christ's name during the Tribulation, respond with a shout of affirmation: "Yes, Lord God Almighty, true and just are your judgments" (verse 7).

BIBLICAL BOILS

Malignant, painful sores appear several times in the Bible. In the days of Moses, God sent a plague of boils on the Egyptians, who had refused to release the Israelites from slavery (Exodus 9:9–11). Job was afflicted with boils in Satan's attempt to force him to turn away from God (Job 2:1–13), and Jesus told about a poor beggar named Lazarus, who was covered with the same sores (Luke 16:21). The pain from just one boil is incredible. In the Tribulation, beast-worshipers will be covered with such sores.

The world oppresses God's people and then wonders why God brings judgment. Evil men and women go day after day without acknowledging God's existence or thanking him for his goodness—and then are surprised at his judgment. Most people want a God who is kind, not a God who is just. They want God to keep promises of blessing but ignore any promises of judgment. Then, when the judgment comes, they respond not with repentance but with cursing. The fact that the world faces God's condemnation without repentance or sorrow reveals how deep the rebellion against God runs in our spiritual DNA. Those who consistently choose now to live apart from God will make the same choice when confronted with his hand of judgment.

In Other Words

The plagues of scorching sun and darkness (16:8 – 10) recall the Old Testament plague of darkness, a judgment on Egypt's sun-deity, Amon-Re .... That the darkness actually causes pain (16:10) may reflect the darkness of Moses' day, which could be "felt" (Ex. 10:21; cf. Ps. 107:10).

Craig Keener, in *Revelation* (NIV Application Commentary; Grand Rapids: Zondervan, 2000), 394.

We wonder if some of those who, under the sixth seal, called unto the rocks and the mountains to fall upon them (Revelation 6:16) because they thought those little judgments were the great day of wrath, can remember back to those days of little distress and compare them with the horror of what they are now going through. Their bodies were covered with sores, the stench of death in seas and rivers fills their nostrils with the odor of corruption, their bodies are scorched with fire, and then suddenly they are precipitated into the utmost blackness.

Donald Grey Barnhouse, in *Revelation: An Expositional Commentary* (Grand Rapids: Zondervan, 1971), 299.

Three Down, Four to Go

When the fourth *trumpet* judgment sounded from heaven, the sun and the moon were darkened. Now as the fourth *bowl* is poured out, the opposite effect is produced. The sun's fiery power is intensified beyond anything humans have ever experienced. A massive solar flare erupts, and the earth is scorched by the heat. God had promised believers who died under the Antichrist's persecution that the sun would never beat down on them again (Revelation 7:16). Now their persecutors are burned by the sun's fire.

Unbelievers know exactly where the judgment comes from. They don't curse the sun as its heat intensifies; they curse the one who controls the sun, the one greater than the sun. Mankind will curse the name of God and refuse to repent. They refused to turn to God when he offered his grace, they refused when he left room for mercy, and they will still refuse when his judgments come in full strength. Those who worship the beast will find their hearts hardened by God's judgment, not softened into repentance and faith. They compound their guilt by their refusal to believe even when they see God's power up close and personal.

God now presses his judgment to the throne of the Antichrist, to the center of Satan's rule on earth. The fifth bowl is poured out on the Antichrist's throne, the central place of his governmental rule—and the entire kingdom of the Antichrist is plunged into supernatural, catastrophic darkness. This is not just a storm-darkened afternoon or even a moonless, starless night. This is a powerful blackness in which no one

---

Help File

ANGELCAREERBUILDER.COM

Revelation tells us more about the specific ministries of angels than any other biblical book. Here in chapter 16 we find an angel who is in charge of the waters. In chapter 14 we came upon an angel with power over fire (14:18). Angels restrain the winds in Revelation 7:1, and in 9:1 an angel opens the Abyss, a compartment in hell.

God may have placed angelic beings in charge of certain aspects of the natural world at the time of creation. As human beings turned away from God's truth and embraced idolatry (as outlined in Romans 1:20–23), the perversions of mythology arose. Instead of a holy angel in charge of the waters, mythology proposes a spirit in the waters or in the trees, a "Mother Nature" or earth goddess in control of the natural world. Most pagan teaching has its roots in a twisting of God's truth.

Bible Networking

Deuteronomy 32:22

> For a fire will be kindled by my wrath,
>   one that burns to the realm of the dead below.
> It will devour the earth and its harvests
>   and set afire the foundations of the mountains.

Malachi 4:1

"Surely the day is coming; it will burn like a furnace. All the arrogant and every evildoer will be stubble, and that day that is coming will set them on fire," says the LORD Almighty.

---

can see a thing and no one dares to move. The darkness is so intense that people experience pain and express their anguish by gnawing their tongues in agony.

One reason I believe that these bowl judgments fall in rapid order is because John says the people in this intense darkness are still suffering the pain of the sores from the first bowl judgment. The sores, the lack of water, the burning of the sun, and now a shroud of absolute darkness are more than these men and women can bear. But in their agony, they don't cry out for God's mercy or ask for his deliverance. Instead, they curse God and refuse to repent of their evil acts. In the context of this passage, their evil acts are worshiping the beast (13:4) and murdering believers (16:6).

These are the words I find hardest to accept in the whole book of Revelation—not the descriptions of God's judgments, but the refusal of men and women to repent in the face of such incredible judgment. They know that the plagues come from the God of heaven, but they turn back to the darkness rather than come to the light. They embrace the full extent of God's wrath rather than run to him for mercy. This is the last acknowledgment in Revelation that people refuse to repent. From this point on, we can take for granted that the followers of the Antichrist have hardened their hearts beyond any thought of repentance or remorse.

Preparing for Armageddon (Revelation 16:12–16)

> The sixth angel poured out his bowl on the great river Euphrates, and its water was dried up to prepare the way for the kings from the East. Then I saw three evil spirits that looked like frogs; they came out of the mouth of the dragon, out of the mouth of the beast and out of the mouth of the false prophet. They are demonic spirits that perform signs, and they go out to the kings of the whole world, to gather them for the battle on the great day of God Almighty.
>
> "Look, I come like a thief! Blessed are those who stay awake and keep their clothes on, so that they may not go naked and be shamefully exposed."
>
> Then they gathered the kings together to the place that in Hebrew is called Armageddon.

The Euphrates River in modern Iraq is the focus of the sixth bowl judgment. This plague causes the river to dry up to prepare the way for the kings of the East. We first met these kings back in chapter 9 when four angels were released to gather an army of two hundred million men. I believe that those verses (9:13–16) should be linked with the sixth bowl judgment here in chapter 16.

The Euphrates River marked the eastern boundary of the Roman Empire in the first century, and it will mark the eastern boundary of the

Rome's Darkness

Those Bible students who take a preterist approach to Revelation believe that the darkness described in Revelation 16 refers to the political turmoil that swept over the city of Rome and the whole Roman Empire after Emperor Nero's suicide in AD 68. The civil war that erupted nearly tore apart the empire. The year AD 69 became known as "the year of four emperors," as a series of self-appointed Caesars tried to claim the throne. The preterist view is that Revelation predicts the destruction of Jerusalem and the fall of Rome in the past, not end-times events still in the future.

Exodus 10:21 – 22

Then the LORD said to Moses, "Stretch out your hand toward the sky so that darkness spreads over Egypt—darkness that can be felt." So Moses stretched out his hand toward the sky, and total darkness covered all Egypt for three days.

Amos 5:20

Will not the day of the LORD be darkness, not light—
pitch-dark, without a ray of brightness?

Mark 13:24 – 25

But in those days, following that distress,

"the sun will be darkened,
and the moon will not give its light;
the stars will fall from the sky,
and the heavenly bodies will be shaken."

Help File

A BLOODY VALLEY

The area around Megiddo was the scene of several conflicts in the Old Testament. Deborah and Barak fought here against the Canaanites (Judges 4), and Gideon staged the spectacular defeat of the Midianites here (Judges 6). This was also the region where King Saul's sons were killed by a Philistine army (Saul was wounded in this same skirmish, after which he took his own life; 1 Samuel 31). King Ahaziah died here after Jehu had wounded him (2 Kings 9:27), and King Josiah died in battle against the Egyptian army (2 Kings 23:29–30). In the modern age, Napoleon's march from Egypt to Syria ended in disaster in the valley of Megiddo, and in 1917 the British defeated the Turks in the same valley. None of these conflicts will compare, however, to the final war of the Tribulation when the nations of the world fight each other and ultimately wage war against God himself.

Antichrist's empire in the future. The Antichrist will have little control over the nations of "the East" (that is, the modern nations of India and China, and other nations in Southeast Asia). The leaders of those nations will gather a massive army to wage war against the Antichrist (at least it will begin that way). As they gather and march westward toward the Antichrist's throne in Jerusalem, this army will leave nothing but devastation in its path. One-third of the earth's population will die— hundreds of millions of people (9:15).

The Euphrates River will not be the only obstacle to the army's movement, but it will be the last natural barrier between the East and the land of Israel, the ultimate destination. The army and its equipment will not bottleneck at bridges but will be able to cross the riverbed almost anywhere. They will enter the Antichrist's territory unhindered.

The kings of the East are drawn to the Antichrist's kingdom by demonic power. John sees three evil spirits that look like frogs spring from the mouths of the dragon, the Antichrist, and the false prophet. The members of this unholy trinity all speak words of challenge and defiance that release powerful demonic angels, who pull the Eastern nations to the final great war. These demons have the ability to perform satanic miracles—actual miracles, but from Satan and not from God. All their evil power is focused on drawing not just the kings of the East but the kings of the whole earth "for the battle of the great day of God Almighty."

The word John uses for "battle" implies more than a single encounter. A better word might be "war" or "campaign." The final conflict of the Tribulation will be a series of battles that will end only when Jesus returns

THE EUPHRATES RIVER

The Bible refers directly or indirectly to the Euphrates more than twenty-five times. The 1,700-mile river rises in central Turkey and flows southeast through Syria and Iraq to the Persian Gulf. It is the longest river in western Asia. As the coalition army of Eastern nations makes its way toward Israel in the middle of the Tribulation, they will be surprised to discover that the Euphrates River has dried up, making it easy to cross. The final military campaign of the Tribulation will be the armies of the Antichrist against the armies of the kings of the East and will engulf the entire region of Israel and its neighbors.

Armageddon

Students of Revelation have proposed lots of other interpretations of the battle of Armageddon. Some futurist interpreters think that "the kings from the East" are not *enemies* of the Antichrist but *allies* of the Antichrist (or perhaps the Antichrist himself), who destroy the rebuilt city of Babylon (see Revelation 18) and then march against Israel to destroy the Jews. One Bible scholar (who holds that view) writes:

> In the Bible, "East" refers to the region of Mesopotamia (Assyria and Babylon), and the drying up of the river will allow the forces of the Antichrist to assemble out of Babylon, his capital. The armies joining him will be those of the seven remaining kings out of ten described in Daniel 7:24–27 and Revelation 17:12–13. Their goal will be the final destruction of the Jews.
>
> Thomas Ice, "Armageddon," in *The Popular Encyclopedia of Bible Prophecy*, ed. Tim LaHaye and Ed Hindson (Eugene, Ore.: Harvest House, 2004), 39.

Historicist interpreters have tried to find a "Battle of Armageddon" someplace in modern history. Since they believe that Revelation gives us an outline of human history during the church age, they believe it has to fit in somewhere before Jesus' eventual return. Alexander Hardie, writing in 1926, concluded that World War 1 fit the biblical prediction:

> The last Great War of 1914–1918, which convulsed and disgraced humanity, was doubtless the predicted Armageddon.
>
> Alexander Hardie, *A Study of the Book of Revelation* (Los Angeles: Times-Mirror Press, 1926), v.

I'm sure his view was revised when World War II came along twenty years later.

Idealist interpreters believe that Armageddon is not a single future battle but a symbol for God's deliverance against overwhelming odds. William Hendriksen summarizes this perspective:

> Har-Magedon is the symbol of every battle in which, when the need is greatest and believers are oppressed, the Lord suddenly reveals his power in the interest of his distressed people and defeats the enemy.
>
> William Hendriksen, *More Than Conquerors: An Interpretation of the Book of Revelation* (1940; reprint, Grand Rapids: Baker, 1998), 163.

Bible Networking

Isaiah 11:15

The LORD will dry up
   the gulf of the Egyptian sea;
with a scorching wind he will sweep his hand
   over the Euphrates River.
He will break it up into seven streams
   so that anyone can cross over in sandals.

to the earth as the conquering King. As the demons work, the Antichrist's enemies and allies will all begin to make their way toward Israel.

Christians reading this passage in the first century or today or in the future Tribulation might be troubled by what John describes. The armies of the earth gathered against God seem to be a daunting force, and we might wonder if God's power is enough to stand against such an army. Even John may have trembled at the thought. And so God, right on cue, issues one short word of assurance and warning:

> "Look, I come like a thief! Blessed are those who stay awake and keep their clothes on, so that they may not go naked and be shamefully exposed."
>
> Revelation 16:15

This seems to be Jesus' voice warning the world of his soon return. His coming will be like the arrival of a thief to those who are unprepared. They will be shocked by that event. In contrast, those who are ready for his return, those already clothed in the garments of salvation, will not suffer shame or loss. This warning applies both to Jesus' coming for his church in the rapture and to his coming in glory at the end of the Tribulation. At either time, those who are unprepared will suffer loss, and those who are prepared will be rewarded.

The Antichrist will kill most of the men and women who believe in Jesus during the Tribulation, but he won't kill them all. Some will survive, and they will look forward to Jesus' return with hope and anticipation. Jesus tells them to hold on just a little longer.

In Other Words

Even as the saints are worthy of rest and reward, so the wicked are worthy of divine chastening and judgment. The bloodletting during the Great Tribulation, as saints are slaughtered by the thousands, is without parallel in the history of the race.

John Walvoord, in *The Revelation of Jesus Christ* (1966; rev. ed., Chicago: Moody, 1989), 234.

Help File

BATTLE PLAN

The final war of Armageddon will envelop the entire land of Israel. The kings from the East initially will come to fight against the Antichrist. The Antichrist either defeats the Eastern coalition or persuades those rulers and armies to join him in his war of annihilation of the Jewish people. The Bible identifies three main centers in the final conflict:

Jerusalem

The prophet Zechariah summarized the campaign of Armageddon like this:

I [the LORD] will gather all the nations to Jerusalem to fight against it; the city will be captured, the houses ransacked, and the women ravished. Half of the city will go into exile, but the rest of the people will not be taken from the city. Then the LORD will go out and fight against those nations, as he fights on a day of battle. On that day his feet will stand on the Mount of Olives, east of Jerusalem, and the Mount of Olives will be split in two from east to west, forming a great valley, with half of the mountain moving north and half moving south.

Zechariah 14:2–4

God will allow the armies of the Antichrist to capture Jerusalem and to take half the people captive. But then Jesus will arrive on earth. His feet will touch the Mount of Olives to the east of Jerusalem, and the mountain will split, creating an enormous valley. The surviving Jews will use that valley to flee from Jerusalem. In that moment, every Jew still alive in Jerusalem will believe in Jesus as the true Messiah. "All Israel will be saved," as Paul writes in Romans 11:26. They will flee from the city by way of the newly formed escape route, and Jesus will fight for them. Jerusalem will be the scene of intense fighting before and at the return of Jesus in glory. (We will talk more about that event when we get to Revelation 19.)

The final statement about the sixth bowl judgment takes us back to the kings of the earth. The rulers and their armies are drawn by demonic power and by God's divine plan to a place called Armageddon. In Hebrew the word is a combination of *har*, meaning mountain or hill, and *mageddon*, probably referring to the ancient city of Megiddo.

Armageddon is usually taken to refer to the wide valley that lies next to the mount of Megiddo, fifty miles north of Jerusalem. The valley of Megiddo (also called the plain of Esdraelon or the valley of Jezreel) will be the staging area for the final war of the Tribulation. The war will engulf the entire region, but Armageddon will be the place where the armies of the world will congregate.

BATTLE PLAN (CONTINUED)

Megiddo

The final war begins north of Jerusalem on the plain of Jezreel near the city of Megiddo. The armies loyal to the Antichrist and the armies of the kings from the East clash in a bloody campaign. John had written earlier that blood would soak the ground for about 180 miles (Revelation 14:20). Megiddo, or the place John calls Armageddon, will be the location of fierce fighting.

Edom

In the writings of the prophet Isaiah, the Lord is pictured as pouring out his wrath and vengeance on the enemies of his people, beginning south and east of Jerusalem in the territory of Edom. The Deliverer is portrayed as coming from Edom as he treads the winepress of his wrath.

Who is this coming from Edom,
from Bozrah, with his garments stained crimson?
Who is this, robed in splendor,
striding forward in the greatness of his strength?
"It is I, speaking in righteousness,
mighty to save."
Why are your garments red,
like those of one treading the winepress?
"I have trodden the winepress alone;
from the nations no one was with me.
I trampled them in my anger
and trod them down in my wrath;
their blood spattered my garments,
and I stained all my clothing....
I trampled the nations in my anger;
in my wrath I made them drunk
and poured their blood on the ground."
Isaiah 63:1–3, 6

The entire land of Israel is engulfed in this war. It comes to an end only when Jesus returns in such majesty and power that all Israel believes in him and all God's enemies are destroyed.

Bible Networking

Daniel 11:42, 44 - 45

He [the Antichrist] will extend his power over many countries .... But reports from the east and the north will alarm him, and he will set out in a great rage to destroy and annihilate many. He will pitch his royal tents between the seas at the beautiful holy mountain. Yet he will come to his end, and no one will help him.

Joel 3:2, 9, 12, 16

> I will gather all nations
>   and bring them down to the valley of Jehoshaphat.
> There I will enter into judgment against them
>   concerning my inheritance, my people Israel ....
> Proclaim this among the nations:
>   Prepare for war! ...
> "Let the nations be roused;
>   let them advance into the Valley of Jehoshaphat,
> for there I will sit
>   to judge all the nations on every side...."
> The LORD will roar from Zion
>   and thunder from Jerusalem;
>   the earth and the heavens will tremble.
> But the LORD will be a refuge for his people,
>   a stronghold for the people of Israel.

Psalm 2:1 - 2

> Why do the nations conspire
>   and the peoples plot in vain?
> The kings of the earth rise up
>   and the rulers band together
>   against the LORD and against his anointed.

The valley is fourteen miles wide and twenty miles long, but it will not be the only place of battle or the only location where military forces are in place. Armageddon, however, will be a central point of the conflict and gives its name to the entire final war.

The Seventh Bowl (Revelation 16:17 – 21)

> The seventh angel poured out his bowl into the air, and out of the temple came a loud voice from the throne, saying, "It is done!" Then there came flashes of lightning, rumblings, peals of thunder and a severe earthquake. No earthquake like it has ever occurred since the human race has been on earth, so tremendous was the quake. The great city split into three parts, and the cities of the nations collapsed. God remembered Babylon the Great and gave her the cup filled with the wine of the fury of his wrath. Every island fled away and the mountains could not be found. From the sky huge hailstones, each weighing about a hundred pounds, fell on people. And they cursed God on account of the plague of hail, because the plague was so terrible.

As the seventh angel pours the contents of his bowl into the air, a series of final catastrophes pummel the earth. A loud voice (probably God's voice) shouts, "It is done!" God's Tribulation judgments are now completed. This is God's final act before the return of Jesus in power.

In Other Words

The only ones who escape the judgment are those who have refused to obey the edict of the beast, those few individuals who trust in Christ in those evil days.

John Walvoord, in *The Revelation of Jesus Christ* (1966; rev. ed., Chicago: Moody, 1989), 232.

How appropriate that a grievous sore should be the first of these judgments. Medically speaking, a sore is the outward sign of some inner corruption, and it would, therefore, be entirely fitting that the corruption of the hearts of these rebels should be manifest before all.

Donald Grey Barnhouse, in *Revelation: An Expositional Commentary* (Grand Rapids: Zondervan, 1971), 289.

In Other Words

The unmistakable impression of the Scriptures is that the whole world is being brought to the bar of justice before Christ as King of kings and Lord of lords. There is no escape from divine judgment except for those who avail themselves of the grace of God in that day by faith in Jesus Christ.... Even the lake of fire will not produce repentance on the part of those who have hardened their hearts against the grace of God.

John Walvoord, in *The Revelation of Jesus Christ* (1966; rev. ed., Chicago: Moody, 1989), 242.

The world has an appointment with destiny. It is on the road to Armageddon. When we put our trust in Jesus Christ as our Savior, God graciously transfers us from the road to Armageddon to the road to glory. The good news is that Jesus is coming someday, perhaps today, to take his own out of this world to heaven before the road to Armageddon dead-ends.

Mark Hitchcock, in *101 Answers to the Most Asked Questions about the End Times* (Sisters, Ore.: Multnomah, 2001), 198.

Help File

DESPERATE DAYS

The Bible refers to the last great war with titles that convey judgment and doom:

- a day of vengeance (Isaiah 34:8)
- treading the winepress of God's anger (Isaiah 63:2; Joel 3:13; Revelation 14:19–20)
- the day that will burn like a furnace (Malachi 4:1)
- the great and dreadful day of the LORD (Joel 2:31; Malachi 4:5)
- the harvest (Joel 3:13; Revelation 14:15–16)
- the battle on the great day of God Almighty (Revelation 16:14)

Bible Networking

Isaiah 24:18 - 21

The floodgates of the heavens are opened,
  the foundations of the earth shake.
The earth is broken up,
  the earth is split asunder,
  the earth is violently shaken.
The earth reels like a drunkard,
  it sways like a hut in the wind;
so heavy upon it is the guilt of its rebellion
  that it falls—never to rise again.
In that day the LORD will punish
  the powers in the heavens above
  and the kings on the earth below.

Just like when the seventh *seal* on the scroll was broken (Revelation 8:5) and when the seventh *trumpet* was blown (Revelation 11:19), the seventh *bowl* judgment produces lightning, rumbles of thunder, and an earthquake. This final earthquake, however, is the most devastating that the earth has ever experienced.

The massive earthquake causes "the great city" to break into three parts. John doesn't identify the city. Earlier in the book, he called Jerusalem "the great city" (Revelation 11:8). It could also be a reference to the capital city of the Antichrist's empire, called Babylon in chapter 18. Every city in the world comes under stunning devastation as a result of the earthquake.

The entire surface of the earth is changed. Earlier in the Tribulation, an earthquake moved islands and mountains; at the end of the Tribulation, mountains collapse and sink as a result of an earthquake. Whatever human order remains in society collapses with the mountains.

Giant hailstones fall from the sky. Each rock of ice weighs about what one man can carry—about a hundred pounds. The hail destroys whatever is left standing after the earthquake.

IN THE HEADLINES

On December 26, 2004, a massive earthquake in southeast Asia triggered destructive tsunamis through the region. It was the longest lasting quake ever recorded and produced the longest rupture in the earth's surface. A small earthquake lasts less than a second; a moderate-sized quake lasts a few seconds; the Asian quake lasted 500 to 600 seconds—almost 10 minutes!

The quake, centered in the Indian Ocean, also created the longest gash ever observed—nearly 800 miles long. Scientists estimate that the average ground movement up and down along the fault line was at least 16 feet with some places moving nearly 50 feet. The tremor vibrated the entire planet. No place on earth escaped some movement of the earth's crust. One scientist's conclusion: "There will be more earthquakes like this."

Based on a Web article from CNN.com.

In Other Words

The staggering dimensions of this conflict can scarcely be conceived. The battlefield will stretch from Megiddo in the north (Zechariah 12:11; Revelation 16:16) to Edom on the south (Isaiah 34:5 – 6; 63:1), a distance of approximately two hundred miles. It will reach from the Mediterranean Sea on the west to the hills of Moab on the east, a distance of almost one hundred miles. The center of the entire area will be the city of Jerusalem (Zechariah 14:1 – 2). Into this area the multiplied millions of men will be crowded for the final holocaust. The kings with their armies will come from the north and the south, from the east and from the west. There will be an invasion from hell beneath. And entering the scene at the last moment will be an invasion from space. In the most dramatic sense this will be the "valley of decision" for humanity (Joel 3:14) and the great winepress into which will be poured the fierceness of the wrath of almighty God (Revelation 19:15).

Herman Hoyt, in *The End Times* (Chicago: Moody, 1968), 163.

Points to Remember

- ☑ Seven angels pour out seven bowls of God's wrath on the world at the end of the Tribulation.

- ☑ God's judgments are always just—and come only after his mercy and grace are pushed aside.

- ☑ Demonic spirits draw the rulers and armies of the world toward Jerusalem for the final climactic war of the Tribulation—Armageddon.

- ☑ When the bowl judgments end, the earth and all of human society lie in shambles, waiting for Jesus to return in power and glory.

The vast majority of human beings who remain on the earth still refuse to turn from their evil ways. Instead of pleading with God for mercy, they curse God because of the devastation produced by the hail.

The next event in the time line of Revelation comes in Revelation 19:11—Jesus returns from heaven to destroy his enemies and to establish his kingdom on earth. Chapters 17 and 18 give us more details about specific events that occur in the Tribulation's last days, but as the seven bowl judgments end, Jesus returns.

CHAPTER 17

The Mother of All Evil

The Mother of All Evil

Revelation 17

> ▸ A prostitute in dazzling dress rides a seven-headed scarlet beast.
> ▸ A powerful false religious system emerges in the Tribulation.
> ▸ For a while, apostate religious leaders support the Antichrist.
> ▸ Ultimately, the Antichrist destroys the harlot religion.

Access Codes

Key Codes: Level 17

→ Prostitute: A person who trades sex for money; a picture in Scripture of someone who abandons the true God to worship false gods

→ The scarlet beast: The Antichrist

→ Mystery: Something hidden or unknowable, but then revealed by God

→ Babylon the Great: Revelation's code phrase for the political, economic, and religious empire of the Antichrist

→ The Abyss: A compartment in hell where demons are imprisoned; used in Revelation 17 to describe Satan's control of the Antichrist

Press Pause

After describing the final wave of God's judgment on the earth, John the apostle pauses the action to give us more information and deeper insight into a couple of special aspects of the story. Back in verse 19 of chapter 16, just one mention was made of Babylon the Great. Now one of the bowl-carrying angels comes over to John and explains what Babylon is and how it fits into the scenario of the future Tribulation.

A little review of what has brought us to this point in God's future might help:

- After the rapture, when Jesus removes true believers from the earth, those who remain will find themselves in a seven-year period of time called the Tribulation.
- Three great waves of judgment will sweep the earth during those years. Early in the Tribulation, God unleashes seven *seal* judgments; in the middle of the Tribulation, seven *trumpet* judgments fall; and in the final days of the Tribulation, seven *bowl* judgments crash down on the earth.
- As the dust clears from the bowl judgments, Jesus returns to earth in triumph to overthrow his enemies and to set up a kingdom of justice and peace on the earth.
- Before John sees Christ's return in Revelation 19, he draws us aside and explains some things about how the Antichrist will dominate human society during the Tribulation.
- Satan's master plan in the Tribulation centers on a man—the beast —who will rise to prominence during the first half of the Tribulation as the powerful leader of a ten-nation Western confederation.
- In the middle of the Tribulation, the Antichrist invades Israel and sets himself up as god in the temple of Jerusalem. The inhabitants of the Antichrist's empire must worship him or they will be killed.
- Only those who worship the beast and receive his mark will be able to buy or sell or to hold a job.

In Other Words

While the beast is the political ruler of the empire, the woman represents the blasphemous religion that seduces the nations and the economic system that draws them into its luxury.

Grant Osborne, in *Revelation* (Grand Rapids: Baker, 2002), 610.

It is probable that the events of chapter 17 occur at the beginning of the Great Tribulation [the last three and a half years of the Tribulation]. The revelation is given to John, however, subsequent to the revelation of the vials [or bowls]. It must be remembered that from John's point of view all of the events of the book of Revelation were future, and it pleased God to reveal various aspects of future events in other than their chronological order.

John Walvoord, in *The Revelation of Jesus Christ* (1966; rev. ed., Chicago: Moody, 1989), 243.

2 Thessalonians 2:1 – 3

Concerning the coming of our Lord Jesus Christ and our being gathered to him, we ask you, brothers and sisters, not to become easily unsettled or alarmed by the teaching allegedly from us—whether by a prophecy or by word of mouth or by letter—asserting that the day of the Lord has already come. Don't let anyone deceive you in any way, for that day will not come until the rebellion occurs and the man of lawlessness is revealed, the man doomed to destruction.

James 4:4

You adulterous people, don't you know that friendship with the world means enmity against God? Anyone who chooses to be a friend of the world becomes an enemy of God.

Two avenues of power—religious worship and economic control—give the Antichrist a stranglehold on the world. Those two allies of the Antichrist's domination are the focus of Revelation 17 and 18—a false worship system is the theme of chapter 17, and centralized economic control is the theme of chapter 18.

Back to Babylon

Both the religious system and the economic system are called *Babylon*. We will explore several views of what John means by "Babylon," but I take the word to refer to the Antichrist's entire world empire. He rules over a satanic kingdom that God calls Babylon. It's a city; it's a false religion; it's a worldwide economic system—but it's all under Satan's dominion. Satan uses the Antichrist; he uses the false prophet; for a while he uses apostate religious leaders—but in the end, the whole corrupt system comes crashing down.

I think God calls the Antichrist's empire "Babylon" for a very specific reason. In the Old Testament, Babylon is viewed as the source of all false worship and idolatry. After the great flood early in earth's history, mankind disobeyed God's command to fill the earth and instead gathered at a place that would later be called Babylon. (You can read the account yourself in Genesis 11.) Human earth-dwellers decided to build a tower whose top would be like heaven. They would worship their false gods in an astonishing monument to mankind's ability. God, however, confused their languages, and they were forced to disperse through the earth. The place called Bab-El (meaning "gate to God") became Babel (which means "confusion")—and later it was called Babylon. The name became a tag for false worship, worship that offended and nauseated the true God of heaven and earth.

In the future, after the true church is removed from the earth in the rapture, an apostate "church" will emerge. Religious Babylon in the Tribulation will include all corrupt and false Christian and non-Christian religious systems. The word *apostate* means "to stand away from" the place where you once stood. An apostate in biblical language is someone who stands outside of true faith in the Lord Jesus Christ. Since all genuine believers are taken out of the world in the rapture, those religious people left behind will all stand outside the boundaries of biblical truth. The major religious organizations still functioning will dump every distinctive belief and practice for the sake of unity.

The whole religious world will join together in the Tribulation as the alternative to any emerging remnants of faith in Jesus. It's not difficult to see the false prophet rise up as the religious leader of this false religious system. He uses the religious influence of the various groups to promote the Antichrist's agenda until the Antichrist decides that he can no longer tolerate any religious rivals and the apostate church is torn to shreds.

In Other Words

Apostates are consistently characterized by two things in the New Testament: false doctrine and ungodly living. Apostates believe wrong and behave wrong. "They profess to know God, but by their deeds they deny him" (Titus 1:16).

Mark Hitchcock, in *Seven Signs of the End Times* (Sisters, Ore.: Multnomah, 2002), 82.

This open, deliberate, willful repudiation of the truth of the Bible is described in Scripture as one of the major characteristics of the last days of the church on earth.

J. Dwight Pentecost, in *Will Man Survive?* (Grand Rapids: Zondervan, 1980), 58.

Religious Call Girl (Revelation 17:1 – 5)

One of the seven angels who had the seven bowls came and said to me, "Come, I will show you the punishment of the great prostitute, who sits by many waters. With her the kings of the earth committed adultery, and the inhabitants of the earth were intoxicated with the wine of her adulteries."

Then the angel carried me away in the Spirit into a wilderness. There I saw a woman sitting on a scarlet beast that was covered with blasphemous names and had seven heads and ten horns. The woman was dressed in purple and scarlet, and was glittering with gold, precious stones and pearls. She held a golden cup in her hand, filled with abominable things and the filth of her adulteries. This title was written on her forehead:

MYSTERY
BABYLON THE GREAT
THE MOTHER OF PROSTITUTES
AND OF THE ABOMINATIONS OF THE EARTH.

John is invited to witness the punishment of "the great prostitute." Several marks of the future apostate religious system emerge from these verses:

- The future apostate "church" will permeate the Antichrist's empire. Everybody will be touched by the false church's power. The prostitute in John's vision sits by many waters. In verse 15, the angel tells John that the waters represent "peoples, multitudes, nations and languages" who are under the Antichrist's control.
- The apostate religious Babylon will link its power to the political power of the beast. The kings of the earth get in bed spiritually with the prostitute and commit immorality with her. That is the Bible's vivid way of describing spiritual unfaithfulness to God. The future religious movement will make an outward claim of loyalty to God, but in reality they will turn away from the true God and stand away (apostasize) from his Word.
- The future false church becomes an instrument of deception in the Antichrist's hand. The outward religious appearance of false worship brings a spiritual drunkenness over the world. They are intoxicated to the point where they can't tell the difference between God's truth and Satan's lie.

As John accepts the angel's invitation, he is carried away in his vision to a desert place where he can get the full picture of the woman's evil

The Great Prostitute

As you would expect, those who hold to differing views of how to interpret Revelation differ on who or what the great prostitute represents. Here's a summary of those differing perspectives:

- Interpreters who take a *historicist* view of Revelation believe that John's prophecy predicts how the history of the church age will unfold. It's a road map (in their minds) of the time between Christ's first coming to Bethlehem and his second coming in the future. Almost all historicist commentators take the prostitute Babylon as a reference to the apostate Roman Catholic Church. They believe that chapter 17 of Revelation pictures the destruction of the corrupt Catholic Church just before Jesus returns.

- Some *futurist* interpreters also see Babylon as the Roman Catholic Church—but in its apostate form after the rapture. All remaining Protestants (in their view), along with Mormons and others, join with the Catholic Church to form an apostate superchurch.

- Christians who hold to a *preterist* view of Revelation believe that the prophecies in the book were fulfilled in the past in the destruction of Jerusalem and in the ultimate collapse of the Roman Empire. Chapter 17 (in their view) does not describe a future corrupt church, but rather God's judgment on an empire that persecuted the Christians.

- Those who take an *idealist* view believe that John's visions can be applied to any age of the church. Babylon (in their view) represents any political, religious, or economic power that is arrayed against God and his people. Babylon is the sinful corrupt world that seeks to seduce and destroy the followers of Christ.

role in the Antichrist's kingdom. The woman sits on a scarlet beast that is covered with offensive, God-mocking names—a reflection of the beast's true character. The beast is the same one introduced back in chapter 13. He is the Antichrist, the leader of a revived Western alliance of nations. The fact that the woman rides on the beast indicates that the false religious system is supported by the political power of the Antichrist. It also shows that, to an extent, the woman controls the beast.

John's vision of the woman riding the beast seems to describe the situation during the *first* half of the Tribulation, before the Antichrist emerges as the betrayer and claims all worship for himself in the

Bible Networking

1 Timothy 4:1

The Spirit clearly says that in later times some will abandon the faith and follow deceiving spirits and things taught by demons.

2 Timothy 3:1 – 5

But mark this: There will be terrible times in the last days. People will be lovers of themselves, lovers of money, boastful, proud, abusive, disobedient to their parents, ungrateful, unholy, without love, unforgiving, slanderous, without self-control, brutal, not lovers of the good, treacherous, rash, conceited, lovers of pleasure rather than lovers of God—having a form of godliness but denying its power. Have nothing to do with such people.

middle of the seven years. During the first three and a half years, after the true church is raptured out, the false church emerges as a controlling force in human society. Religious differences and conflicts are put aside in order to participate in the political power of the Antichrist's empire. The Antichrist uses the religious system to exalt himself and to solidify his control over the nations of his kingdom. The false church is his ally for a while. The beast carries the woman and supports her false worship.

The future religious system is not only powerful but also fabulously wealthy. The woman is dressed in scarlet and purple—expensive colors to produce in the ancient world. Gold, precious stones, and pearls hang from her neck and wrists. This woman loves to show off her money. The cup in her hand is pure gold, but the contents of the cup are filth. She's carrying garbage in a cup worth thousands of dollars. As beautiful and enticing as the woman may appear to the world, in God's eyes she is filled with nauseating filth. She makes God gag!

The woman's name is a "mystery." That doesn't mean it's creepy or mysterious. It means the name is hidden until God reveals it. God calls her "Babylon the Great." The title does not refer to the literal city of Babylon or the Babylonian Empire that was so prominent in the Old Testament. God uses the term in its religious sense. This woman is the source of false worship, just as Babylon was the source of all false religion and idolatry in the Old Testament. Instead of being a woman of beauty and grace, she is called "THE MOTHER OF PROSTITUTES" by God. Spiritual unfaithfulness to God is a sin that is singled out for some of the most severe condemnation in Scripture. False worship toward the true God, along with the corrupt worship of false gods, turns God's stomach. He calls it an "abomination."

A False Church with a Purpose (Revelation 17:6–14)

I saw that the woman was drunk with the blood of God's people, the blood of those who bore testimony to Jesus.

When I saw her, I was greatly astonished. Then the angel said to me: "Why are you astonished? I will explain to you the mystery of the woman and of the beast she rides, which has the seven heads and ten horns. The beast, which you saw, once was, now is not, and will come up out of the Abyss and go to its destruction. The inhabitants of the earth whose names have not been written in the book of life from the creation of the world will be astonished when they see the beast, because it once was, now is not, and yet will come.

"This calls for a mind with wisdom. The seven heads are seven hills on which the woman sits. They are also seven kings. Five have fallen, one is, the other has not yet come; but when he does come, he must remain for a little while. The beast who once was, and now is not, is an eighth king. He belongs to the seven and is going to his destruction.

"The ten horns you saw are ten kings who have not yet received a kingdom, but who for one hour will receive authority as kings along with the beast. They have one purpose and will give their power and authority to the beast. They will make war against the Lamb, but the Lamb will triumph over them because he is Lord of lords and King of kings — and with him will be his called, chosen and faithful followers."

In Other Words

The startling feature of this scene is that the [prostitute] is sitting on the beast, indicating that she will have power over the man of sin. This event must occur during the first part of the tribulation before the man of sin overthrows religion and requires everyone to worship him.

Charles Ryrie, in *Revelation* (Chicago: Moody, 1968), 264.

The leaders of this future religious system will have some very specific goals in mind. They will seek first to destroy all the followers of the true God. The woman John sees is intoxicated with the blood of God's people (verse 6). The Antichrist's religious system will unite under the banner of love and tolerance, but it will be totally intolerant of anyone whose allegiance is to Jesus. The people who come to faith in the early years of the Tribulation will find themselves hunted down by religious leaders.

False religion has always been the enemy of true faith in the true God, but in the Tribulation, false religious Babylon will have the backing of civil authority and the power to arrest and execute God's people. The Christians who first read the book of Revelation knew what this was all about. The Roman emperors who persecuted the early Christians had them arrested on religious charges, along with the civil charges of treason and sedition against the government. Because the Christians worshiped no images, they were accused of being *a-theists* — worshipers of no god. Because they refused to acknowledge Caesar as Lord, the Christians were viewed as enemies of the state.

Religious Babylon will search out Tribulation believers and hunt for Tribulation witnesses and then slaughter them in such numbers that this prostitute, Babylon, becomes drunk on their blood.

ROME'S SEVEN HILLS

The ancient city of Rome was built on seven hills near the Tiber River. Their names echo through Rome's history— Palatine, Aventine, Caelian, Esquiline, Viminal, Quirinal, and Capitoline. Other hills were added as the city expanded, but Rome was always known as "the city of seven hills." The title was used repeatedly by Roman writers, very much like American journalists use the phrase "inside the Beltway" to refer to Washington, D.C. In the apostle John's day, the Romans held a festival every year (the *Septimontium*— "seven mountain" festival) to celebrate their magnificent city.

Some interpreters of Revelation have tried to link the future false church and even the Antichrist himself to the pope and the Roman Catholic Church. I do not agree with that view. The apostate church will have a lot of Catholics in it, but it will have a lot of Protestants and others too. Those who have put their faith in Jesus, regardless of denomination, will be taken up in the rapture. Those who are only outwardly religious will be left behind.

Satan gives the false church a free ride during the first part of the Tribulation, but in the end, he rips the church to shreds. That's how Satan always works. In the beginning he is alluring and supportive and makes great promises. He tells the married woman who is tempted by the flirtations of a coworker that she deserves a little fun in her life. He tells the man surfing the Internet that just looking at that porn site won't hurt anyone. Satan greets us at the front door of sin with a warm hug and the promise of happiness ahead. In the end, however, he turns against us and rips our lives to shreds. He beats us up and kicks us into the alley to bear—all alone—the shame and consequences of our sin. That's often where Jesus finds us. He cleans us up, heals our wounds, puts us back in a place of service, and restores our joy. Satan destroys those who are his; Jesus never gives up on those who are his.

Exalt the Beast!

The second purpose of the apostate religious system of the Tribulation is to exalt the beast. I will warn you before we start that verses 7 through 13 of Revelation 17 are one of the most difficult passages in the New Testament. I won't have the final answers. But the one clear fact we need to keep focused on is in verse 13: "They have one purpose and will give their power and authority to the beast." As John explains the mystery of the woman and of the beast she rides, he doesn't want us to miss the fact that the goal of evil, corrupt people in the Tribulation is to exalt their hero. Just as Christians want glory and honor to go to Jesus, sinful Tribulation-dwellers will give up everything for the Antichrist. With that in mind, let me try to unravel a few strands in these verses.

The angel tells John that the beast he saw "once was, now is not, and will come up out of the Abyss and go to its destruction" (verse 8). I think that the angel is referring to the fatal wound that the Antichrist suffers in the middle of the Tribulation (Revelation 13:3, 14). When the Antichrist invades Israel at the midpoint of the seven-year Tribulation, he suffers a fatal wound, perhaps an assassination, but he survives—or, more likely, he comes back from the dead—to the astonishment of the

world. That miraculous "resurrection" sets the stage for his takeover of the temple of God in Jerusalem and his proclamation that he is "God."

What we learn here in Revelation 17 is that during that time of his death, the beast descends into the Abyss, most likely to be fully joined in mind and purpose with Satan. Then he comes back to life as the Satan-man — a man fully dominated and indwelt (possessed) by Satan. He is the beast who once was (on earth), but now is not (as he goes through death), and will come up out of the Abyss (in a satanic miracle of resurrection). It is *that* beast who carries the great prostitute on his back.

This beast also possesses incredible political power. He has seven heads and ten horns. The heads, according to the angel in verse 9, are seven hills on which the woman sits. For centuries before John wrote this, Rome was known as the seven-hilled city. The religious power of the apostate church will be centered in Rome.

The city of Rome may also be the *political* center of the Antichrist's empire — the great city that splits into three pieces in the final earthquake of the Tribulation (Revelation 16:19). Since the beast reigns over a revived form of the old Roman Empire, the city of Rome would be a natural choice for his capital. Rome may even be the "Babylon" of Revelation 18, the *economic* center of the Antichrist's empire. What seems most clear is that Rome is the center of *religious* activity, at least during the first half of the Tribulation.

THE PROPHECIES OF ST. MALACHY

Some of the most curious predictions ever recorded are the prophecies of Saint Malachy. The prophecies are a list of 111 short statements that claim to describe each pope from the time of Celestine II (who was pope from 1143 to 1144) down to the last pope. St. Malachy supposedly received these revelations and wrote them down before his own death in 1148. The problem is that the prophecies did not surface until 1595—150 years later. The "official" explanation is that the prophecies were misplaced inside the Vatican archives.

Whether they are forgeries or not, some of the predictions about popes even since 1595 are surprisingly accurate. John Paul I, whose brief papacy lasted just thirty-three days on both sides of a full moon in 1978, is described as *De medietate lunae* ("from the middle of the moon"). Clement XIV (1769–1774) is called "a swift bear" by Malachy, and his coat of arms featured a running bear.

Malachy's list is getting close to its end. The current pope, Benedict XVI, is called *Gloria olivae* ("the glory of the olive"). The list then ends with a curious prediction: the last pope will be a new Peter, and the Roman church will suffer a final persecution. After that, the city of Rome will be destroyed and the last judgment will come. Malachy's words are: "In the last persecution of the Holy Roman Church there shall reign Peter the Roman, who will feed the sheep amid great tribulations; and when these are passed, the city of the seven hills will be utterly destroyed and the terrible judge will judge the people."

The seven heads on the scarlet beast also represent seven kings (verse 10)—"five have fallen, one is, the other has not yet come." No wonder the angel says we will need a wise mind to figure this out. If I tried to explain all the interpretations of this verse, I would fill another book. So let me give you the one that I think fits best: The five kings past are five imperial rulers who could have been the Antichrist if the Tribulation had started in John's day. The emperor who sent John into exile (the man's name was Domitian) was the sixth ruler. The ruler yet to come (the seventh) is the Antichrist, the final Roman emperor who will rule during the Tribulation.

What makes this even more difficult is that the angel mentions an *eighth* ruler: "The beast who once was, and now is not, is an eighth king. He belongs to the seven and is going to his destruction" (verse 11). Perhaps the Antichrist is both the seventh and the eighth ruler. During the first half of the Tribulation, his policies seem to be focused on peace and the good of mankind. After he suffers the fatal wound and emerges

290 The Book of Revelation Made Clear

as Satan's embodiment, he reveals his true evil character. The same person takes on two roles as both the seventh ruler and the eighth.

The ten horns on the beast also represent ten kings (verse 12), but these are the kings of the ten kingdoms that form the center of the Antichrist's empire. These kings all rule during the Tribulation and give their authority to the beast. They rule only a brief time in God's scheme of things ("one hour"). Their single goal, however, their whole purpose in life, is to exalt the beast.

War against the Lamb

The false church's final purpose is to make war against Jesus and against the followers of Jesus. Everything the Antichrist does, every move he makes, every satanic law he enacts, is directed against Jesus. In the end he will gather the armies of the world, not so much to attack Israel as to make war with the Lamb. But the Lamb will triumph! That phrase in verse 14 is the theme of the whole book. No matter what opposition Satan and his followers can mount, Jesus *will* triumph. Jesus wins!

The Woman Destroyed (Revelation 17:15 – 18)

Then the angel said to me, "The waters you saw, where the prostitute sits, are peoples, multitudes, nations and languages. The beast and the ten horns you saw will hate the prostitute. They will bring her to ruin and leave her naked; they will eat her flesh and burn her with fire. For God has put it into their hearts to accomplish his purpose by

In Other Words

Obviously, mystery Babylon, the apostate pagan church of the last days, will not develop overnight. Such an ecumenical organization, involving many diverse religious groups, will be created by negotiation and conferences over a number of years leading up to the beginning of the seven-year Tribulation period. It is therefore quite probable that we will witness the initial steps toward this one-world church of the last days before the rapture takes the Christians home to heaven.

Grant Jeffrey, in *The Final Warning: Economic Collapse and the Coming World Government* (Colorado Springs: WaterBrook, 1995), 151.

agreeing to give the beast their power to rule, until God's words are fulfilled. The woman you saw is the great city that rules over the kings of the earth."

In the first half of the Tribulation, the prostitute church will gain unbelievable power and influence. The religious leaders will ride in wealth on the back of the Antichrist. They will play a prominent role in his empire. But the day will come when the Antichrist and his political allies will tear religious Babylon to shreds.

We aren't told when that happens, but it seems likely that the false church is destroyed in the middle of the Tribulation. When the Antichrist sets himself up as God in the temple, he will tolerate no competition, no rivalry for worship. At that point he will strip the apostate church of her power, devour her wealth, and burn whatever is left.

The Antichrist will think he is accomplishing his own purposes in destroying religious Babylon, but in reality he will be doing God's will. The beast and the ten kings hate the woman and destroy her only because God puts that desire in their hearts, and by their actions they accomplish God's purpose. The one in control is *not* Satan or the Antichrist; the one in control of a world that seems out of control is a sovereign God. He can use even the raging of wicked political leaders to fulfill his word and to accomplish his purposes.

The day is coming when the false religious system of this world will seek worldwide power by an alliance with the last of the Caesars. Their plan will succeed for a while. The prostitute church will think she can control the Antichrist, but she will find out too late that he has used her for his own ends. The beast takes all that he can and then smashes the false church in hatred and rage. His goal is to exalt himself as the object of the world's worship.

Points to Remember

- ☑ A universal false religious movement will rise to great power in the first half of the Tribulation.

- ☑ The apostate "church" will exalt the Antichrist and execute followers of Jesus.

- ☑ In the middle of the Tribulation, the Antichrist will destroy the prostitute religion—and exalt himself as God.

CHAPTER 18

The End of the End

The End of the End

- ▶ More angels show up.
- ▶ A mighty city is destroyed.
- ▶ Kings and captains cry over lost wealth.
- ▶ A big stone makes a big splash.

MR. BLOCKHEAD
HEADS UP

Access Codes

Key Codes: Level 18

→ Babylon the Great: The capital city of the Antichrist's empire

→ Demons: Sinful angels under Satan's authority

→ Adultery: Unfaithfulness; used in this chapter to picture people who abandon the true God for false gods

→ Millstone: A large, round stone used for grinding grain into flour

→ Prophets: Men and women who speak God's message

The Great City Collapses

As chapter 18 of Revelation opens, seven bowls of God's wrath have already been poured out on the earth in devastating judgment (Revelation 16). Mankind's day on earth is coming to an end.

The armies of the world are gathered in and around Israel for the final conflict. Jesus stands on the edge of heaven, ready to return to earth in triumph. John has just one more task before he sees Jesus' return. He has a vision of the destruction of the Antichrist's great city. Babylon falls in one hour's time (verse 10).

In Revelation 17, Babylon was the name given to the prostitute riding on the seven-headed beast. That was the false religious Babylon that will emerge in the early years of the Tribulation. But John uses "Babylon" in other ways too. Here in Revelation 18, Babylon is the name of a great city that God destroys. We had a hint of that in verse 18 of chapter 17: "The woman you saw is the great city that rules over the kings of the earth."

Babylon is a term used in Revelation to refer to the Antichrist's empire in all its forms. It's a code word for all that stands against God. The beast will rule over an entire system—political, religious, economic, cultural—that is based on hatred toward God. The Antichrist will not be an atheist; he will acknowledge that God exists, but he will hate God and oppose God's plan in every way possible.

The Antichrist's power will center in one magnificent city. John calls it "Babylon the Great." I understand the city to be the capital of the Antichrist's revived Roman Empire. The heart of the Antichrist's

WHAT ABOUT NOSTRADAMUS?

The young lion will overcome the old one,
On the field of battle in a single combat;
He will put out his eyes in a cage of gold;
Two fleets one, then to die, a cruel death.

Michel de Notredame (1503–66), better known as Nostradamus, was a French physician who developed an interest in astrology and prophecy. He wrote prophetic four-line verses (such as the one above) and arranged them in ten books of one hundred verses each. His book, titled *Centuries*, claims to predict events from his time to the year 3797.

The verses are not in chronological order. They jump back and forth throughout history, supposedly prophesying events at different points in time. His predictions, however, are couched in obscure phrases and symbols and can be interpreted pretty much according to the whims of the reader. Nostradamus

further complicates matters by not dating any of his prophecies. When the two World Trade Center towers were attacked and collapsed in September 2001, supporters of Nostradamus found what they thought was a clear prediction of that event in one line that read, "The twins will fall." Most of Nostradamus's predictions "fit" only after the event when a suitable line or two of his writings can be pulled out and applied to the situation. James Randi, author of *The Mask of Nostradamus*, claims that in the 103 cases in which Nostradamus specifically mentions identifiable persons or dates, he was wrong 100 percent of the time!

Nostradamus reflected the secularism of the French Renaissance. Before his time, almost all end-times thinkers had expected that God would bring an end to the world. Nostradamus focused on a secular end to human history. He thought that mankind would wipe itself out by war or disease. Nostradamus never spoke of divine judgment, heaven, or hell.

WHERE IN THE WORLD IS BABYLON?

One of the significant interpretive questions in the book of Revelation centers on the term *Babylon*. Is it the literal city of Babylon on the Euphrates River, or is the term used symbolically (as a code) for another city? It might help to look at the arguments on both sides.

Those who believe that Babylon refers to the literal city of Babylon in Iraq make the following points:

- The Bible says "Babylon"—and if we are to interpret Scripture in its normal sense, we should accept it at face value. Most interpreters take John's references to the Euphrates River near Babylon literally, so why not the references to Babylon itself?
- God predicted the destruction of Babylon in the Old Testament, but those predictions have yet to be *completely* fulfilled. (The passages cited most often are Isaiah 13 and 47; Jeremiah 50–51; and Zechariah 5.)
- The ancient city of Babylon will be rebuilt as a magnificent city and will become the political and economic center of the Antichrist's empire—all within the years leading up to the Tribulation or within the first half of the Tribulation.

Those who believe that Babylon refers to another city rely on other arguments:

- The Old Testament predictions of Babylon's destruction *were* fulfilled when the Persians conquered and later destroyed the city. Attempts at rebuilding the city (most recently by Saddam Hussein) have all failed. For 2,500 years, Babylon has been nothing but ruins.
- Rebuilding the actual city of Babylon would take decades—especially if it is to become the economic and political hub of the entire Western world under the Antichrist. Do we have to wait for Babylon to be rebuilt before Jesus comes for believers in the rapture?
- John makes it clear that he doesn't want us to take "Babylon" as a reference to the city in Iraq. He calls it "mystery Babylon" (17:5) and says it is a city drunk with "the blood of God's people, the blood of those who bore testimony to Jesus" (17:6). Furthermore, the city sits on seven hills (17:9)—a clear reference in John's day to the city of Rome.
- The earliest Christian writers commenting on the book of Revelation took "Babylon" to refer to Rome.
- The Antichrist will rule over a revived Roman/Western empire from a powerful city. John calls it "Babylon"; we know it (most likely) as Rome. Some believe that the city could be New York or another great city, but the evidence seems to point most directly to Rome.

MARKS OF THE ANTICHRIST'S "BABYLON"

Here are some marks to watch for:

- rich and prosperous (17:4)
- immoral and drunk with spiritual false-hood (17:2)
- intimately connected to Satan and the beast (17:7–8)
- a city that rests on seven hills (17:9)
- the political capital of a ten-nation confederation (17:10–13)

- an empire that rules over many peoples and nations (17:15–18)
- the center of international commerce (18:3, 11–13)
- a city dependent on supplies from sea merchants (18:17–18)
- an entertainment and pleasure capital (18:22–23)
- destroyed by fire in one hour (18:9–10, 17, 19)

political and economic power will be a ten-nation confederation that encompasses the old Roman Empire. Perhaps that will be expanded to a Western empire that includes nations that are linked by history and culture to Rome — nations like the United States, Canada, Latin America, and Australia. One city will be the capital city, the hub of the world's economy, and the place of the Antichrist's throne.

God Says, "Enough" (Revelation 18:1 – 8)

After this I saw another angel coming down from heaven. He had great authority, and the earth was illuminated by his splendor. With a mighty voice he shouted:

"'Fallen! Fallen is Babylon the Great!'
She has become a dwelling for demons
and a haunt for every evil spirit,
a haunt for every unclean bird,
a haunt for every unclean and detestable animal.
For all the nations have drunk
the maddening wine of her adulteries.
The kings of the earth committed adultery with her,
and the merchants of the earth grew rich from her excessive luxuries."

Then I heard another voice from heaven say:

"'Come out of her, my people,'
so that you will not share in her sins,
so that you will not receive any of her plagues;
for her sins are piled up to heaven,

In Other Words

Two thousand years of church history verify that apocalyptic "Babylon" is Rome. It is either pagan Rome, papal Rome, or a future revived Rome — but it is Rome!

Ed Hindson, in *The Book of Revelation: Unlocking the Future* (Chattanooga, Tenn.: AMG, 2002), 156.

I believe the references to Babylon in Revelation 17 – 18 refer to a literal, rebuilt city of Babylon in modern-day Iraq on the Euphrates River, which God will destroy at the end of the Tribulation.

Mark Hitchcock, in *The Second Coming of Babylon* (Sisters, Ore.: Multnomah, 2003), 103.

and God has remembered her crimes.
Give back to her as she has given;
   pay her back double for what she has done.
   Pour her a double portion from her own cup.
Give her as much torment and grief
   as the glory and luxury she gave herself.
In her heart she boasts,
   'I sit enthroned as queen.
I am not a widow;
   I will never mourn.'
Therefore in one day her plagues will overtake her:
   death, mourning and famine.
She will be consumed by fire,
   for mighty is the Lord God who judges her.

Heaven is filled with magnificent, powerful angels. In this scene, still another one comes down from heaven, and the earth is lit up by his splendor. People who are expecting quiet organ music in heaven will be startled by the sounds of Revelation. This radiant angel shouts in a mighty voice, "Fallen! Fallen is Babylon the Great!"

The Antichrist's capital city will become the focus of world attention over the seven years of the Tribulation, but with one stroke, God will destroy the city. Babylon falls because her sins are piled up to heaven and because God remembers her crimes.

The city will become the dwelling place for demons. Every evil spirit on earth will find rest in Babylon. Demonic domination results in corruption among the people who live in the city. God's voice from heaven promises to pay back double for her violence, exploitation, and greed.

The people in the Antichrist's city think that the party will never end. They think that God's judgment will never be able to touch their lives — but they are wrong! Politicians commit spiritual adultery with Satan and his demons. Stock traders and merchants live in excessive luxury. Materialism, greed, pride, and self-promotion are all marks of the inhabitants of the beast's city. In response, God sends death, mourning, and famine. God's fire destroys the city in one hour. What it took human beings centuries to build is gone in one puff of God's angry breath. The survivors will be happy to trade a Cadillac for a crust of bread.

Before God judges the city, however, he warns his own people to flee: "Come out of her, my people" (verse 4). My question is, Why are any followers of Jesus in this sinful city to begin with? The righteous man Lot lived in Sodom (Genesis 19:1; 2 Peter 2:6–9), and true believers will be in the Antichrist's city even at the end. God warns them to flee, and as soon as they escape, judgment comes.

Bible Networking

Isaiah 13:19 – 20

Babylon, the jewel of kingdoms,
   the pride and glory of the Babylonians,
will be overthrown by God
   like Sodom and Gomorrah.
She will never be inhabited
   or lived in through all generations;
there no nomads will pitch their tents,
   there no shepherds will rest their flocks.

Who Feels Sorry for Babylon? (Revelation 18:9 – 20)

"When the kings of the earth who committed adultery with her and shared her luxury see the smoke of her burning, they will weep and mourn over her. Terrified at her torment, they will stand far off and cry:

"'Woe! Woe to you, great city,
    you mighty city of Babylon!
In one hour your doom has come!'

"The merchants of the earth will weep and mourn over her because no one buys their cargoes anymore—cargoes of gold, silver, precious stones and pearls; fine linen, purple, silk and scarlet cloth; every sort of citron wood, and articles of every kind made of ivory, costly wood, bronze, iron and marble; cargoes of cinnamon and spice, of incense, myrrh and frankincense, of wine and olive oil, of fine flour and wheat; cattle and sheep; horses and carriages; and human beings sold as slaves.

"They will say, 'The fruit you longed for is gone from you. All your luxury and splendor have vanished, never to be recovered.' The merchants who sold these things and gained their wealth from her will stand far off, terrified at her torment. They will weep and mourn and cry out:

A TOURIST'S GUIDE TO BABYLON

In Revelation 17 we saw the rise and fall of a future religious system that will deceive the world. In chapter 18 we are confronted with another Babylon—an economic and political system centered in a great city. A few summary points will help us keep the two "Babylons" straight.

RELIGIOUS BABYLON	COMMERCIAL BABYLON
Destroyed by the kings of the earth (17:16)	Destroyed by judgment from God (18:8)
When the prostitute church falls, the kings of the earth rejoice (17:16)	When the city falls, the kings cry (18:9)
Destroyed (most likely) in the *middle* of the Tribulation	Destroyed at the *end* of the Tribulation
Described in symbolic language—"a woman sitting on a scarlet beast" (17:3)	Described in literal language—"you mighty city of Babylon" (18:10)

Bible Networking

2 Peter 2:6 - 9

If [God] condemned the cities of Sodom and Gomorrah by burning them to ashes, and made them an example of what is going to happen to the ungodly; and if he rescued Lot, a righteous man, who was distressed by the depraved conduct of the lawless (for that righteous man, living among them day after day, was tormented in his righteous soul by the lawless deeds he saw and heard)—if this is so, then the Lord knows how to rescue the godly from trials and to hold the unrighteous for punishment on the day of judgment.

'Woe! Woe to you, great city,
   dressed in fine linen, purple and scarlet,
   and glittering with gold, precious stones and pearls!
In one hour such great wealth has been brought to ruin!'

"Every sea captain, and all who travel by ship, the sailors, and all who earn their living from the sea, will stand far off. When they see the smoke of her burning, they will exclaim, 'Was there ever a city like this great city?' They will throw dust on their heads, and with weeping and mourning cry out:

"'Woe! Woe to you, great city,
   where all who had ships on the sea
   became rich through her wealth!
In one hour she has been brought to ruin!'
"Rejoice over her, you heavens!
   Rejoice, you people of God!
   Rejoice, apostles and prophets!
For God has judged her
   with the judgment she imposed on you."

Three groups are devastated by Babylon's fall:

- First, the *kings of the earth*, the political leaders who survive or escape the city's collapse, weep and mourn for their destroyed empire. They call Babylon the "mighty city" (verse 10). The political leaders are upset because their strength and power and influence are gone. They have invested all their political hope and confidence in the beast and in his satanic power. They have been

Bible Networking

Jeremiah 51:60-64

Jeremiah had written on a scroll about all the disasters that would come upon Babylon—all that had been recorded concerning Babylon. He said to Seraiah, "When you get to Babylon, see that you read all these words aloud. Then say, 'LORD, you have said you will destroy this place, so that neither people nor animals will live in it; it will be desolate forever.' When you finish reading this scroll, tie a stone to it and throw it into the Euphrates. Then say, 'So will Babylon sink to rise no more because of the disaster I will bring on her. And her people will fall.'"

Luke 6:24-25

But woe to you who are rich,
    for you have already received your comfort.
Woe to you who are well fed now,
    for you will go hungry.
Woe to you who laugh now,
    for you will mourn and weep.

Living Wisely

God calls any believers living in the doomed city of Babylon to "come out of her" (Revelation 18:4). When a society or nation is too corrupt to listen to God, judgment soon follows. That has been God's consistent pattern all through history. In the Bible, God sent a flood (in Noah's day), fire from heaven (on Sodom and Gomorrah), and an invading army (on Assyria and Babylon). God still raises up nations and brings down nations as he sovereignly desires. But before judgment comes, God warns his people to leave. He had Noah build an ark as a place of safety. God had Lot flee from Sodom. When the ancient city of Babylon fell, God protected Daniel in the middle of it. Christians today are to seek justice and work for integrity in our culture, but if God ever warns us to leave, we had better leave. Those who fail to heed God's warning or who look back with longing on a condemned culture will share in its destruction.

at the forefront as the Antichrist's empire has been controlled from his capital. Now, in one hour, it all collapses.

The Antichrist himself is not in the capital city when God's destructive judgment strikes. He is in Israel, at the place called Armageddon, getting his armies ready for the last war against God and against God's people. I'm certain that the news of the collapse of Babylon will be a shock to him, but it will not turn him away from his decision to bring one final blow to God's plan. The news of Babylon's fall will simply harden the Antichrist's heart and fuel his rage against God even more.

- The second group to mourn for Babylon is the *merchants*. They are upset because their wealth is gone—"no one buys their cargoes anymore" (verse 11). The merchants look at the smoldering ruins of the city and weep for their lost inventory. The stuff we think is so important will mean nothing when God's final judgment falls.

- *Seamen* who earn their living transporting goods to Babylon are crying too. They had become rich because of Babylon, but now their jobs are gone forever. They stand on ships out in the sea and see the smoke rising from the rubble, and they cry their hearts out.

All three groups testify to the suddenness of Babylon's fall—"in one hour" the city and its wealth were brought to ruin. They all testify to the intensity of Babylon's destruction too. They all stand at a distance, terrified by what they have seen.

In Other Words

I often have students or churches read through this list [in Revelation 18:12 – 13] of what was incredible luxury in Roman times and ask themselves this question: How many of these do I have in my home? This is a good lesson in the materialism of our own day.

Grant Osborne, in *Revelation* (Grand Rapids: Baker, 2002), 647.

Today, as in John's day, profit margins matter more to some people than justice. God has promised to set those matters straight.

Craig Keener, in *Revelation* (NIV Application Commentary; Grand Rapids: Zondervan, 2000), 446.

304 The Book of Revelation Made Clear

Some students of Revelation believe that the Antichrist's city is destroyed by nuclear attack. So much devastation in such a short time, they argue, must point to a nuclear bombardment. But Revelation links Babylon's destruction to the direct judgment of God: "She will be consumed by fire, for mighty is the Lord God who judges her" (verse 8). God "rained down burning sulfur on Sodom and Gomorrah," and no one survived (Genesis 19:24). God could bring the same awesome judgment on the future Babylon and in one hour destroy the entire city and everyone in it.

Those who dwell on earth may mourn and weep over Babylon, but the people in heaven rejoice. We won't rejoice because so many people die but because God is bringing this justice to bear on an empire that has killed so many Christians:

> "Rejoice over her, you heavens!
>   Rejoice, you people of God!
>   Rejoice, apostles and prophets!
> For God has judged her
>   with the judgment she imposed on you."
>
> Revelation 18:20

When Babylon is destroyed, hope ends for the Antichrist and all his followers. All they can do is gather at Armageddon and make one last desperate attempt to defeat Jesus in war.

In Other Words

This event comes late in the Great Tribulation, just prior to the second coming of Christ, in contrast to the destruction of the harlot of chapter 17 which seems to precede the Great Tribulation and paves the way for the worship of the beast.

John Walvoord, in *The Revelation of Jesus Christ* (1966; rev. ed., Chicago: Moody, 1989), 259.

Satan sails a sinking ship. His doom is announced and will be carried out. Sin cannot win, and faith cannot fail. If you are a lover of Babylon, you are following a lost cause. Babylon will be destroyed by a devastating collapse. It will happen cataclysmically fast. And its destruction will be utterly complete.

Adrian Rogers, in *Unveiling the End Times in Our Time* (Nashville: Broadman & Holman, 2004), 201.

The Final Word (Revelation 18:21 – 24)

Then a mighty angel picked up a boulder the size of a large millstone and threw it into the sea, and said:

"With such violence
the great city of Babylon will be thrown down,
never to be found again.
The music of harpists and musicians, pipers and trumpeters,
will never be heard in you again.
No worker of any trade
will ever be found in you again.
The sound of a millstone
will never be heard in you again.
The light of a lamp
will never shine in you again.
The voice of bridegroom and bride
will never be heard in you again.
Your merchants were the world's important people.
By your magic spell all the nations were led astray.
In her was found the blood of prophets and of God's people,
of all who have been slaughtered on the earth."

A Preterist Perspective

Christians who believe that most of the book of Revelation was fulfilled in the *past* rather than the *future* are called *preterists* (from a Latin word meaning "past"). They claim that John's prophecies center on the destruction of Jerusalem in AD 70, not on a still-future Tribulation.

Preterists are divided on how they view "Babylon" in Revelation 17 and 18. Some believe that Babylon stands for the city of Jerusalem, which was "suddenly" destroyed by the Roman armies; others believe that Babylon represents the Roman Empire that came under God's judgment and "fell" in AD 476.

The objection to the identification of Babylon with ancient Rome is that Rome did not fall suddenly or permanently. The objection to equating Babylon with first-century Jerusalem is that Jerusalem was not a major commercial center, nor did its fall create an economic crisis for the kings and merchants of the earth.

As if to drive home the certainty of Babylon's destruction one more time, a mighty angel emerges from heaven and gives John an object lesson, an acted-out parable. The angel picks up a huge boulder the size of a grinding "wheel" that weighed several tons and throws it into the sea. In the future, Babylon will be thrown down, just like that stone. She will sink and never rise again.

All the sparkling attractions of that city will be gone. The music of her symphonies and nightclubs will never be heard again. The sounds of industry and commerce will be silent. Family life stops. Even light refuses to shine. Future evil Babylon will become as dark and as silent as hell.

God points out three reasons for Babylon's total annihilation. First, material wealth is worshiped instead of God—"your merchants were the world's important people" (verse 23). Second, demons were in control, not the Lord—"by your magic spell all the nations were led astray" (verse 23). Finally, Babylon is crushed because godly men and women were killed without mercy—"in her was found the blood of prophets and of God's people" (verse 24).

Points to Remember

- ☑ A brilliant angel announces the destruction of Babylon, the political and commercial capital of the Antichrist's empire.

- ☑ The city is destroyed by fire from God in one hour.

- ☑ Political leaders and business-people weep and mourn for the loss of their wealth and power.

- ☑ Another angel throws a huge stone in the sea to represent Babylon—a big splash, then gone forever.

CHAPTER 19

Finally — Jesus Comes Again!

Finally — Jesus Comes Again!

- ▶ Shouts of praise thunder through heaven!
- ▶ John falls down in worship at an angel's feet but is told to stop.
- ▶ Heaven opens, and Jesus returns to earth.
- ▶ The Antichrist meets his match—and his judge.

Key Codes: Level 19

- ➜ Hallelujah: A Hebrew word used as a shout of praise to God in the Old Testament
- ➜ Twenty-four elders: A symbol of all church-age believers
- ➜ Wedding supper: A joyful reception after the wedding ceremony
- ➜ Scepter: A decorated rod symbolizing the king's power and authority
- ➜ Fiery lake of burning sulfur: Hell

Keep on Shoutin'! (Revelation 19:1–10)

After this I heard what sounded like the roar of a great multitude in heaven shouting:

"Hallelujah!
Salvation and glory and power belong to our God,
 for true and just are his judgments.
He has condemned the great prostitute
 who corrupted the earth by her adulteries.
He has avenged on her the blood of his servants."

And again they shouted:

"Hallelujah!
The smoke from her goes up for ever and ever."

The twenty-four elders and the four living creatures fell down and worshiped God, who was seated on the throne. And they cried:

"Amen, Hallelujah!"

Then a voice came from the throne, saying:

"Praise our God,
   all you his servants,
you who fear him,
   both great and small!"

Then I heard what sounded like a great multitude, like the roar of rushing waters and like loud peals of thunder, shouting:

"Hallelujah!
   For our Lord God Almighty reigns.
Let us rejoice and be glad
   and give him glory!
For the wedding of the Lamb has come,
   and his bride has made herself ready.
Fine linen, bright and clean,
   was given her to wear."
(Fine linen stands for the righteous acts of God's people.)

Then the angel said to me, "Write: 'Blessed are those who are invited to the wedding supper of the Lamb!'" And he added, "These are the true words of God."

At this I fell at his feet to worship him. But he said to me, "Don't do that! I am a fellow servant with you and with your brothers and sisters who hold to Jesus' testimony. Worship God! For the testimony of Jesus is the Spirit of prophecy."

Chapter 19 changes everything in the book of Revelation. The destruction of the Antichrist's capital in chapter 18 marks the end of the

HANDY HEBREW WORDS

Revelation 19 is the only place in the New Testament where the word *Hallelujah* appears. The other Hebrew word in the passage, *Amen*, is used at least thirty times in the New Testament (most often by the apostle Paul; never by Jesus, unless you count the closing word of the Lord's Prayer in Matthew 6:13 [see TNIV text note]). "Amen" appears eight other times in Revelation (1:6, 7; 3:14; 5:14; 7:12 [twice]; 22:20, 21). Two other Hebrew words used in the New Testament are *Hosanna*, which means "Save us" (see Matthew 21:9), and *Marana tha* (an Aramaic word meaning "Come, Lord," see 1 Corinthians 16:22).

Tribulation. Dreadful judgment gives way to joy-filled songs of praise. The darkness of the Antichrist's oppression is removed by the brilliant light of the returning King. Satan's day and mankind's day on earth end, and God's day begins.

Just before the sky bursts open and Jesus returns to earth, the inhabitants of heaven explode in loud shouts of praise to God. Four times we hear the word "Hallelujah!" (or, in some Bible translations, "Alleluia!"). Hallelujah is a Hebrew word used often in the Old Testament, especially in the Psalms. It means "praise to Yahweh," or "praise to the LORD." Some Christians get a little nervous when someone says "Hallelujah!" in a church service, but actually it's good practice for heaven. We will hear and shout the word repeatedly in heaven's throne room.

The first "Hallelujah" comes like a roar of thunder from a great multitude in heaven. I think that these are Tribulation believers who have suffered under the Antichrist and have been killed for their faith in Jesus. Back in Revelation 6, they began to cry out for God to avenge their blood (6:10), and now God has destroyed the evil city of Babylon. These faithful witnesses to Jesus praise God for his deliverance (salvation) and his glory and his power. They praise him for the justice of his judgment on a wicked, unrepentant world that had massacred his followers.

The Tribulation believers are so excited that they shout it again— "Hallelujah!" The smoke of the great prostitute Babylon will go up before God forever. Their statement can't refer to the city's burning forever; it must refer to the eternal judgment of the people who carried out the evil schemes of the Antichrist. God's judgment on them is right and true to his promise to avenge the blood of his servants.

The shout of praise is picked up next by the twenty-four elders and the four living creatures around God's throne. We were introduced to the elders back in Revelation 4. I think that the elders represent the

In Other Words

This is an occasion for every true servant of God to praise the Lord.... Hence it reads, "Keep on praising our God, all his servants who fear him, small and great." The verb "praise" is in the present tense and is therefore a command to "keep on praising" the Lord.

John Walvoord, in *The Revelation of Jesus Christ* (1966; rev. ed., Chicago: Moody, 1989), 270.

Bible Networking

2 Corinthians 11:2

I promised you to one husband, to Christ, so that I might present you as a pure virgin to him.

Ephesians 5:25

Husbands, love your wives, just as Christ loved the church and gave himself up for her.

church—all the believers in Jesus whose bodies were resurrected or changed at the time of the rapture. The four living creatures are the magnificent angels who stand at attention around the throne of God. We fall down before the living God and shout, "Amen, Hallelujah!"

Amen is another Hebrew word. We think of it as the proper way to close a prayer, but it means much more than that. The word means "may it be." When we end a prayer with "Amen," we are asking God to bring about all that we have prayed for. We are calling on God to accomplish all that he desires in our lives and in our world. The multitude of Christians in heaven who were taken out before the beginning of the Tribulation hear the shout of victory from those who died under the Antichrist, and we say, "Amen! May it be! Praise to the Lord!"

We say these words as we fall down in worship and adoration. As I read that, I tried to remember the last time I had fallen down in praise and adoration of God. I've kneeled down a few times recently. I've been on hands and knees before the Lord a few times in life. Only once or twice can I remember falling facedown before him. I haven't practiced much for heaven.

It's been a while since I said "Amen" to God's will too. I've asked him to do what I wanted in my life or in a certain situation, but I'm not very prone to say, "Amen, Lord. Do what *you* plan, accomplish what *you* purpose, carry out *your* will—and whatever good and right things you choose to do, I will praise you." Watching God bring judgment on the world in the Tribulation will bring us to the place of absolute confidence in his wisdom and sovereign power. We won't have any suggestions to make.

The next sound John hears is a voice from God's throne. The words come most likely from an angel: "Praise our God, all you his servants."

Then everyone in heaven—Tribulation martyrs, church-age believers, angels, Old Testament believers—shouts, "Hallelujah! For our Lord God Almighty reigns."

Come to the Wedding!

The servants of God in heaven rejoice, not because the Lord will defeat the Antichrist, but because the wedding supper of the Lamb is about to begin. Jesus is not only the conquering King in this chapter; he is also the groom leading a joyful wedding procession. The Lamb's bride is dressed in the finest, brightest, cleanest linen, a picture of her rewards,

JESUS' SECOND COMING

At the rapture, Jesus appears in the clouds to take his people out of the world. At his return in power, everyone on earth will see him. Here are the details that we can glean from the Bible about his return to earth:

- Jesus will return *personally*. The angels who spoke to Jesus' followers when Jesus ascended into heaven said that Jesus would "come back in the same way" (Acts 1:11).
- Jesus will appear *visibly*. Jesus himself said that the people of the earth would "see the Son of Man coming on the clouds of heaven, with power and great glory" (Matthew 24:30). Earlier in Revelation, John had written, "every eye will see him, even those who pierced him" (Revelation 1:7).
- Jesus will come *suddenly*. "For as lightning that comes from the east is visible even in the west, so will be the coming of the Son of Man" (Matthew 24:27).
- Jesus will come in *majesty*. Jesus said, "For the Son of Man is going to come in his Father's glory" (Matthew 16:27).
- Jesus will come with his *angels*. He specifically promised in Matthew 16:27 that he would come "with his angels" and later that he would send his angels out as reapers into the world (Matthew 24:31; Matthew 13:39).
- Jesus will return with his *church*. Paul in Colossians 3:4 writes, "When Christ, who is your life, appears, then you also will appear with him in glory." The Old Testament prophet Zechariah in 14:5 adds, "Then the LORD my God will come, and all the holy ones with him."
- Jesus' feet will touch the *Mount of Olives*. "On that day his feet will stand on the Mount of Olives" (Zechariah 14:4). The spot where Jesus ascended will be the spot where he returns.
- Jesus will reign in *victory* at his return. Zechariah predicted, "The LORD will be king over the whole earth" (14:9).

the righteous acts done in obedience and love for Christ. The bride is the church—all the men and women who had believed in Jesus from the beginning of the church in Acts 2 until the moment of the rapture. Tribulation martyrs are not the bride; Old Testament believers such as Abraham and David are not the bride. They will all have their place in God's program and their reward for faithfulness. The church, however, is the bride, engaged to Jesus now but in the future to be linked to him even more closely. We will be displayed to heaven and earth as Jesus' chosen bride, those he loved and laid down his life to redeem.

The wedding day has arrived. The vows of commitment have been spoken. Now (as was the custom in John's day) the bride and groom and their friends make a noisy procession to the couple's new home for the reception. John calls it "the wedding supper." Those invited to the supper are blessed.

So who will be there?

- *The bride.* The church
- *Old Testament believers.* Jesus makes it clear that we will sit down in the kingdom with Abraham and Isaac. Old Testament followers of the Lord will receive their resurrected bodies soon after Jesus'

GOING TO GET MARRIED

Jewish marriage customs are reflected in the New Testament description of Jesus and his bride, the church. First-century Jews saw three distinct stages in the marriage process:

- First, *the prospective bride and groom are engaged.* They make a public commitment to each other that requires a divorce to dissolve. The "engagement" between Jesus and his bride takes place in this life when we by faith commit ourselves to Jesus as Savior and Lord, and he, in his Word, promises to receive all who will believe in him. Paul pictures the church as a virgin

waiting for her bridegroom to come (2 Corinthians 11:2).

- The second stage of marriage takes place when *the groom comes to take his engaged bride to the home of his parents for a marriage ceremony.* Jesus comes for his bride at the rapture. He takes us to the Father's house (heaven) for the marriage ceremony.
- Finally, *the bride and groom and their guests make a noisy procession to their new home for a wedding feast.* That procession is what we have in Revelation 19. Jesus and the church return to earth to set up the kingdom and to share in a joyous feast with their guests.

return to the earth and will join in the festivities on a cleansed earth, an earth ready to receive the kingdom rule of Jesus.

- *Tribulation believers* who died during the seven-year Tribulation will also be invited. They will receive resurrection bodies after Jesus' return to earth too and will find rest and peace during the time of Jesus' reign on earth.
- *Followers of Jesus who survive the Tribulation* will be there too. They will not be resurrected but will attend as normal human beings, the first human residents of Jesus' earthly kingdom.
- *The groom* will be the center of everything at the wedding supper. Praise and honor and glory will resound to him from every guest. Jesus told his disciples before he died that he would "not drink of this fruit of the vine from now on until that day when I drink it new with you in my Father's kingdom" (Matthew 26:29). It may be that we will share in the greatest Communion service of all time as we rejoice together at the marriage supper of the Lamb in the opening days of Jesus' kingdom on earth.

John is so stunned by the power of this multitude's shout that he forgets that he is supposed to be writing it all down. The angel that seems to have accompanied John throughout the book of Revelation gives him a little verbal nudge. "Write," he says. "'Blessed are those invited to the wedding supper.'" Then he adds, "These are the true words of God" (or, "All God's words are true").

John is overwhelmed. He does something no human should ever do. He falls down in worship to an angel! Now it's the angel's turn to be stunned. He grabs John and pulls him up and says, "Don't do that! God alone is worthy of worship. I am a fellow servant with you." As glorious

In Other Words

Instead of the normal seven-day Jewish wedding ceremony, this one presumably lasts seven years (during the Tribulation period). The marriage is completed in heaven (Revelation 19:7), but the marriage supper probably takes place later on earth where Israel is awaiting the return of Christ and the church.

Ed Hindson, in *The Book of Revelation: Unlocking the Future* (Chattanooga, Tenn.: AMG, 2002), 192.

Bible Networking

Matthew 8:11

"I say to you that many will come from the east and the west, and will take their places at the feast with Abraham, Isaac and Jacob in the kingdom of heaven."

Isaiah 59:19

From the west, people will fear the name of the LORD,
　　and from the rising of the sun, they will revere his glory.
For he will come like a pent-up flood
　　that the breath of the LORD drives along.

as angels are, they are never to be worshiped. We may honor faithful angels, just as we honor faithful Christians or godly pastors, but we are never to give them reverence or worship. God alone is the object of our worship and adoration.

Then the angel makes one of the most important statements in Scripture about biblical prophecy: "The testimony of Jesus is the Spirit of prophecy" (verse 10). The whole purpose of prophecy in the Bible is to unfold and reveal the majesty and glory of Jesus. Don't get so wrapped up in the Antichrist or the mark of the beast that you miss Jesus! John writes this book as the unveiling of who Jesus really is—and he is about to give us the most powerful description in all of Scripture of the true character and mission of Jesus in the plan of God. Jesus is the conquering King. He has conquered the hearts of those who believe in him. He has conquered death by the power of his resurrection. He has conquered all the devastation that sin has left in our lives. But the day will come when Jesus will conquer the world. He will sweep away every remnant of human order and human government and replace it with the glory and peace of his sovereign reign. It's a day that John the apostle longed for; it's a day that every Christian looks for; it's the day that all of creation waits for in eager anticipation. Jesus comes to earth a second time. Not as a humble baby in Bethlehem, but as the King over every king!

Help File

DANIEL'S STONE

In the Old Testament book of Daniel, God gave the Babylonian king Nebuchadnezzar a glimpse of what the arrival of Jesus' kingdom on earth would be like. The king saw an enormous statue of a man representing succeeding world empires— Babylon, the head of gold; Persia, the chest and arms of silver; Greece, the stomach and hips of bronze; Rome, the legs of iron; and the final empire of ten toes of iron and ceramic, the ten-nation empire of the Antichrist. Suddenly something flew toward the statue—a huge stone not carved by human hands. The stone struck the statue on the feet and crushed the entire structure into dust. God was showing Nebuchadnezzar that the sudden arrival of God's kingdom would blow away every remnant of human authority and power. Jesus won't just fix up what's here; he will replace everything with a whole new order. (You can read about Nebuchadnezzar's dream and Daniel's interpretation of the dream in Daniel 2.)

Revelation 360°

Rapture.alt
No War, No Way!

Not everyone agrees that Jesus will return as a warrior to destroy the Antichrist and his armies. Yehezkel Landau, a Jewish theologian in Israel, believes that Christians should be working for justice in the Middle East, not waiting for Armageddon—the time when the "children of darkness" will be "vanquished by the virtuous defenders of the true faith."

Most Christians (in his view) pervert biblical prophecy to produce this twisted version of John 3:16: "God so loved the world that he sent World War III." (Note: the quotations are taken from an editorial in *The Jerusalem Post* [November 1983] titled "The President and the Prophets.")

Bible scholar Barbara Rossing takes a similar view: "Peace and peace plans in the Middle East are a bad thing, in the view of fundamentalist Christians, because they delay the countdown to Christ's return ... that is the most terrifying aspect of this distorted theology. Such blessing of violence is the very reason why we cannot afford to give in to [this] version of the biblical story line" (*The Rapture Exposed* [New York: Basic Books, 2004], 46).

The Lord Is a Warrior (Revelation 19:11–16)

> I saw heaven standing open and there before me was a white horse, whose rider is called Faithful and True. With justice he judges and makes war. His eyes are like blazing fire, and on his head are many crowns. He has a name written on him that no one knows but he himself. He is dressed in a robe dipped in blood, and his name is the Word of God. The armies of heaven were following him, riding on white horses and dressed in fine linen, white and clean. Coming out of his mouth is a sharp sword with which to strike down the nations. "He will rule them with an iron scepter." He treads the winepress of the fury of the wrath of God Almighty. On his robe and on his thigh he has this name written:
>
> KING OF KINGS AND LORD OF LORDS.

John has seen some amazing scenes as the book of Revelation has unfolded—gruesome beasts rising from the sea and earth, hundred-pound hailstones pounding the earth, demon locusts swarming from the pit of hell. But nothing compares with what he sees now. John's jaw must have dropped as he saw the skies split open. The barrier between earth and heaven was ripped away—and right there in front of him was a white horse.

The white horse always held a conqueror. Earlier in the book, John saw a different rider on a white horse (6:1–2). That conqueror led the world down a path of destruction and judgment. That rider was a deceiver, an instrument of Satan. The rider on this white horse has a completely different character. He is called Faithful and True. The rider is Jesus Christ, God the Son, the conquering King and Lord of all.

Jesus' purpose in returning in majesty is clear—he comes to judge and to make war on those who oppose him. His eyes are like fire, penetrating every hidden motive, seeing everything with perfect understanding. He is crowned with all of God's authority. Many diadems give him the right to reclaim the world. In addition to the names we do know ("Faithful," "Word of God"), Jesus has a name that no one knows. A person's *name*, especially as it relates to God, reflects that person's character. Jesus' unrevealed name reflects the depth of character as God—a depth only he can comprehend. There is a lot about who Jesus is that you and I will never be able to understand or know. We are human beings; he is the eternal God.

The armies of heaven follow him, also riding white horses and clothed in brilliant garments. The army's clothing is the same as the bride's clothing in verse 8. So "the armies of heaven" are most likely church-age believers who ride along with the Warrior-King in victory. The army could also include Old Testament believers and Tribulation believers who are yet to be resurrected before the kingdom age begins. It's possible, too, that the armies include the holy angels. Jesus himself said that when he returned, "all the angels" would come with him (Matthew 25:31).

The odd thing about this army is that they have no weapons. The only weapon mentioned is a gigantic sword protruding from Jesus' mouth. That sword is the only weapon Jesus needs. The same "word" that brought galaxies of stars into existence instantly and effortlessly will destroy the Antichrist and the armies of the earth.

The robe "dipped in blood" is not a reminder of the cross. This is not redemptive blood, but the blood of judgment and justice. This is a fulfillment of the prediction back in Revelation 14:20 that the blood of God's enemies would spatter to the horses' bridles.

The end of injustice and the establishment of God's kingdom on earth will not come from good intentions or human effort or by means of pro-Christian legislation. Human beings will not bring God's day to earth; Jesus will. The kingdom will be ushered in by the powerful intervention of God the Son. That doesn't mean, however, that we should just throw up our hands and give up on our deteriorating culture. Until Jesus comes, we are called to be salt and light in a decaying, darkening world. We are to work for a just society, a righteous government, and a compassionate culture, in spite of the fact that human culture will continue to drift further and further from God. We can't stop calling attention to God's righteous standards, and we certainly can't stop praying for God's kingdom to come. Every area of our culture—the media, government, education, health care, industry, technology, finance, the arts—needs Christians who will raise their voices to speak for what is right and good. But we aren't surprised when, in spite of our most fervent efforts, the society around us becomes more and more hostile to Christ and to those who follow him.

The name that sets Jesus apart from everyone else in this scene is the name "KING OF KINGS AND LORD OF LORDS." Jesus is the supreme King and the only Lord. His name is exalted above every other name in the universe.

The Final Conflict (Revelation 19:17 – 21)

And I saw an angel standing in the sun, who cried in a loud voice to all the birds flying in midair, "Come, gather together for the great supper of God, so that you may eat the flesh of kings, generals, and the mighty, of horses and their riders, and the flesh of all people, free and slave, great and small."

Then I saw the beast and the kings of the earth and their armies gathered together to make war against the rider on the horse and his army. But the beast was captured, and with him the false prophet who had performed the signs on his behalf. With these signs he had deluded those who had received the mark of the beast and worshiped his image. The two of them were thrown alive into the fiery lake of burning sulfur. The rest were killed with the sword coming out of the mouth of the rider on the horse, and all the birds gorged themselves on their flesh.

As Jesus returns, the armies of the world have already gathered in and around Israel. The armies loyal to the Antichrist and the armies of

In Other Words

For the essence of prophecy is to give a clear witness to Jesus.

New Living Translation, Revelation 19:10.

We can serve the kingdom. We can prepare for the kingdom. We can pray, "Thy kingdom come." But the kingdom of God will come only through God's power and because he wills it. We will not usher in God's reign.

Joel Green, in *How to Read Prophecy* (Downers Grove, Ill.: InterVarsity, 1984), 121.

If you read Revelation and don't come to know and to love Jesus more, you have missed it all.

Adrian Rogers, in *Unveiling the End Times in Our Time* (Nashville: Broadman & Holman, 2004), 211.

Bible Networking

2 Thessalonians 2:8

Then the lawless one will be revealed, whom the Lord Jesus will overthrow with the breath of his mouth and destroy by the splendor of his coming.

2 Thessalonians 1:6 – 8

God is just: He will pay back trouble to those who trouble you and give relief to you who are troubled, and to us as well. This will happen when the Lord Jesus is revealed from heaven in blazing fire with his powerful angels. He will punish those who do not know God and do not obey the gospel of our Lord Jesus.

the kings of the East turn from fighting each other to fighting against the Lord. The Antichrist's goal is to destroy the people of Israel. If he can't stop God, at least he wants to thwart God's plan to keep his promises to Abraham and David. If he can wipe out the Jews, there would be no one in Abraham's line to receive the kingdom. Jesus' return stops the Antichrist in his tracks. With one breath, Jesus lays waste the vast armies gathered against Jerusalem.

The Jews had already realized that the Antichrist was a liar and deceiver when he took over Israel's temple and set himself up as the object of the world's worship. Israel had turned from the Antichrist, but they have not yet turned to Jesus as their Messiah. When they see Jesus coming to earth in glory, however, the hearts of the nation will be turned to him in faith. They will look on the one they had pierced so long ago and will believe that he is their Messiah. Cleansing and forgiveness will flow like water.

The first thing Jesus does is capture the Antichrist and the deceiving false prophet. They are thrown alive into the lake of fire. They don't die but are cast, body and spirit, into the final hell, into the place Jesus originally made for the devil's confinement. The beast and the false prophet are not annihilated in the lake of burning sulfur. They don't cease to exist. One thousand years later, when Satan is finally cast into the same place, John says it is the place where the beast and the false prophet still reside (Revelation 20:10). All three members of the evil false trinity will be tormented in that place forever and ever.

With their leader taken out, the armies of the world fall into complete disarray, but no one escapes. They are killed by the sword that comes out of Jesus' mouth—a symbol of his power. Instantly, Jesus destroys millions of people who have gathered in battle against him. The Old Testament prophet Zechariah gives us a clue as to how the armies will be slain:

> This is the plague with which the LORD will strike all the nations that fought against Jerusalem: Their flesh will rot while they are still standing on their feet, their eyes will rot in their sockets, and their tongues will rot in their mouths. On that day people will be stricken by the LORD with great panic. They will seize each other by the hand and attack one another.
>
> Zechariah 14:12–13

One word from Jesus—and the whole battle ends. Then an angel calls the birds of the whole region to the battlefield for a feast of flesh (Revelation 19:21).

For a thousand years after this, there will be no more war. Human beings will convert their weapons into implements of productivity and peace. The words of war will drop out of the human vocabulary. Jesus will reign as the righteous King over all the earth.

Only one way is provided to escape the coming time of God's wrath. The writer of Psalm 2 calls us to "kiss [the LORD's] son." We only escape by believing on and following after the Son of God, Jesus Christ. His anger and justice will be ignited someday soon, and no one will escape. We are safe only when we come to him in faith and find protection in his mercy and forgiveness.

Points to Remember

☑ The inhabitants of heaven will shout in praise because God's kingdom is about to come.

☑ The second coming of Jesus to earth is marked by his visible return with the inhabitants of heaven behind him.

☑ The Antichrist and the false prophet will be cast bodily into the lake of burning sulfur—the first human occupants of the final hell.

☑ Christ will destroy the armies of the world with one breath, one spoken word of power—and the birds will feast on the bodies of those who have fallen.

CHAPTER 20

A Peaceable Kingdom

A Peaceable Kingdom

- ▶ Satan is put away—for a thousand years.
- ▶ Jesus reigns over the earth.
- ▶ Catch a glimpse of a final rebellion and the final judgment.
- ▶ The reality of hell!

MR. BLOCKHEAD
HEADS UP

Access Codes

Key Codes: Level 20

➡ Abyss: A compartment of hell where evil angels are confined

➡ The beast: The Antichrist; a future world dictator

➡ His mark: The sign of a person's allegiance to the Antichrist; a visible mark

➡ Gog and Magog: An Old Testament phrase that describes nations in rebellion against God

➡ The book of life: A record in heaven of those who have believed in Jesus

➡ Hades: The place where the spirits of unbelievers reside after death

➡ Lake of fire: The final and eternal place of torment and separation from God

Making Sense of the Kingdom

Revelation 20 is one of the great dividing lines in biblical prophecy. Your view of the first part of this chapter will determine how you interpret pretty much everything else in the Bible related to prophecy. The pivotal issue is how you interpret the phrase "a thousand years." It seems pretty straightforward, but it's not that simple. Christians have argued for centuries about what the "thousand years" stands for and when it occurs.

The issue centers on the view you take of the millennium. That word comes from two Latin words—*mille* meaning "one thousand" and *annum* meaning "year." The term *millennium* then, in Christian theology, refers to the thousand years described here in Revelation 20:1–7. Everyone agrees that the millennium is a long period of time. The key questions are, What exactly happens during the millennium, and when does it occur?

Three main millennial views have emerged among Christians—premillennialism, postmillennialism, and amillennialism. (Try reading *that* sentence three times as fast as you can!) I won't go into all the arguments for each position, but a summary might help:

- *Premillennialists* believe that the thousand years comes directly after Jesus' return to earth in power and victory. (The "pre" in premillennial refers to Jesus' return *before* the millennium.) During the millennium Jesus will reign over the earth—so the millennium is sometimes called "the kingdom age" or "the millennial kingdom." Satan will be confined; the curse of sin will be lifted; peace and prosperity will cover the earth. Premillennialists believe that the promises to Israel in the Old Testament of an earthly kingdom will be literally fulfilled in the future millennial reign of Christ.

- *Postmillennialists* believe that Jesus will return to earth *after* ("post-") the thousand years of Revelation 20. This view teaches that the message of the gospel will continue to spread with such power that eventually our world will be "Christianized" and a golden age of peace and righteousness will emerge. At the end of that age (the kingdom age), Jesus will return and bring human history to a close. Postmillennialism is being repackaged in Christian circles today and called the Reconstructionist view or the Dominion view. Many Americans who hold this view teach that Christians should be working to make the United States into a Christian theocracy rather than to be governed as a secular democracy.

- *Amillennialists* believe that the kingdom age is right now. The promises to Israel of an earthly, eternal kingdom have been transferred from old Israel to the church—the new Israel—and the promises are fulfilled in a spiritual kingdom in which Jesus reigns in the church and in our hearts right now. He will not reign over an earthly kingdom in the future. "Amillennial" means "no millennium" or "no visible earthly kingdom." The phrase "one thousand years" in this view is not to be taken literally but in the sense of "a long time."

MILLENNIAL VIEWS: HOW THEY STACK UP

View	*When* Jesus Will Reign	*How* Jesus Will Reign	*Where* Jesus Will Reign
Amillennial	In the present age — *between* Jesus' first coming and second coming	Spiritual reign over the church and in the hearts of believers	In heaven
Postmillennial	In the future but *before* his return to earth	Spiritual and political reign through Christians on earth	In heaven
Premillennial	In the future but *after* his return to earth	Literal, personal reign over the kingdom for a thousand years	On earth from his throne in Jerusalem

The view reflected in this book is the premillennial view. I hold this position for several reasons:

- Premillennialism is the only view that takes Revelation 20:1–7 in its normal sense. Six times in the passage the Bible says that Jesus will rule over a kingdom that lasts one thousand years.
- The normal reading of Revelation 19 and 20 shows that the kingdom comes *after* Jesus visibly returns to earth in power.
- The premillennial view allows us to accept at face value the Old Testament predictions about a visible kingdom on earth. God promised Abraham (the human father of the nation of Israel, the Jews) the land of Canaan as a permanent dwelling place (Genesis 12:1–3; 15:18–19). The Jews have held the land at various times for varying lengths of time, but never permanently. God promised King David that one of his descendants would rule Israel forever (2 Samuel 7:12–16; 1 Chronicles 28:5, 7). The promises of an earthly kingdom given in Isaiah and Zechariah and Daniel

have never been fulfilled, so God will fulfill those promises in the future.

While I hold this particular position, I also realize that godly, committed Christians hold other views. I can respect and love them and still disagree. This is not a test of the genuineness of our faith. We will all give an account of ourselves to Jesus—and we will *all* receive reward and honor from him.

The Dragon Tackled (Revelation 20:1–3)

> And I saw an angel coming down out of heaven, having the key to the Abyss and holding in his hand a great chain. He seized the dragon, that ancient serpent, who is the devil, or Satan, and bound him for a thousand years. He threw him into the Abyss, and locked and sealed it over him, to keep him from deceiving the nations anymore until the thousand years were ended. After that, he must be set free for a short time.

After witnessing the destruction of the Antichrist's armies in chapter 19, John's eyes are again drawn toward heaven as a mighty angel comes down, armed with a key and a chain. Satan, the dragon, the energizing force behind the Antichrist and the false prophet, is captured and confined in the Abyss. We've seen the Abyss opened and closed before

CHARACTERISTICS OF THE KINGDOM

Here are some of the benefits of Jesus' future kingdom, according to the prophets:

- War will disappear, and human beings will focus on peaceful, productive pursuits (Zechariah 9:10; Isaiah 2:4; 9:7).
- Social justice, moral purity, and racial harmony will permeate human culture (Psalm 72:1–4, 12–14; Isaiah 42:3).
- Disability, deformity, and disease will be eradicated from earth (Isaiah 33:24; 35:5–6; 61:1–2).
- Long life will be normal (Isaiah 65:20–22).
- The earth will be abundantly productive (Psalm 72:16; Isaiah 35:1–2; Amos 9:13).
- Wild animals will not be threatening to human beings (Isaiah 11:6–9; 65:25).
- The knowledge of the true God will extend to every person on earth (Isaiah 66:23).

Sign me up!

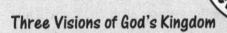

Three Visions of God's Kingdom

Amillennial View: Anthony Hoekema

Amillennialists believe that the millennium of Revelation 20 is not exclusively future but is now in the process of realization.... (156)

Chapters 20–22 [of Revelation] comprise the last of the seven sections of the book of Revelation and therefore do not describe what follows the return of Christ. Rather, Revelation 20:1 takes us back once again to the beginning of the New Testament era. (159–60)

Premillennial View: George Eldon Ladd

Premillennialism is the doctrine stating that after the Second Coming of Christ, he will reign for a thousand years over the earth before the final consummation of God's redemptive purpose in the new heavens and the new earth of the Age to Come. This is the natural reading of Revelation 20:6. (18)

Postmillennial View: Loraine Boettner

Postmillennialism is that view of the last things which holds that the kingdom of God is now being extended in the world through the preaching of the gospel and the saving work of the Holy Spirit in the hearts of individuals, that the world eventually is to be Christianized, and that the return of Christ is to occur at the close of a long period of righteousness and peace. (117)

All quotations are taken from *The Meaning of the Millennium: Four Views*, ed. Robert Clouse (Downers Grove, Ill.: InterVarsity, 1977)

in Revelation, but now Satan (and by implication all his evil angels) are confined in that dark, seemingly bottomless pit of hell. For the thousand years of Jesus' reign, the deceiver will be locked away.

The kingdom will start out with an interesting population. At least five different groups will inhabit and enjoy Christ's earthly reign:

- *Gentile believers who survive the Tribulation.* As much as the Antichrist will try to destroy every follower of Jesus during the Tribulation, he will not succeed. A few believers will survive the

Bible Networking

Isaiah 11:6 – 9

The wolf will live with the lamb,
   the leopard will lie down with the goat,
the calf and the lion and the yearling together;
   and a little child will lead them.
The cow will feed with the bear,
   their young will lie down together,
   and the lion will eat straw like the ox.
Infants will play near the hole of the cobra;
   young children will put their hands into the viper's nest.
They will neither harm nor destroy
   on all my holy mountain,
for the earth will be filled with the knowledge of the LORD
   as the waters cover the sea.

Amos 9:13

"The days are coming," declares the LORD,

   "when the reaper will be overtaken by the one who plows
      and the planter by the one treading grapes.
   New wine will drip from the mountains
      and flow from all the hills."

Tribulation and will enter the kingdom in their normal human bodies. They will be able to marry and reproduce in the millennium. In fact, Isaiah implies that child-bearing years will be extended for those who enter the kingdom (Isaiah 65:20). In Matthew's gospel, Jesus talked about those who survive the Tribulation:

When the Son of Man comes in his glory, and all the angels with him, he will sit on his glorious throne. All the nations will be gathered before him, and he will separate the people one from

MEET THE PLAYERS

The *amillennial* view of God's kingdom is held by the Roman Catholic Church, Eastern Orthodox churches, and many Protestants. The foundations of this view are usually traced back to Augustine, a fifth-century church leader and teacher (AD 354–430). The Protestant Reformers John Calvin and Martin Luther also taught an amillennial view of the kingdom.

The Augsburg Confession (Lutheran) and Westminster Confession are basically *postmillennial* in outlook. Lutheran, Presbyterian, and Reformed groups have tended to teach this position. The present-day Christian Reconstructionist movement is also postmillennial.

The view that Jesus will return to reign over a thousand-year kingdom on earth was the view of the early church. Almost all the church leaders in the first three centuries after Jesus' resurrection held to a *premillennial* view. The fifth-century teacher Augustine was the one who suggested that the kingdom of God was really a spiritual kingdom made visible in the earthly church (the amillennial view). His teaching soon replaced premillennialism as the majority view. Premillennialism made a comeback in the middle of the nineteenth century and is currently a very widely held view of end-time events. Some well-known premillennialists are Charles Ryrie, John Walvoord, Hal Lindsey, Tim LaHaye, Chuck Swindoll, and John MacArthur Jr. *The Scofield Reference Bible* and the *Ryrie Study Bible* are strongly premillennial in their interpretation of biblical prophecy.

another as a shepherd separates the sheep from the goats. He will put the sheep on his right and the goats on his left.

Then the King will say to those on his right, "Come, you who are blessed by my Father; take your inheritance, the kingdom prepared for you since the creation of the world."

Matthew 25:31–34

- *Jewish believers who survive the Tribulation.* There will be Jewish believers in Jesus who survive the Tribulation. The 144,000 Jews who are sealed by God early in the Tribulation are supernaturally protected from the Antichrist's onslaughts (Revelation 7:1–8; 14:1–5). The remnant of Israel who sees Jesus return in glory believes in him as Messiah and will survive the final war and enter the kingdom. These Jewish believers will be in normal human bodies and will help to repopulate the earth in the millennium.
- *Glorified church-age believers.* Christians who were taken to heaven in the rapture before the Tribulation will return with

Christ and will reign with him during the kingdom. We will be in resurrected bodies so we will not reproduce, but we will enjoy the blessings of Jesus' kingdom on earth.

- *Resurrected Old Testament believers.* The men and women who believed in the true God in the Old Testament age will not be resurrected at the rapture. Paul says those "in Christ" are resurrected at the rapture. The hope of Old Testament believers was the kingdom of the Messiah. They are resurrected when Jesus returns in glory. We will sit down with Abraham, Isaac, and Jacob (and all the other Old Testament believers) *in* the kingdom of God (Matthew 8:11). Those Old Testament saints will be in resurrected bodies so they will not marry or reproduce, but they will enjoy the fulfillment of God's promise of a kingdom.
- *Resurrected Tribulation martyrs.* As we will see in the next section of Revelation 20, those followers of Jesus who were killed during the Tribulation will be resurrected when Jesus returns, and they will reign with Jesus during the kingdom. They are another group in resurrected, eternal bodies—so no babies.

The earthly kingdom will be populated by both resurrected believers in glorified bodies and Tribulation-surviving believers in normal bodies. Some of us will reign with Jesus and have responsibilities for oversight in the kingdom, and some will do the work of replenishing the earth and gathering in its abundance. We will all enjoy the wonderful blessings of a world without war or sickness or want.

ONE WILL BE TAKEN AND THE OTHER LEFT

Jesus' explanation of how the angels will remove all unbelievers from the world helps us understand another statement from Jesus—a statement that is usually misinterpreted. Here is what Jesus says:

> That is how it will be at the coming of the Son of Man. Two men will be in the field; one will be taken and the other left. Two women will be grinding with a hand mill; one will be taken and the other left.
>
> Matthew 24:39–41

You will hear this passage quoted as a description of the rapture, but it is not about the rapture. It is a statement about the harvest at the end of the age. The one taken out is the unbeliever, not the Christian. God's angels will remove every follower of the Antichrist, and only believing survivors of the Tribulation will enter the kingdom.

Future FAQs

What about the Jews?

Angels will separate unbelieving Gentiles (non-Jews) out of the world, but millions of Jewish people will also survive the Tribulation. Some, like the 144,000 witnesses, will believe in Jesus early in the Tribulation. Many will believe when they see Jesus return to Jerusalem at the end of the Tribulation. But in the transition to the kingdom, Jews from around the world will be gathered to the land of Israel and judged by the Lord.

The prophet Ezekiel describes that dramatic scene when Israel comes face-to-face with their Messiah:

> I [the LORD] will bring you from the nations and gather you from the countries where you have been scattered—with a mighty hand and an outstretched arm and with outpoured wrath. I will bring you into the wilderness of the nations and there, face to face, I will execute judgment upon you. As I judged your ancestors in the wilderness of the land of Egypt, so I will judge you, declares the Sovereign LORD. I will take note of you as you pass under my rod, and I will bring you into the bond of the covenant. I will purge you of those who revolt and rebel against me. Although I will bring them out of the land where they are living, yet they will not enter the land of Israel. Then you will know that I am the LORD.
>
> Ezekiel 20:34–38

The Jews who have believed on Jesus will enter the kingdom; those who refuse to believe will die. Ezekiel also spells out the blessings that will come to those who receive the kingdom:

> For I [the LORD] will take you out of the nations; I will gather you from all the countries and bring you back into your own land. I will sprinkle clean water on you, and you will be clean; I will cleanse you from all your impurities and from all your idols. I will give you a new heart and put a new spirit in you; I will remove from you your heart of stone and give you a heart of flesh. And I will put my Spirit in you and move you to follow my decrees and be careful to keep my laws. Then you will live in the land I gave your ancestors; you will be my people, and I will be your God.
>
> Ezekiel 36:24–28

Amos 9:15

"I will plant Israel in their own land,
   never again to be uprooted
   from the land I have given them,"
      says the LORD your God.

Daniel 7:13 – 14

"In my vision at night I looked, and there before me was one like a son of man, coming with the clouds of heaven. He approached the Ancient of Days and was led into his presence. He was given authority, glory and sovereign power; all nations and peoples of every language worshiped him. His dominion is an everlasting dominion that will not pass away, and his kingdom is one that will never be destroyed."

Not everyone who survives the Tribulation, however, will enter the kingdom. The prophet Daniel implies that there will be a time of transition after Jesus returns (Daniel 12:11 – 12). During that transition, Jesus will judge those human beings who survive the Tribulation. Those who have believed in Jesus will enter the kingdom; those who followed the Antichrist will die.

Jesus makes it clear several times in the gospel accounts that at the end of the age, when Jesus returns to earth in glory, there will be a separation made between believers and unbelievers. Here's how he explains it in Matthew 13:

> The Son of Man will send out his angels, and they will weed out of his kingdom everything that causes sin and all who do evil. They will throw them into the blazing furnace, where there will be weeping and gnashing of teeth. Then the righteous will shine like the sun in the kingdom of their Father.
>
> Matthew 13:41 – 43

In the same passage, Jesus also used the picture of a fishing expedition to describe the separation of the wicked out of his kingdom. When the fishing net is full, the fishermen pull it to shore and sort the fish.

The good fish are collected in baskets; the worthless fish are thrown away. Jesus adds:

> This is how it will be at the end of the age. The angels will come and separate the wicked from the righteous.
>
> Matthew 13:49

The transition between the Tribulation and the beginning of the kingdom includes several steps of renewal and judgment:

- Jesus returns to earth and destroys the armies gathered against him.
- The Antichrist and false prophet are sent to the lake of fire. Satan and his demons are confined to the Abyss.
- Old Testament believers and Tribulation believers who died before Jesus' return will be resurrected.
- Angels will fan out over the world and remove every surviving unbeliever from the earth.

A Thousand-Year Reign (Revelation 20:4 – 6)

> I saw thrones on which were seated those who had been given authority to judge. And I saw the souls of those who had been beheaded

Bible Networking

1 Corinthians 15:42 – 44

So will it be with the resurrection of the dead. The body that is sown is perishable, it is raised imperishable; it is sown in dishonor, it is raised in glory; it is sown in weakness, it is raised in power; it is sown a natural body, it is raised a spiritual body.

John 11:25 – 27

Jesus said to [Martha], "I am the resurrection and the life. Anyone who believes in me will live, even though they die; and whoever lives by believing in me will never die. Do you believe this?"

"Yes, Lord," she told him, "I believe that you are the Messiah, the Son of God, who was to come into the world."

because of their testimony about Jesus and because of the word of God. They had not worshiped the beast or his image and had not received his mark on their foreheads or their hands. They came to life and reigned with Christ a thousand years. (The rest of the dead did not come to life until the thousand years were ended.) This is the first resurrection. Blessed and holy are those who have part in the first resurrection. The second death has no power over them, but they will be priests of God and of Christ and will reign with him for a thousand years.

John's attention is drawn next to a series of thrones occupied by "those who had been given authority to judge" (verse 4). Interpreters of Revelation have proposed several ideas about who these people are, but the best view (I think) is that these are resurrected church-age believers who returned with Jesus. The twenty-four elders in Revelation 4:4 and 11:16 represent the church, and they may now sit as a tribunal. Their job (most likely) is to judge Tribulation believers whose bodies are now resurrected and glorified. They had been faithful in their loyalty to Jesus, even to the point of death, and now they receive rewards for their faithfulness. Church-age believers had already been rewarded at the judgment seat of Christ, and now we sit in judgment on Tribulation believers.

John uses an interesting word in verse 4 to describe how most of these Tribulation believers died. He says they "had been beheaded." Apparently as the Antichrist and his followers seek out Christ-followers during the Tribulation, they will execute those they find by cutting off their heads. Perhaps public executions like those the Roman Empire imposed on the early Christians will be used again to warn and deter others who may be thinking of following Christ. The Tribulation believers who die in such a horrible way had refused to worship the beast or his image

In Other Words

The very ones who were beheaded for the witness of Jesus — the Greek word is that they were *hatcheted*— are the ones who live and reign with Christ. So all of the believers from righteous Abel down through the very last of the saints of God in the Tribulation period will share in the triumph of the Son of God. His is the victory, won at Calvary, but he shares it with all of his redeemed ones.

Donald Grey Barnhouse, in *Revelation: An Expositional Commentary* (Grand Rapids: Zondervan, 1971), 383.

and had refused his mark on their foreheads or hands. They died at the hands of the Antichrist but now are raised in eternal bodies to live and reign with Christ over his kingdom on earth. The people who put them to death are now dead themselves, confined to Hades. The Antichrist is in the lake of fire. Jesus lives and reigns as earth's conquering King.

The "rest of the dead," all the unbelievers of all the ages, will not be raised until the thousand years are over. The spirits in the torment of Hades will ultimately be judged, but not until the golden years of Christ's kingdom have come to an end.

John's declaration is, "This is the first resurrection" (verse 5). He repeats it in verse 6: "Blessed and holy are those who have part in the first resurrection." John is not referring to the first resurrection *in time*, since there have been other resurrections before this. He is saying that what these Tribulation believers experienced was the first *kind* of resurrection, a resurrection to life. The second kind of resurrection will be what unbelievers experience, a resurrection to condemnation and eternal separation from God. All believers—church-age believers at the rapture, Old Testament believers at the beginning of the kingdom, Tribulation believers at Jesus' return—will experience the resurrection to life, the first resurrection. We will never die again. We will have bodies that are designed for eternity. These bodies will never grow old, never get sick, never need surgery, never need food or rest to sustain them—glorious bodies that will never wear out.

The Final Rebellion (Revelation 20:7–10)

When the thousand years are over, Satan will be released from his prison and will go out to deceive the nations in the four corners of the

GOG AND MAGOG

Students of Revelation have scratched their heads over a reference to "Gog and Magog" in verse 8 of Revelation 20. The prophet Ezekiel had predicted a battle in which Gog (a leader) and his people, Magog, attack Israel. In response, God sends a great earthquake and pours out rain, hail, and burning sulfur on the army and destroys them. (You can read about it in Ezekiel 38.)

Is this the battle Ezekiel predicted?

Most interpreters think that the Gog and Magog battle comes during (or just before) the Tribulation. So John reaches back here in Revelation 20 and uses the names of some of Israel's old enemies to give us some indication of the hatred toward God and his people that will continue through-out the centuries of the millennium.

earth—Gog and Magog—and to gather them for battle. In number they are like the sand on the seashore. They marched across the breadth of the earth and surrounded the camp of God's people, the city he loves. But fire came down from heaven and devoured them. And the devil, who deceived them, was thrown into the lake of burning sulfur, where the beast and the false prophet had been thrown. They will be tormented day and night for ever and ever.

For a thousand years, human beings will live in a world of peace and incredible blessing—no sickness, no hunger, no hurricanes or tsunamis. Those who enter the kingdom in normal human bodies will marry and reproduce and fill the earth. They will live long lives—hundreds of years and perhaps even the entire length of the millennium. Sin's curse will be lifted, and mankind will enjoy an age of opportunity and goodness the likes of which no one has known since the garden of Eden.

The children born during the kingdom, however, will be born with an inner bent to sin—just like children who are born today. Their parents may be committed followers of Jesus and the world they enter will be perfect, but their hearts will still love darkness rather than light. There will not be the opportunities for sinful behavior in the kingdom that we have in our world today, and Satan will not be around during the kingdom to tempt human beings; but the sinful heart will still require God's transforming grace. Children born during the millennium will still need to believe in Jesus and be born again.

Many inhabitants of the kingdom will believe and will follow Jesus obediently and joyfully; others will outwardly obey but inwardly refuse to believe. Satan is released at the end of the thousand years to test those who were born during the kingdom. Just as God used Satan to test the faith and commitment of Adam and Eve in the original garden

In Other Words

I'm sure this doesn't bring any joy to God's heart. This creature, Satan, was God's most beautiful creation, and here he ends in terrible infamy.

Hal Lindsey, in *There's a New World Coming* (Eugene, Ore.: Harvest House, 1984), 262.

Hebrews 9:27

People are destined to die once, and after that to face judgment.

2 Thessalonians 1:8 – 9

[Jesus] will punish those who do not know God and do not obey the gospel of our Lord Jesus. They will be punished with everlasting destruction and shut out from the presence of the Lord and from the glory of his might.

Jesus in Matthew 25:41

"Depart from me, you who are cursed, into the eternal fire prepared for the devil and his angels."

No matter what view you take of when and how the millennium happens, one fact is clear from Revelation 20: we will spend eternity with Christ—in his presence, in his service, in his glory. Those who reject God's grace, those who refuse to believe that Jesus is the Savior, even those who outwardly conform to God's standards but ultimately join the rebellion against God, will be justly judged and separated from God's blessing and life forever. Those who in humble faith have accepted God's gift of salvation will spend eternity in joyful adoration of the Lamb. Which group will you be in? There's still time to accept Jesus as your Savior and to follow him in obedient faith. If you've never made that commitment, today is God's appointed time for you to believe in Jesus. Ask him in faith to forgive you and to make you his child. He has already promised to receive all who come to him.

of Eden, God will use Satan to test the loyalty of all who have experienced the perfections of Christ's earthly kingdom.

As soon as Satan is released, he's right back at his old tricks. A thousand years in the Abyss won't change his nature. He sweeps through human society and finds a multitude of people ready to rebel against the Lord. They have lived in a perfect world, with every need met and unlimited opportunity to pursue life's dreams, but they turn away from the light and truth of Jesus to follow the great deceiver.

Satan's tactics against God won't change over the thousand years either. He organizes this rebellious mob into an army and sets out to make war against the camp of God's people. This is most likely a reference to the city of Jerusalem, where Jesus will personally reign over his kingdom. Satan's army gathers, but no battle is fought. No shot is fired. Fire falls from heaven and devours the army in one blast.

The End of an Evil Career

Satan, the evil leader of the final rebellion, is not devoured by fire from heaven. Instead he is taken before Jesus, and he bows his knee (hatefully) to Jesus as Lord. Satan's tongue confesses (spitefully) that Jesus is the only King. Then Satan is cast into the lake of burning sulfur to join the Antichrist and the false prophet in torment forever.

Satan is sometimes pictured (in cartoons and even in our minds) as the ruler of hell, the king of the place of torment, but that is not

In Other Words

What are we to think of this doctrine [the eternal conscious punishment of the wicked]? It is hard — and it should be hard — for us to think of this doctrine today. If our hearts are never moved with deep sorrow when we contemplate this doctrine, then there is a serious deficiency in our spiritual and emotional sensibilities. . . .

The reason it is hard for us to think of the doctrine of hell is because God has put in our hearts a portion of his love for people created in his image, even his love for sinners who rebel against him.

Wayne Grudem, in *Systematic Theology* (Grand Rapids: Zondervan, 1994), 1151–52.

true. Satan is not the king of hell; he's just another inmate. Jesus said that eternal fire was originally prepared for the devil and his angels (Matthew 25:41). From God's perspective, ever since Satan's original rebellion against God, his final end was certain. God, for his own purposes, allows Satan and sin to run their course, but the outcome was never in doubt. Satan's final place of judgment is the lake of fire.

No Place to Hide (Revelation 20:11–15)

Then I saw a great white throne and him who was seated on it. The earth and the heavens fled from his presence, and there was no place for them. And I saw the dead, great and small, standing before the throne, and books were opened. Another book was opened, which is the book of life. The dead were judged according to what they had done as recorded in the books. The sea gave up the dead that were in it, and death and Hades gave up the dead that were in them, and everyone was judged according to what they had done. Then death and Hades were thrown into the lake of fire. The lake of fire is the second death. All whose names were not found written in the book of life were thrown into the lake of fire.

This is one of the most sobering passages in the Bible. Every person who has refused to accept the grace and mercy that Jesus offers gets a glimpse in these verses of what their ultimate encounter with God will be like. It's not a passage to be read with glee, but with tears.

Help File

A SECOND DEATH?

John writes in Revelation 20:14, "The lake of fire is the second death." The concept of death in the Bible always involves separation. *Physical death* is the separation of the spirit from the body. *Eternal death* is the separation of a person from the conscious presence of God forever. That's the death John is talking about here—the second kind of death. The first kind of death, physical death, is temporary. Every person will ultimately be brought back to life. Believers will be resurrected in eternal bodies; unbelievers will be revived in decaying bodies—but body and spirit are ultimately reunited for everyone. The second kind of death, however, is never reversed. Unbelievers are separated from any sense of God's presence forever. Believers in Christ will never experience the second death: "The second death has no power over them" (Revelation 20:6).

At the very end of earth's history, every unbeliever will be raised from the dead. They will not be raised in a holy, glorified body, but in the same body they had at death. The only change will be that their bodies will now exist forever. The spirits of unbelievers have been in conscious torment in Hades. In the future, Jesus will revive their bodies and reunite their spirits with their bodies. Their bodies may have decayed into dust thousands of years earlier. They may have died at sea and been scattered over the ocean. Some may have even tried to escape the final judgment by having their ashes thrown to the wind. But God will bring every unbeliever from every age and place back to life to stand before him for judgment.

The great white throne judgment is not a judgment that will determine if a person is saved or lost. Only unbelievers will be there. Believers in Jesus will face another judgment, the judgment seat of Christ, to establish their rewards. No believer will stand before God at this final judgment. The unbelieving through the ages have rejected God's truth and salvation in life, and now they will bear his condemnation.

Unbelievers are judged from two sources—"the books" and "the book of life." First they are shown that their name does not appear in the book of life, the record of all those who have put their faith in Jesus alone for forgiveness and cleansing. Every unbeliever will be shown that, in spite of God's abundant grace and in spite of several opportunities to believe, they consistently refused God's offer. Unbe-

Points to Remember

- ☑ At the time of Jesus' return to the earth, Satan will be bound and confined to the Abyss for a thousand years.

- ☑ Believers who died during the Tribulation will be resurrected, rewarded for their faithfulness, and will reign with Christ throughout the centuries of the millennium.

- ☑ Jesus' kingdom on earth will be a time of peace, blessing, and prosperity.

- ☑ At the end of the thousand years, Satan is released and is allowed to test those who live on the earth. A multitude of people will gather to make war against God and will be destroyed by fire from heaven.

- ☑ Jesus will sit on a magnificent throne and judge all unbelievers of all the ages. Those whose names are not written in the book of life will be separated from God forever in the lake of fire.

lievers will not be there to debate or negotiate with God. The apostle Paul says that every mouth will be silenced and the whole world held accountable to God (Romans 3:19).

Unbelievers will also be judged from the books—from a record of their deeds on earth. Their deeds will not save them; we are saved only by grace through faith in Jesus. Their deeds will determine their degree of punishment in eternity. Some unbelievers who have had a greater knowledge of God than others will suffer more severe punishment than those with less knowledge and less opportunity. Those unbelievers who pursued evil will be treated more harshly than those whose debt of sin is less.

Every unbeliever will bow their knee to Jesus and will confess that Jesus is Lord, but it will be too late to change their destiny. There will be no second chance at the great white throne judgment, just the awful condemnation of their own sin before a holy God. Those whose names are not found in the book of life are ushered into eternal hell.

No Christian thinks about hell with joy. It's a very hard truth to accept, but we are convinced by the overwhelming testimony of Scripture that those who reject Christ are separated from the conscious presence of God forever.

CHAPTER 21

Tripping through Heaven

Tripping through Heaven

> ▸ John sees a new universe—and a magnificent city.
> ▸ Tears are wiped away.
> ▸ Gates of pearl and streets of gold—for real!

Key Codes: Level 21

→ Alpha and Omega: First and last letters in the Greek alphabet
→ Fiery lake of burning sulfur: Hell
→ Jasper: A brilliant, translucent stone; building material of the new Jerusalem
→ Twelve tribes of Israel: The sons of Jacob who became the leaders of the twelve extended families ("tribes") that make up the people of Israel
→ Stadia: A unit of measure about 200 feet (65 meters)—two-thirds the length of a football field

Finally Home

For a Christian, home is a place we've never been. We've all had an earthly home, but it doesn't take much to remind us of how temporary and fragile that place can be. A fire, a hurricane, a job transfer is all it takes. One place is left behind or lost—and we look for another place to live.

Our true home, however, is heaven. The apostle Paul says in 2 Corinthians 5 that when we are absent from this body, when our spirit separates from our body in physical death, we are then "at home" with the Lord (verse 8). We will enjoy a conscious, close relationship with Jesus forever.

The final heaven is what John sees in Revelation 21 and 22. Earth's history has come to a conclusion with a glorious millennium of peace and abundance. A short, final rebellion is followed by the final judgment. (We saw all that in Revelation 20.) Then God will take all the redeemed of all the ages and seat us in some cosmic grandstand for the final act of the human drama.

This old earth (and the universe that it sits in) will pass away. When the Bible says a *new* heaven and a *new* earth are made, I take that to mean that this earth and the heavens that surround it are destroyed and something new is created. Here's how the apostle Peter describes the end of our planet:

> But the day of the Lord will come like a thief. The heavens will disappear with a roar; the elements will be destroyed by fire, and the earth and everything done in it will be laid bare. Since everything will be destroyed in this way, what kind of people ought you to be? You ought to live holy and godly lives as you look forward to the day of God and speed its coming. That day will bring about the destruction of the heavens by fire, and the elements will melt in the heat. But in keeping with his promise we are looking forward to a new heaven and a new earth, where righteousness dwells.
>
> 2 Peter 3:10–13

Our world will not end in a nuclear holocaust or by natural disasters brought on by global warming. It won't end as a frozen chunk of ice when the sun burns out. The world began as an act of God, and it will end that way. The energy held within the molecules of earth will be released, and the world as we know it will be gone. "The present heavens and earth," Peter writes, "are reserved for fire" (2 Peter 3:7). The same word from God that spoke our universe into existence will bring about its end. But in its place something new emerges—a creation more beautiful than anything we can imagine!

THE FIRE OF ROME

The first-century Roman emperor Nero most likely hired street thugs to burn a portion of Rome near the royal palace where Nero wanted to do some expansion work. When the fire got out of hand and destroyed a large swath of the city, Nero began to look for someone to blame. He finally settled on the Christians. What proved so condemning to the Christians was their belief that, following Jesus' return, the earth would be purged by fire. These overzealous Christians, Nero claimed, were simply trying to get things started early.

When We All Get to Heaven (Revelation 21:1-8)

Then I saw "a new heaven and a new earth," for the first heaven and the first earth had passed away, and there was no longer any sea. I saw the Holy City, the new Jerusalem, coming down out of heaven from God, prepared as a bride beautifully dressed for her husband. And I heard a loud voice from the throne saying, "Look! God's dwelling place is now among the people, and he will dwell with them. They will be his people, and God himself will be with them and be their God. 'He will wipe every tear from their eyes. There will be no more death' or mourning or crying or pain, for the old order of things has passed away."

He who was seated on the throne said, "I am making everything new!" Then he said, "Write this down, for these words are trustworthy and true."

He said to me: "It is done. I am the Alpha and the Omega, the Beginning and the End. To the thirsty I will give water without cost from the spring of the water of life. Those who are victorious will inherit all this, and I will be their God and they will be my children. But the cowardly, the unbelieving, the vile, the murderers, the

A BIOGRAPHY OF EARTH

The present earth and our surrounding universe have gone through a series of changes over the ages:

- *Creation*: The world was created as a work of God's perfection and as a home for human beings. The first humans, Adam and Eve, were placed in a garden and given a job—to care for the garden as an act of worship to God.
- *Fall*: Adam and Eve were created as holy human beings, but their holiness and loyalty to God were untested. God tested their obedience by designating one tree as off-limits. When

Adam and Eve disobeyed God's command, they became sinful in their character—they "fell" from their lofty place in God's creation. The entire creation suffered the consequences of their sin. Death became part of the human condition. Paul says that the whole creation is in bondage to decay and groans in pain as it waits for God's lifting of sin's curse during the millennium (Romans 8:20-22).

- *Flood*: The global flood of Noah's day brought about a major change in the earth's surface. Ocean bottoms and mountain ranges were altered by the catastrophic pressures of huge sexually immoral, those who practice magic arts, the idolaters and all liars—they will be consigned to the fiery lake of burning sulfur. This is the second death."

The final heaven is a new earth. If a believer in Jesus dies today, that person goes to heaven to be with Christ. That heaven, God's heaven, is called "my Father's house" in John 14:2 (NIV). But that heaven, and the heaven John sees all throughout the book of Revelation up to this point, is a temporary home. Our *eternal* dwelling place will be a newly created earth, unscarred by sin's decay or disease or disaster. John introduces the new universe in verses 1–8 of Revelation 21 and then goes into more detail about the city we will live in (21:9–27) and the paradise that surrounds the city (22:1–5).

The only description John gives of the new earth at this point is that "there was no longer any sea." Our present earth is covered with water over more than half of its surface. Seas and oceans divide continents and countries. Cultural divides are wide between Africa and North America, or Asia and Latin America. The new earth will not be marked by those political or social divisions. We will maintain our ethnic distinctions in heaven (John saw people in heaven from every language and ethnic

A BIOGRAPHY OF EARTH (CONTINUED)

amounts of water (Genesis 6–9; Psalm 104:6–9). The apostle Peter says, "The world of that time was deluged and destroyed" (2 Peter 3:6). The same earth emerged from the flood, but it was radically different on its surface than the preflood world.

- *Kingdom*: During Jesus' one-thousand-year reign over the earth, sin's curse will be lifted. The earth will produce abundantly; sickness will be eradicated; human life will be extended. Even wild animals will live together in peace. The only outward remnant of sin's curse will be the serpent—it will still crawl on its stomach and eat dust as a reminder of God's original judgment on Satan (Genesis 3:14; Isaiah 65:25).

- *Fire*: After the kingdom and the final judgment of unbelievers, the present universe will be destroyed and removed by fire. Some Christians believe that this will be a surface change similar to that produced by the flood—a cleansing by fire. But the language of 2 Peter 3:10–12 implies that the present universe will pass off the scene as a newly made heaven and earth takes its place.

Philippians 1:21 – 24

For to me, to live is Christ and to die is gain. If I am to go on living in the body, this will mean fruitful labor for me. Yet what shall I choose? I do not know! I am torn between the two: I desire to depart and be with Christ, which is better by far; but it is more necessary for you that I remain in the body.

2 Corinthians 5:6 – 9

Therefore we are always confident and know that as long as we are at home in the body we are away from the Lord. We live by faith, not by sight. We are confident, I say, and would prefer to be away from the body and at home with the Lord. So we make it our goal to please him, whether we are at home in the body or away from it.

1 Corinthians 15:51 – 52

Listen, I tell you a mystery: We will not all sleep, but we will all be changed—in a flash, in the twinkling of an eye, at the last trumpet. For the trumpet will sound, the dead will be raised imperishable, and we will be changed.

group), but we will not be separated by religious suspicion, national rivalry, or economic prosperity. The new earth will have some smaller bodies of water (like the river mentioned in 22:1), but no dividing oceans. It's also possible that John uses the term "sea" in its symbolic sense of the evil, churning nations from which the Antichrist comes forth in Revelation 13:1. Evil nations that persecuted God's people and opposed God's plan will be missing from the new earth.

John also sees a beautiful city descend to the earth—"the Holy City, the new Jerusalem." He will give us more details about the city later in the chapter, but at this point the city appears as a bride clothed in a shining white gown, dazzling to all who see it.

Then a voice from heaven's throne—God's voice or an angel's voice—announces that the longing of every human heart since Adam and Eve were expelled from the garden of Eden has finally been fully satisfied. God will now dwell with his people—not as a shining cloud that guides Israel in the Old Testament, not veiled in human flesh like

Jesus in the Gospels, and not as an invisible Spirit residing in the hearts of believers. God will dwell with human beings in bodily form as Jesus, but his glory and majesty as God will be visible. We will walk with God in face-to-face fellowship, like Adam and Eve did in the original creation.

God's personal presence will transform human existence. Death, sorrow, pain, and hurt will be no more. God will wipe away every tear. I think that means past tears as well as future tears. We will finally have God's perspective on some of the experiences of this life that brought us so much pain. We will fully understand his purposes behind the loss of a job or the death of a child or the cancer that took our mate's life. We may not understand now why God allows certain things to touch our lives, but someday we will understand—and those tears we shed throughout lonely nights or in pain-filled days will be wiped away. Everything will be made new.

In verse 5 of Revelation 21, God begins to speak. He confirms and affirms everything that John has witnessed and recorded. He assures John, and every reader of the book, of his sovereign reign as King: "I am the Alpha and the Omega, the Beginning and the End." That expression means that God started human history in creation, he will end human history in the final events John has witnessed, and he has guided human history at every point in between. God has never been caught off guard or been surprised. God is not sitting in heaven wringing his hands and

In Other Words

This chapter deals with the history of the new earth and the new heaven; no longer are we dealing with Adam's sinful race, now we are dealing with all the redeemed of the ages who, at last, find themselves in God's Utopia — the Holy City, the new Jerusalem.

Donald Grey Barnhouse, in *Revelation: An Expositional Commentary* (Grand Rapids: Zondervan, 1971), 400.

Not just the book of Revelation but the whole Bible has pointed to this moment. Since Adam and Eve lost their place in Paradise and sin reigned on earth (Romans 5:12 – 21), the divine plan has prepared for the moment when sin would finally be eradicated and the original purpose of God when he created humankind would come to pass.

Grant Osborne, in *Revelation* (Grand Rapids: Baker, 2002), 726.

wondering what he will do next. He sits above the flow of history and sees and directs it all—and, best of all, we are in his hands!

God's promise is very clear. The person who believes in Jesus and who remains faithful by God's grace will inherit all that is promised in Revelation 21. Eternity on a wonderful new earth is not just "pie in the sky." The promise of eternal life is motivation to live obediently and joyfully for the Lord in this life. We will never thirst in heaven. Every desire and longing of the human spirit will be fully satisfied. Some people think of heaven as kind of boring—sitting around, strumming on harps. That's not what God designed us for, and it's not what he designed eternity to be. We will be occupied in engaging, stimulating

THE NEW JERUSALEM "TRAVEL GUIDE"

LOCATION

- It descends from God's heaven to rest on or above the new earth.
- It is a cube-shaped or pyramid-shaped city 1,500 miles on each side (length, width, height).
- It covers approximately the distance from present-day New York to Florida and from the Mississippi River to the Atlantic coast; it stands one-eighth of the way to our moon.

ACCESS

- The massive city wall (200 feet high) has twelve gates—three in each direction; the gates are never closed.
- The city rests on twelve foundation stones.

SIGHTS TO SEE

1. Each gate is like an enormous pearl, inscribed with the name of one of the twelve families that make up the nation of Israel. Ancient people considered the pearl to be the most valuable precious stone because its beauty comes entirely from nature. Human effort or craftsmanship cannot improve its quality.
2. Saint Peter won't be standing at the gate; angels will.
3. The names of Jesus' original followers, the apostles, are written on the twelve foundation stones.
4. Once inside the city, be sure to look down. The streets are made of gold.

WHAT? NO DIAMONDS?

It surprises some readers that no mention is made of a diamond foundation for the new Jerusalem. A diamond might be hidden in that list of gems because we don't know with certainty what some of these precious stones were. The fact is, however, that diamonds weren't known or used as gems in John's day. They don't start showing up in jewelry and on crowns until around AD 1200.

THE NEW JERUSALEM "TRAVEL GUIDE" (CONTINUED)

LITTLE-KNOWN FACTS

- Each foundation stone is a gemstone. Eight of the stones appear on the breastplate of the high priest in Old Testament Israel (Exodus 28:17–20; 39:10).
  - Jasper: The walls of the city are made of jasper; a white, translucent stone.
  - Sapphire: A blue stone; could also be lapis lazuli—traditionally the stone on which the Ten Commandments were written.
  - Agate (or chalcedony): A green form of quartz.
  - Emerald: Green, translucent stone; only mention of the stone in the New Testament.
  - Onyx (or sardonyx): Another variety of quartz; reddish-white; prominent in some of the crown jewels of England.
  - Ruby (or sardius): The first stone in the breastplate of Israel's high priest; often used to carve ancient seals that were pressed into clay or wax to secure a letter or document.
  - Chrysolite: A dark-colored yellow gem sometimes found in meteorites or volcanic lava.
  - Beryl (also called aquamarine): Blue or blue-green crystal.
  - Topaz: Imperial yellow-orange or green gem; largest uncut stone ever found weighed six hundred pounds.
  - Turquoise: A blue stone with silver flecks.
  - Jacinth: Perhaps the orange gem zircon or a blue stone such as lapis lazuli.
  - Amethyst: A deep-purple crystal; the large amethyst on the English royal crown is the oldest of the crown jewels.
- We are dazzled today by a small stone in a ring or necklace. The new Jerusalem, however, will rest on enormous stones of gemlike brilliance.

Future FAQs

How can nations and kings exist in heaven?

Verse 24 of Revelation 21 has been a difficult verse for students of Revelation: "The nations will walk by [God's] light, and the kings of the earth will bring their splendor into [the city]." Nations in heaven? Instead of boring you with all the suggestions that interpreters have proposed, let me give you a couple of explanations that make the most sense.

This could be John's way of explaining that the whole new earth will be occupied, not just the new Jerusalem. All the people who fill the new earth will live in the light that emanates from God. The "kings" John refers to are those believers who reign with Christ, even in the eternal state.

John tells us in Revelation 22:5 that we "will reign for ever and ever." Other interpreters suggest that church-age believers will live in the great city, while Old Testament believers and millennial-age believers will occupy the rest of the earth.

Another possibility is that those who live in natural human bodies through the years of the millennium will enter the new creation in bodies that are different from the resurrected, glorified bodies. Those people would be like Adam and Eve were in the original creation — uncontaminated by sin but in bodies designed to care for the new earth, as Adam and Eve were to care for the original earth. Because they have access to the tree of life (Revelation 22:2), they can live forever in their human bodies. Those millennial believers dwell on the new earth in organized groups or "nations" and are the people over whom glorified believers will reign forever. Just a thought.

activity and ministry forever. We will never be bored and never exhaust the limitless creativity of God.

Because John (and all of us reading Revelation) still live in the present world, God emphasizes that evil and impurity will have no place in the world to come. Those whose spiritual separation from God is evidenced by lives of immorality, violence, or disobedience to God will have already been sent to another place, a horrible place of darkness and torment.

Bible Networking

Isaiah 65:17 – 19

See, I [the LORD] will create
 new heavens and a new earth.
The former things will not be remembered,
 nor will they come to mind.
But be glad and rejoice forever
 in what I will create,
for I will create Jerusalem to be a delight
 and its people a joy.
I will rejoice over Jerusalem
 and take delight in my people;
the sound of weeping and of crying
 will be heard in it no more.

Jesus in Mark 13:31

"Heaven and earth will pass away, but my words will never pass away."

Hebrews 13:14

For here we do not have an enduring city, but we are looking for the city that is to come.

A Guided Tour of Heaven (Revelation 21:9 – 27)

One of the seven angels who had the seven bowls full of the seven last plagues came and said to me, "Come, I will show you the bride, the wife of the Lamb." And he carried me away in the Spirit to a mountain great and high, and showed me the Holy City, Jerusalem, coming down out of heaven from God. It shone with the glory of God, and its brilliance was like that of a very precious jewel, like a jasper, clear as crystal. It had a great, high wall with twelve gates, and with twelve angels at the gates. On the gates were written the names of the twelve tribes of Israel. There were three gates on the east, three on the north, three on the south and three on the west. The wall of the city had twelve foundations, and on them were the names of the twelve apostles of the Lamb.

Bible Networking

Isaiah 44:6

"This is what the LORD says—
  Israel's King and Redeemer, the LORD Almighty:
I am the first and I am the last;
  apart from me there is no God."

Galatians 4:26

But the Jerusalem that is above is free, and she is our mother.

Hebrews 11:10

[Abraham] was looking forward to the city with foundations, whose architect and builder is God.

The angel who talked with me had a measuring rod of gold to measure the city, its gates and its walls. The city was laid out like a square, as long as it was wide. He measured the city with the rod and found it to be 12,000 stadia in length, and as wide and high as it is long. He measured its wall and it was 144 cubits thick, by human measurement, which the angel was using. The wall was made of jasper, and the city of pure gold, as pure as glass. The foundations of the city walls were decorated with every kind of precious stone. The first foundation was jasper, the second sapphire, the third agate, the fourth emerald, the fifth onyx, the sixth ruby, the seventh chrysolite, the eighth beryl, the ninth topaz, the tenth turquoise, the eleventh jacinth, and the twelfth amethyst. The twelve gates were twelve pearls, each gate made of a single pearl. The great street of the city was of gold, as pure as transparent glass.

I did not see a temple in the city, because the Lord God Almighty and the Lamb are its temple. The city does not need the sun or the moon to shine on it, for the glory of God gives it light, and the Lamb is its lamp. The nations will walk by its light, and the kings of the earth will bring their splendor into it. On no day will its gates ever be shut, for there will be no night there. The glory and honor of the nations will be brought into it. Nothing impure will ever enter it, nor will anyone who does what is shameful or deceitful, but only those whose names are written in the Lamb's book of life.

I enjoy reading travel guides, especially the ones with lots of pictures of the attractions in a new city. I've never been to Rome or London, but I've enjoyed some interesting hours reading tour books written by people who have been there. It makes me wish that John had been able to pull out a digital camera and take some pictures of the new Jerusalem to add to what he writes. He does his best trying to use present-world language to describe next-world sights, but we can only begin to imagine the splendor and beauty of the great city where we will spend eternity.

What You Won't Find in the New Jerusalem

John sees no temple in the new creation. God himself dwells directly with his people, so in reality the whole earth is a temple. We won't have church buildings in eternity, because our whole existence will be an act of worship and adoration to God. You won't find any denominational offices in heaven either. We will all join in perfect unity before the Lord.

Darkness will be a thing of the past too. A new sun and moon may exist as part of the new creation, but John says there is no need for them. The glory of God lights the city and the entire new earth. No streetlights, porch lights, flashlights, or security lights are needed. We will live in never-ending daylight.

Future FAQs

Will there be animals in heaven?

Of all the questions I've ever been asked about heaven, this one is asked most often. The Bible never tells us directly whether animals will be part of the new creation, but I am confident they will be. God filled the original earth with animals and declared them to be good. The new creation will contain many of the same things that our present earth contains—rivers, trees, fruit—so why not animals? When the question relates to a family pet, it gets a little more difficult. Animals do not have an eternal spirit like human beings have. There's no hint in Scripture of a resurrection for animals. At the same time, God loves to give good gifts to his children. He is extravagant in his grace. He may surprise us all by giving us back some pets we have cherished on earth.

The first seven verses of Revelation 21 should be read at every Christian's funeral. The focus of our lives is not on the separation and sorrow of death but on the glory and joy of heaven. The heartaches and disappointments we experience in life on earth will someday fade away as we see God's great purpose for our lives coming to completion. We will finally understand all that God was doing to bring us to maturity in Christ — and the tears will dry up. That's not just "pie in the sky" theology; that future hope changes how we live every day. We live with confident trust that God has a plan and a purpose that he is fulfilling through us. We may not see the grand design right now, but eternity will reveal fully what we can only see today in shadowy pieces.

In Other Words

Imagine there's no heaven.

> John Lennon, from his song "Imagine" (Lenono Music, 1971, 1999).

Human history begins in a garden and ends in a city.

> Warren Wiersbe, in *Be Victorious* (Wheaton, Ill.: Victor, 1985), 145.

The Christian life is meant to be like heaven on earth. Believers regularly taste the sweetness of the same heaven to which someday we will go to dwell forever. Praising and loving God with all your being, adoring and obeying Christ, pursuing holiness, cherishing fellowship with other saints — those are the elements of heavenly life we can begin to taste in this world. Those same pursuits and privileges will occupy us forever, but we can begin to practice them even now.

> John MacArthur, in "Heaven," in *The Popular Encyclopedia of Bible Prophecy*, ed. Tim LaHaye and Ed Hindson (Eugene, Ore.: Harvest House, 2004), 130.

Impurity will be missing from the new Jerusalem too. No police officers will be needed; no jails, no courts, no lawmakers. The desire and capacity to sin will be removed from our hearts, and we will walk in perfect, joyful obedience to God. Places that cater to and exploit sinful desires will certainly be missing—no adult theaters, casinos, bars, or drug dealers.

Human sickness and death are no longer part of the human condition in heaven. That means no clinics or hospitals or funeral homes or cemeteries.

Oddly enough, the pursuit of material wealth will be a thing of the past too. The commodities we hold in highest esteem will be used as building supplies in heaven. We won't have to think about retirement plans or 401k plans—which means no banks, stock markets, or commodity exchanges in heaven—and no collection agencies or pawn shops either.

A lot of things we accept as commonplace in this world will be missing in the next world—and we won't miss any of them.

Points to Remember

- ☑ God creates a new universe and a new earth as our eternal dwelling place.

- ☑ A magnificent city descends to the new earth—the brilliant city of God.

- ☑ God will personally dwell with his people.

- ☑ Sorrow, sickness, sadness, and separation are gone forever.

CHAPTER 22

The Never-Ending Story

The Never-Ending Story

- The new earth is a paradise.
- John tells the whole truth and nothing but the truth.
- Jesus' final promise: "I am coming soon!"

Key Codes: Level 22

→ The river of the water of life: Drinking water on the new earth

→ The tree of life: Food for the immortal

→ Dogs: John's term for those who have refused God's grace

→ The Root and the Offspring of David: A title for Israel's promised Messiah, Jesus

→ The bride: The true church; all those who have believed in Jesus

→ Amen: A Hebrew word that means "so let it be"

Paradise Restored

In the original creation, God placed the first human beings in a beautiful "garden of delight" (which is what the word "Eden" means). Adam and Eve were placed in the garden not just to enjoy it but to take care of it as an act of worship to God. They walked with God in the cool part of the day and saw him face-to-face. When Adam and Eve disobeyed God's command and sinned, they were driven out of the garden into a changed world, one marked now by death and sorrow and pain—a world languishing under the curse of sin.

Adam and Eve's removal from the garden was not simply a consequence of their sin. God was also graciously barring them from eating from the tree of life that grew in the garden. Eating from that tree would have caused them to live forever—but they would have lived in sinful, deteriorating bodies. God knew that his plan of redemption would include the resurrection and transformation of human bodies, so he kept Adam and Eve (and their descendants) from the tree.

As John the apostle looks into the future, however, he sees a new garden surrounding the heavenly city of God—and the tree of life is accessible again!

The River, the Tree, and the Throne (Revelation 22:1–5)

> Then the angel showed me the river of the water of life, as clear as crystal, flowing from the throne of God and of the Lamb down the middle of the great street of the city. On each side of the river stood the tree of life, bearing twelve crops of fruit, yielding its fruit every month. And the leaves of the tree are for the healing of the nations. No longer will there be any curse. The throne of God and of the Lamb will be in the city, and his servants will serve him. They will see his face, and his name will be on their foreheads. There will be no more night. They will not need the light of a lamp or the light of the sun, for the Lord God will give them light. And they will reign for ever and ever.

As John's eyes move from the magnificent city to the new world on which it rests, he sees a cool, refreshing river flowing from God's throne—"the river of the water of life." God has already promised to give believers "water without cost from the spring of the water of life" (Revelation 21:6). The river pictures the life-giving presence of God among his people. God is pure and holy and transparent in his nature, like the crystal-clear water in the river. Nothing is hidden or secret or shameful in God's character.

OL' MAN RIVER

Rivers also play a prominent role in Jesus' thousand-year kingdom on earth. The prophet Ezekiel pictured an ever-widening river flowing out of the temple in the kingdom age. The water in the river turns fresh everything it touches, even saltwater, so that animals and fish flourish in its path (Ezekiel 47:1–12). Trees will thrive along its banks and will produce fruit all year long. The prophet Zechariah adds that during the kingdom, "living water will flow out from Jerusalem, half of it east to the Dead Sea and half of it west to the Mediterranean Sea, in summer and in winter" (14:8).

Bible Networking

Joel 3:18

In that day the mountains will drip new wine,
   and the hills will flow with milk;
   all the ravines of Judah will run with water.
A fountain will flow out of the LORD's house
   and will water the valley of acacias.

Jesus in John 7:37

"Let anyone who is thirsty come to me and drink."

Psalm 46:4 – 5

There is a river whose streams make glad the city of God,
   the holy place where the Most High dwells.
God is within her, she will not fall;
   God will help her at break of day.

Jesus used the image of "living water" to refer to himself and his life-changing power (John 4:10). He also pictured the Holy Spirit as "rivers of living water" that will flow from within the believer (John 7:38).

John also sees a wonderful tree (or possibly several trees lining both sides of the river) — the tree of life. These trees produce twelve kinds of fruit, one kind maturing each month of the year. We sometimes think of heaven or eternity as the place where time has ended, but John says we will calculate *months* on the new earth. The problem is, How will we do that? There will be no day-and-night cycle, so we can't count days. If there's no sun or moon, how can we calculate months or years? I don't have an answer, except that the Bible indicates we will somehow still record the passage of time in eternity.

Another question that comes out of this passage is the reference to the leaves of the tree providing "healing" for the nations. If all sickness is removed, no one will need physical healing; if sin and its power are removed, we won't need spiritual healing; if all unbelievers are removed, no one will need redemptive healing. So why healing leaves?

The Greek word John uses is the root of the English word "therapy." The leaves of the tree of life provide "health-giving" power to the residents of the new Jerusalem. The leaves do not correct physical problems, because we won't have any. Instead, the leaves promote the enjoyment of life throughout eternity.

The third great blessing of the new earth will be the absence of sin's curse. The curse will be lifted during Jesus' kingdom, but it will still be possible to sin and rebel against the Lord (Revelation 20:7–9). In the eternal place of rest, there will be no curse at all to contend with—no sickness, no disasters, no sorrow.

We will enjoy an immediate, face-to-face relationship with God. His name, his mark of ownership and blessing, will be on our foreheads. The Antichrist forced his mark on people in the Tribulation, but we will receive God's name with joy and gratitude. The light that John saw illuminating the city will also shine over the whole earth. The light of God's glory will banish darkness and eliminate the need for any other source of light.

In Other Words

There shall be no more curse — perfect restoration. But the throne of God and of the Lamb shall be in it — perfect administration. His servants shall serve him — perfect subordination. And they shall see his face — perfect transformation. And his name shall be on their foreheads — perfect identification. And there shall be no night there; and they need no candle, neither light of the sun; for the Lord giveth them light — perfect illumination. And they shall reign forever and ever — perfect exultation.

A. T. Pierson, cited in J. B. Smith, *A Revelation of Jesus Christ* (Scottdale, Pa.: Herald, 1961), 295.

To the person who simply wants more, who is impatient of limits, who is bored with what he or she has and wants diversion from it, St. John's vision of heaven will not serve well. This is not a paradise for consumers.

Eugene Peterson, in *Reversed Thunder: The Revelation of John and the Praying Imagination* (New York: HarperSanFrancisco, 1988), 184–85.

Bible Networking

Isaiah 60:19

The sun will no more be your light by day,
nor will the brightness of the moon shine on you,
for the LORD will be your everlasting light,
and your God will be your glory.

Psalm 118:27

The LORD is God,
and he has made his light shine on us.

Believers will be occupied with at least two activities in eternity, according to these verses: we will serve God as his servants (verse 3), and we will reign with him forever (verse 5). I don't know all that this will involve, but I do know that we will be engaged in fulfilling, challenging activity forever. Heaven will be a place of rest and worship, but also a place of ministry and responsibility—without the frustration of fatigue, misunderstanding, or sinful motives. Work will be a joy in heaven, an act of worship to God.

These Words Are True (Revelation 22:6 – 11)

The angel said to me, "These words are trustworthy and true. The Lord, the God who inspires the prophets, sent his angel to show his servants the things that must soon take place."

"Look, I am coming soon! Blessed are those who keep the words of the prophecy in this scroll."

I, John, am the one who heard and saw these things. And when I had heard and seen them, I fell down to worship at the feet of the angel who had been showing them to me. But he said to me, "Don't do that! I am a fellow servant with you and with your fellow prophets and with all who keep the words of this scroll. Worship God!"

Then he told me, "Do not seal up the words of the prophecy of this scroll, because the time is near. Let those who do wrong continue to do wrong; let those who are vile continue to be vile; let those who do right continue to do right; and let those who are holy continue to be holy."

The final section of the book of Revelation contains a series of statements made by three individuals—the angel who has guided John, John himself, and Jesus. They repeat some of the important themes of the book and help us respond appropriately to what we've read and heard. The first response of our hearts should be to believe what God has revealed through the angel to John. The angel who has been John's tour guide for most of the book emphasizes that the words John has written are true and worthy of our complete trust. That's because the source of the words is God—not John, not the angel, but God. John didn't cook all this up as he sat in exile on the prison island of Patmos. God is the one who sent the angel and moved in John as he saw and recorded the visions. The end result of God's work is not an inspired *prophet* but an inspired *book*. Revelation (like all of Scripture) is God-breathed, the product of God himself.

John is so overwhelmed (and even exhausted) by the end of the book that he does a foolish thing. He falls down at the angel's feet and begins to give the angel the kind of worship that is due God alone.

Try, Try Again

1975

The year 1975 was a big year for end-of-the-world predictions. The president of the Jehovah's Witnesses, John Knorr, had done some calculations based on Bishop Ussher's dating of the earth's creation and came up with 1975 as the six-thousandth year since Adam's creation—and definitely the year of the return of Christ. The War of Armageddon would wipe out everyone on earth except good Jehovah's Witnesses. Some of his more committed followers began to sell their houses and quit their jobs in anticipation of the end, but 1975 came and went with no world war and no glorious kingdom. Thousands of people left the Jehovah's Witnesses movement.

A prophecy buff named James Taylor also liked 1975. He claimed that Jesus would return on the Jewish New Year, Rosh Hashanah, of that year. When the fall observance of Rosh Hashanah passed without the rapture, James decided that the real date must be 1976 ... later changed to 1980 ... then 1982—you get the picture.

Bible Networking

Isaiah 55:1

> Come, all you who are thirsty,
>   come to the waters;
> and you who have no money,
>   come, buy and eat!
> Come, buy wine and milk
>   without money and without cost.

Jesus in John 14:6

"I am the way and the truth and the life. No one comes to the Father except through me."

JESUS' LAST WORDS . . .

The Bible records some other "last words" of Jesus:

ON THE CROSS

"Father, into your hands I commit my spirit."   Luke 23:46

TO HIS DISCIPLES

"Go into all the world and preach the gospel to all creation."   Mark 16:15

BEFORE HE ASCENDED INTO HEAVEN

"You will receive power when the Holy Spirit comes on you; and you will be my witnesses in Jerusalem, and in all Judea and Samaria, and to the ends of the earth."

Acts 1:8

TO THE CHURCH BEFORE THE RAPTURE

"Whoever has ears, let them hear what the Spirit says to the churches."

Revelation 3:22

The angel's response was immediate and direct: "Don't do that!" The angel knew how tantalizing it would be to accept human adoration and worship. He would be tempted to walk right down the path of Satan, who wanted to be like God and who still tries to get human beings to worship him. Instead, the angel told John to get up and to worship God alone.

John is warned not to seal up what he has written. Daniel in the Old Testament was instructed to close up his book "until the time of the end" (Daniel 12:4). But the fulfillment of these prophecies will soon take place. The problem is it has been nearly two thousand years since John wrote Revelation — far longer than the time between Daniel and John (a mere six hundred years). How can the angel say that the time is near when it would be hundreds of years before any of it happened? I think that the angel's statement (like Jesus' statement later in the chapter that he is coming quickly) points out the fact that the wrap-up of human history could begin at any moment. Paul and John believed that Jesus could return in the air for his people at any moment. That urgency permeates the entire book of Revelation. We are to live (even close to two thousand years after John wrote this book) as though these events could begin to be fulfilled tomorrow.

In fact, in the angel's mind, the urgency is so great that there seems to be little time to repent or to get right with God. Those who do wrong will continue to do wrong, and those who are holy will continue to be holy (verse 11). The point he seems to be pressing home is this: change while there is still time. Believe in Jesus and follow him while he still offers his grace, because the day will soon come when God's judgment will fall. You can't say that you will wait until the end arrives to get right with God because that will be too late.

In Other Words

Worship God and only God. Angels, prophets, and fellow Christians stand on the same level and kneel together on the same ground — as *worshipers*.

Eugene Peterson, in *Reversed Thunder: The Revelation of John and the Praying Imagination* (New York: HarperSanFrancisco, 1988), 187.

Jesus' Final Words (Revelation 22:12 – 17)

"Look, I am coming soon! My reward is with me, and I will give to everyone according to what they have done. I am the Alpha and the Omega, the First and the Last, the Beginning and the End.

"Blessed are those who wash their robes, that they may have the right to the tree of life and may go through the gates into the city. Outside are the dogs, those who practice magic arts, the sexually immoral, the murderers, the idolaters and everyone who loves and practices falsehood.

"I, Jesus, have sent my angel to give you this testimony for the churches. I am the Root and the Offspring of David, and the bright Morning Star."

The Spirit and the bride say, "Come!" And let those who hear say, "Come!" Let those who are thirsty come; and let all who wish take the free gift of the water of life.

THE BEATITUDES OF REVELATION

The Sermon on the Mount is one of the most well-known passages in the Bible. (You can find it in Matthew 5–7.) Jesus gives an extended sermon about what it means to follow him. Jesus begins the sermon with a series of proclamations of blessing—proclamations called the Beatitudes. Here's one: "Blessed are the pure in heart, for they will see God" (Matthew 5:8). The book of Revelation has its own set of beatitudes—proclamations of blessing on those who faithfully follow Jesus:

- "Blessed is the one who reads aloud the words of this prophecy, and blessed are those who hear it and take to heart what is written in it" (Revelation 1:3).
- "Blessed are the dead who die in the Lord from now on" (Revelation 14:13).
- "Blessed are those who stay awake and keep their clothes on, so that they may not go naked and be shamefully exposed" (Revelation 16:15).
- "Blessed are those who are invited to the wedding supper of the Lamb!" (Revelation 19:9).
- "Blessed and holy are those who have part in the first resurrection" (Revelation 20:6).
- "Blessed are those who keep the words of the prophecy in this scroll" (Revelation 22:7).
- "Blessed are those who wash their robes, that they may have the right to the tree of life and may go through the gates into the city" (Revelation 22:14).

Bible Networking

Daniel 12:9–10

[The angel] replied, "Go your way, Daniel, because the words are closed up and sealed until the time of the end. Many will be purified, made spotless and refined, but the wicked will continue to be wicked. None of the wicked will understand, but those who are wise will understand.

Jesus gives his final message to the world in verses 12–19. He emphasizes who he is and that he will return suddenly and soon. Every person's eternal destiny rests on only one thing—their relationship with Jesus.

If you've ever wondered who Jesus really is, he tells us exactly who he is by using a whole series of powerful titles for himself (verses 13, 16).

- "I am the Alpha and the Omega" (meaning Jesus is the one from whom everything started and to whom everything will return).
- "[I am] the First and the Last" (meaning Jesus is the original mover in all of history and the final goal in whom history will be resolved).
- "[I am] the Beginning and the End" (meaning Jesus is the author and originator of everything and the one who will bring everything to a conclusion).
- "I am the Root and the Offspring of David" (meaning Jesus is the Messiah, the giver and fulfiller of all the promises given to David's family and David's nation).
- "[I am] the bright Morning Star" (meaning Jesus' return will signal the dawning of God's new day—a perfect world for eternity).

Jesus certainly leaves no doubt about who he is. Nothing began without him, and nothing will end without his involvement; human history sprouted from his initiative, and it's all moving under his direction to the end that he has determined. If you want in on God's program, you have to come through Jesus. No one else shares the throne; no one else shares the power; no others are mentioned as his equals or alternate saviors or co-redeemers—only Jesus.

HEAVEN AND HELL IN ISLAM

Muslims believe that in the future a final judgment will descend suddenly on the world. The last judgment is also called "the Day of Doom," "the Last Day," "the day of Resurrection," and "the Hour." The final judgment on mankind will be announced by a peal of thunder or a loud trumpet blast, and the natural world will begin to disintegrate.

The Muslim Scriptures, the Qur'an, describe the day of judgment as a time when the normal routines of life are turned upside down:

> When the sun shall be darkened, when the stars shall be thrown down, when the mountains shall be set moving, when the pregnant camels shall be neglected ... when the scrolls shall be unrolled, when heaven shall be stripped off, when hell shall be set blazing, when paradise shall be brought near, then shall a soul know what it has produced.
>
> Qur'an 81:1–4, 10–14

All human beings, whether alive or dead, will be assembled before Allah, the judge. Each human being has a record book that will be examined. The book will be placed in either the person's right hand (a sign of goodness and purity) or left hand (a sign of evil and impurity). Allah is a merciful God, but individuals gain paradise by doing good deeds. A scale will weigh good deeds against evil deeds. Each person will stand before Allah alone. No one can intercede without Allah's permission. Most Muslims believe that Muhammad, their prophet, will be able to intercede in certain cases.

The final outcome is either paradise or eternal hell. The Qur'an describes hell as "the fire," where punishing angels relentlessly torment the lost. Paradise is a luxuriant garden where the saved recline on soft cushions and enjoy a bountiful feast forever. The idea that seventy-two virgins await every man who reaches paradise is a misinterpretation of Islamic teaching. The Qur'an says that all believers, men and women, will enjoy the company of "companions" in paradise. That word in Arabic carries the idea of close friends, not sexual partners.

Muslims believe that at death a person is asked three questions by the angels of death: Who is your God? Who is your prophet? What is your faith? Those who give the right answers will have a comfortable wait until the day of judgment. Those who give the wrong answers will begin to suffer punishment while waiting for the resurrection and Allah's judgment. Only those who die as martyrs for the faith or in "holy war" (*jihad*) go directly to paradise.

Friends or relatives who are dying are turned to face Mecca if possible. The Islamic confession of faith is repeated over and over in hope that the final thought in a dying Muslim's mind will be:

> There is no god but Allah, and Muhammad is his messenger.

Those who wash their robes in the salvation that Jesus provides have the right to enter the city and eat of the tree of life. The rest are outside the realm of God's blessing. Those are the only two options—Jesus, or outside; blessing, or wrath; an eternity of life, or an eternity of death. If you ever wondered about alternate ways to God or whether other religions all lead to the same heaven, Jesus gives you the answer: He is the *only* way to God.

That's what makes his final invitation so urgent. His invitation to everyone who reads or everyone who hears what is said in Revelation is to *come to him.* The Holy Spirit, who works in human hearts to convince them that Jesus is the only Savior, says, "Come." The message of the church, the bride, is to *come to Jesus.* Jesus himself says that if you are thirsty, if you have a desire in your heart to know God personally, come and drink from the water of life. Believe in Jesus, and receive his free gift of new life. Salvation is offered freely to you today. Those who are thirsty are invited—we are welcomed—to come.

No More, No Less (Revelation 22:18–21)

> I warn everyone who hears the words of the prophecy of this scroll:
> If any one of you adds anything to them, God will add to you the

Not every Christian feels comfortable praying "Come, Lord Jesus." We've found it pretty nice in this world. We want heaven, but not for a while. My son once asked me, "Is it wrong to pray that Jesus won't return until after I get married?" I understand his perspective, because I find myself thinking the same way at times. The persecuted church of John's day (and of our day) has a much clearer view of the distinctions between life in a fallen, sinful world and eternity in the presence of God. The things we love in this world may not be wrong in themselves, but if we desire them more than we desire Jesus, our priorities are wrong. Maybe if we prayed that little prayer more often—"Come, Lord Jesus"—we would focus more on what really matters in the here and now.

Deuteronomy 4:2

Do not add to what I [Moses] command you and do not subtract from it, but keep the commands of the LORD your God that I give you.

Proverbs 30:5 – 6

> Every word of God is flawless;
>   he is a shield to those who take refuge in him.
> Do not add to his words,
>   or he will rebuke you and prove you a liar.

1 Thessalonians 3:13

May he [the Lord] strengthen your hearts so that you will be blameless and holy in the presence of our God and Father when our Lord Jesus comes with all his holy ones.

---

plagues described in this scroll. And if any one of you takes words away from this scroll of prophecy, God will take away from you your share in the tree of life and in the Holy City, which are described in this scroll.

He who testifies to these things says, "Yes, I am coming soon."

Amen. Come, Lord Jesus.

The grace of the Lord Jesus be with God's people. Amen.

Revelation opened with a blessing to everyone who would read the book; it closes with a warning: Don't add anything to what God has said—and don't remove anything either. Don't add your interpretation and put it on the same level of authority as God's written words. My views on how to understand various passages have changed over the years. God's truth is unchanging. Some people don't like some of the things they read in Revelation, but taking truth away brings with it some dangerous consequences. God will only rescue two things from this old sin-cloaked earth—his people and his Word. Jesus gave us a very clear perspective on the authority of God's Word: "Heaven and earth will pass away"—you can count on it—"but my words will never pass away" (Matthew 24:35).

If you ever come across a Bible teacher, pastor, or television evangelist who tries to give their own views equal authority with God's Word, look for the nearest exit and run. The same goes for someone who tells you to ignore certain parts of Scripture because "we just don't believe that anymore." Change the channel, put the book back on the shelf, find a new Bible study group. Any person who tries to add or take away from God's truth has placed himself or herself under God's judgment.

Jesus can't let John lay down his pen without one more shout: "I am coming soon." No one reading John's book can say they didn't know that Jesus was coming again. He's repeated the promise over and over—and the heart of every Christian responds as John did. The final prayer of the Bible is a sigh—a deep longing in every believer's spirit: "Amen. Come, Lord Jesus." Come and take us out of this world of sorrow and suffering. Come and judge those who hate your name and distort your truth. Come and establish your kingdom of peace. Come, Lord Jesus. Please come.

Points to Remember

☑ The new Jerusalem is surrounded by paradise—a garden of rivers and the tree of life.

☑ Not everyone is allowed to enter the city, but those who do live in the presence of God.

☑ God issues a warning that no one is to add to or subtract from his words.

☑ The Bible's final prayer is, "Come, Lord Jesus."

Resources for Further Study

Alford, Henry. *Alford's Greek Testament*. 4 vols. 1871. Reprint, Grand Rapids: Baker, 1980.

Barnhouse, Donald Grey. *Revelation: An Expositional Commentary*. Grand Rapids: Zondervan, 1971.

Constable, Thomas. "Notes on Revelation." *www.soniclight.com/constable/notes/pdf/revelation.pdf*. Accessed January 23, 2007.

Couch, Mal. "Trumpet Judgments." In *The Popular Encyclopedia of Bible Prophecy*. Edited by Tim LaHaye and Ed Hindson. Eugene, Ore.: Harvest House, 2004.

Graham, Billy. *Approaching Hoofbeats: The Four Horsemen of the Apocalypse*. Waco: Word, 1983.

Green, Joel. *How to Read Prophecy*. Downers Grove, Ill.: InterVarsity, 1984.

Gregg, Steve, ed. *Revelation: Four Views: A Parallel Commentary*. Nashville: Nelson, 1997.

Grudem, Wayne. *Systematic Theology*. Grand Rapids: Zondervan, 1994.

Hardie, Alexander. *A Study of the Book of Revelation*. Los Angeles: Times-Mirror Press, 1926.

Havner, Vance. *Repent or Else!* Westwood, N.J.: Revell, 1958.

Hendriksen, William. *More Than Conquerors: An Interpretation of the Book of Revelation*. Grand Rapids: Baker, 1967.

Hindson, Ed. *The Book of Revelation: Unlocking the Future*. Chattanooga, Tenn.: AMG, 2002.

Hitchcock, Mark. *101 Answers to the Most Asked Questions about the End Times*. Sisters, Ore.: Multnomah, 2001.

_____. *The Complete Book of Bible Prophecy*. Wheaton, Ill.: Tyndale House, 1999.

_____. *Could the Rapture Happen Today?* Sisters, Ore.: Multnomah, 2005.

_____. *The Four Horsemen of the Apocalypse*. Sisters, Ore.: Multnomah, 2004.

_____. *The Second Coming of Babylon*. Sisters, Ore.: Multnomah, 2003.

_____. *Seven Signs of the End Times*. Sisters, Ore.: Multnomah, 2002.

Hoyt, Herman. *The End Times*. Chicago: Moody, 1968.

Jeffrey, Grant. *The Final Warning: Economic Collapse and the Coming World Government*. Colorado Springs: WaterBrook, 1995.

Jeremiah, David. *Escape the Coming Night*. Dallas: Word, 1997.

Keener, Craig. *Revelation*. NIV Application Commentary. Grand Rapids: Zondervan, 2000.

Kelshaw, Terence. *Send This Message to My Church*. Nashville: Nelson, 1984.

LaHaye, Tim. *Revelation Unveiled*. Grand Rapids: Zondervan, 1999.

LaHaye, Tim, and Ed Hindson, eds. *The Popular Encyclopedia of Bible Prophecy*. Eugene, Ore.: Harvest House, 2004.

Lindsey, Hal. *There's a New World Coming*. Eugene, Ore.: Harvest House, 1984.

Mayhew, Richard. *What Would Jesus Say About Your Church?* Fearns, Scotland: Christian Focus, 1995.

McCall, Thomas. "Problems in Rebuilding the Tribulation Temple" in *Bibliotheca sacra* 129 (January–March 1972).

McGee, J. Vernon. Radio broadcast. *Thru the Bible Radio*, 1983.

Morgan, G. Campbell. *The Letters of Our Lord*. London: Pickering & Inglis, 1945.

Morris, Leon. *The Revelation of St. John*. Grand Rapids: Eerdmans, 1969.

Mounce, Robert. *The Book of Revelation*. Grand Rapids: Eerdmans, 1977.

Osborne, Grant. *Revelation*. Grand Rapids: Baker, 2002.

Pentecost, J. Dwight. *Will Man Survive?* Grand Rapids: Zondervan, 1980.

Peterson, Eugene. *Reversed Thunder: The Revelation of John and the Praying Imagination*. New York: HarperSanFrancisco, 1988.

Phillips, John. *Exploring Revelation*. Neptune, N.J.: Loizeaux, 1991.

Price, Walter K. *The Coming Antichrist*. Chicago: Moody, 1974.

Rogers, Adrian. *Unveiling the End Times in Our Time*. Nashville: Broadman & Holman, 2004.

Ryrie, Charles. *Revelation*. Chicago: Moody, 1968.

Scott, Walter. *Exposition of the Revelation of Jesus Christ*. Reprint, Grand Rapids: Kregel, 1982.

Smith, J. B. *A Revelation of Jesus Christ*. Scottdale, Pa.: Herald, 1961.

Smith, Michael. Unpublished notes on Revelation.

Spilsbury, Paul. *The Throne, the Lamb and the Dragon: A Reader's Guide to the Book of Revelation*. Downers Grove, Ill.: InterVarsity, 2002.

Sproul, R. C. *The Last Days According to Jesus*. Grand Rapids: Baker, 2000.

Stott, John R. W. *What Christ Thinks of the Church*. Grand Rapids: Eerdmans, 1958.

Thomas, Robert. *Revelation 1–7*. Chicago: Moody, 1992.

_____. *Revelation 8–22*. Chicago: Moody, 1995.

Toussaint, Stanley. "The Revelation of John." Unpublished class notes. Dallas: Dallas Theological Seminary, 1970.

Walvoord, John. "Revelation." In *The Bible Knowledge Commentary: New Testament*. Edited by John Walvoord and Roy B. Zuck. Colorado Springs: Victor, 1983.

_____. *The Revelation of Jesus Christ*. 1966. Revised edition, Chicago: Moody, 1989.

Wiersbe, Warren W. *Be Victorious*. Wheaton, Ill.: Victor, 1985.

Wilcox, Michael. *I Saw Heaven Opened: The Message of Revelation*. Downers Grove, Ill.: InterVarsity, 1975.

A Word of Thanks

So many people to thank! The congregation of Parkside Church is a wonderful group of committed followers of Jesus. They love us, encourage us, and bless us as their pastor and as a family. Special thanks go to Bonnie Schreck, my secretary, for following all my squiggles and arrows as she entered the text into the computer. Kyle, my son, did a great job checking all the Scripture references for me. Dr. Michael Smith (now at Liberty University) provided extremely helpful research on the middle chapters of Revelation. His help came just when I needed it most. The team at Zondervan always does superb work. Thanks, Jack Kuhatschek, for your patience on this one. My best fans are my family: Karen, my wife of almost forty years; Kim and Allison (our budding artist); Kevin and Julie; Kyle; and my parents, Paul and Mary Connelly. They have all loved me through thick and thin and are the light of my life every day.

NOTES

Bible Prophecy Made Clear

A User-Friendly Look at the End Times

Douglas Connelly

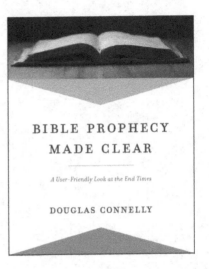

If you have a hard time making sense of the Bible, *Bible Prophecy Made Clear* is for you. It will transform what might seem like gobbledygook into incredible significance—enough to change your life. It can do so because the Bible is more amazing than you've ever dreamed and packed with riches. Making sense of it is no mystery. You'll even have fun as you learn!

Bible Prophecy Made Clear—newly revised and updated—helps you:

- Discover how the Bible's message unfolds from start to finish
- Learn how the Bible developed over many centuries
- Familiarize yourself with the main divisions of the Bible and its 66 individual books
- Find out proven principles for accurately interpreting what you read
- Acquaint yourself with important people, places, and events of the Bible
- Learn key biblical terms and discover the different types of literature represented in the Scriptures
- Get a handle on the Bible's historical and cultural background
- Discover why the Bible among all books is called "God's Word"

Available in stores and online!